Old Notre Dame
Paul Fenlon, Sorin Hall & Me

Old Notre Dame
Paul Fenlon, Sorin Hall & Me

Philip Hicks

Old Notre Dame
Paul Fenlon, Sorin Hall & Me

ISBN: 978-1-7321150-7-1

For bonus material, including photo gallery and
deleted scenes, visit: OldND.com

Published by
CORBY BOOKS
P.O. Box 93
Notre Dame, IN 46556
corbybooks.com

Manufactured in the United States of America

for

Thomas E. Blantz, CSC

Mack R. Hicks

Dennis Wm. Moran
(1943-2018)

Table of Contents

Foreword.. IX

Acknowledgments................................... XI

Introduction...XIII

1. Notre Dame Revisited............................. 1
2. The Professor....................................... 7
3. Visiting Hours...................................... 17
4. The Sorin Seven.................................... 23
5. A Day in the Life.................................. 31
6. Tradition.. 37
7. Starting Out (1896-1916)............................ 45
8. Wheat from Chaff.................................. 55
9. Grand Tour... 61
10. Wartime (1916-19)................................. 69
11. Father O'Neil...................................... 75
12. Teaching (1920-24................................. 83
13. Cheer, Cheer....................................... 93
14. Distinguished Guests.............................101
15. Professors' Alley (1925-29)........................109
16. Out and About....................................115
17. G.K. and Pop (1930...............................123
18. Blizzard 131

19. The Ghost of Washington Hall 139
20. Between the Library and Me 151
21. Who Is Charlie Phillips? (1924-33)..............161
22. Alone..169
23. The Thirties (1931-38) 175
24. The Party 183
25. Mourning 195
26. The Infirmary...203
27. God, Country, Notre Dame (1940-52)..........209
28. More Like a Friend 219
29. It's Alright, Paul..227
30. A Spring Day...237
31. O'Malley's Shadow (1952-74).....................245
32. Waning Days...255
33. Three Watches..263
34. This Good Man...271
35. Getting It Over With.....................................277

Notes...287
Index...289

Foreword

WHEN I MOVED into Sorin Hall in 1979 to serve as assistant rector, I was assigned to the turret room on the second floor near the Basilica. Right underneath me was Professor Paul Fenlon, the last of Notre Dame's bachelor-don professors. Paul taught in the English Department, but he was even better known for his sixty years of residence in Sorin.

Paul was always a gentleman who treated priests with great respect. He was pleased that I lived above him because for a period, a group of students had that room, and they made too much noise, particularly on the weekends. Paul had become accustomed to a calmer, more disciplined dorm setting than prevailed in the 1970s. In fact, before I moved in with Dave Porterfield, who served as rector, Sorin had had five different rectors in five years.

I soon discovered that like most people of his age and pedigree, Paul Fenlon had a quite regular lifestyle and an ample number of idiosyncrasies. Over time, I saw Paul's health decline, and finally he had to move to the Student Health Center before he died. His wake was held in Sorin Hall and his funeral in Sacred Heart Church, attended by his wide circle of friends from near and far. Paul Fenlon was celebrated as a great Notre Dame person and a distinctive representative of the tradition of the Notre Dame bachelor-don professors who resided in all-male undergraduate residence halls.

Phil Hicks, now a history professor at St. Mary's College, was a student in Sorin when I first moved in. I admired the friendship he and a few other students developed with Paul Fenlon. As this wonderful book displays, Phil and Paul became confidants

IX

and sources of mutual support. The fruit of this relationship is this warm account of those years, steeped in the history of the university, during Paul's long and fruitful years in Sorin and on the faculty.

We learn about World War I and how Notre Dame stayed open. We see revealed Paul Fenlon's friendships with Father Dan O'Neil, Charlie Phillips, Ed Fischer, George Shuster, Pat Manion, and Tom Stritch. We have accounts of some famous visitors like Chet Grant and G. K. Chesterton. Interspersed with the serious matters are tales of student antics and misbehaviors, most of which the Professor saw in a poor light.

In the course of his personal time with Professor Fenlon, Phil Hicks learned about his evaluation of various Notre Dame presidents, rectors of Sorin Hall, and fellow bachelor-don professors. Whether accurate or not, they reflect his rather conservative perspective on the Catholic Church, Notre Dame, and the broader American society.

In the final chapters, Phil recounts Paul Fenlon's last weeks and days. Paul was comforted by the range of friends who visited him. He knew inwardly he had given his life in service to the students in his classes and his fellow residents of Sorin Hall. To this very day, Paul Fenlon's legacy is recounted on a plaque in the rear of Sorin Chapel. As we say at Notre Dame, his blood is in the bricks.

Rev. Edward A. Malloy, CSC
President Emeritus
University of Notre Dame

Acknowledgments

SOME PASSAGES in this book first appeared in *Notre Dame Magazine* ("The Last of the Bachelor Dons," Winter 2018-19). I thank its editors, Kerry Temple and John Nagy.

I thank the University of Notre Dame Archives for its assistance over a period of many years and for allowing me to reproduce the photographs used in this book.

For their help in matters large and small, I thank Myron Busby, the late Elizabeth Casey, Tim Creagan, Donna Duzan, Bill Gasdaska, Rev. Gregory A. Green, CSC, Joe Harmon, Theresa Lucas, Tom Masterson, Joe Mulligan, John Sweeney, and Nick Zagotta.

For their support of all my writing projects and for making St. Mary's College such a congenial place to work, I thank my colleagues in the Department of Humanistic Studies: Gail Mandell, John Shinners, Laura Williamson Ambrose, and Jessalynn Bird.

I am grateful to Jim Langford at Corby Books for taking on this project and doing so much to improve the manuscript.

I thank Rev. Edward A. Malloy, CSC, above all for writing the Foreword, but also for making comments on an early draft and sharing his extensive knowledge of Notre Dame with me.

My deep gratitude to Rev. Thomas E. Blantz, CSC, the late Professor Dennis Moran, and my father is expressed in the Dedication. They have each been instrumental in the development of this book over a span of more than four decades. They continue to inspire me.

I am indebted to my mother, Susan, and my brothers, Andy and Doug, for their advice and encouragement.

Closest to home, I thank my wife Joyce and our children Stephen, Reilly, David, and Kathleen. They have been patient with "the Fenlon project" and always there for me. Joyce persuaded me there might be an audience for it beyond my immediate circle of friends and family.

I hope my great debt to Paul Fenlon is obvious from what has been written in the following pages.

Introduction

EARLY IN MY FRESHMAN YEAR at Notre Dame, my roommate and I returned to Sorin Hall after dinner. As we stood in the first-floor lounge watching the evening news, an unfamiliar voice called out from behind us: "Excuse me, boys; say, could one of you help me with my watches?" We turned around. It was the Professor. "They need winding and I can't do it myself. I've got terrible arthritis, you know."

"The Professor," as everyone called him, was a retired faculty member who lived in our dormitory. He was a tall, slender figure with wire-rimmed glasses and thinning white hair brushed straight back. His lanky frame, long face, and especially his voice, with its hint of a drawl and slight singsong, reminded me of Jimmy Stewart, the movie star who grew up just twenty miles from the Professor's birthplace.

While we wound his watches, the Professor asked for our hometowns and then shared anecdotes about former students living in the same parts of the country. As he spoke, I was struck by how funny and "tuned in" he was, not like an old man at all. He'd lived in Sorin nearly sixty years, he told us, most of those in the same room upstairs. He came to Sorin in 1917, decided it was a good hall, and never left.

"Professor," I asked, "is it true that you are the very last of the professors-in-residence?"

"Yes," he said, "though it gives me an uneasy feeling when you realize the last two died just within the last several months, Joe Ryan last spring and two years ago Frank O'Malley—God rest his soul."

Our conversation lasted just long enough to take care of his watches, then two weeks later we had an almost identical encounter in the lounge. As this second visit broke up, the Professor invited us to stop by his room for a chat. "I'm always in," he said. "Just knock."

I'm always in. Just knock: simple words, ordinary phrases, and yet they began a story that would take me forty years to tell, the story of our unlikely friendship.

He was eighty. I had just turned eighteen.

Before meeting him for the first time, I'd exchanged a "hello" in the hallway once or twice. I remembered thinking he must be an interesting person if he'd spent most of his life here. All I'd really heard about him was that he lived in Sorin for a dollar a year. The truth of the matter was that he'd taught English here from 1920 to 1962 and was one of "the giants in Notre Dame history," according to one Notre Dame president. He had a "genius for friendship," and the alumni magazine's profile of him was about to garner the greatest response in the publication's history.

What I could never have known, standing with him there that evening, was that he had enemies attempting to oust him from Sorin, and one day I would play a role in his courageous and sometimes comic effort just to survive.

In the years ahead, he and I would struggle to preserve a Notre Dame institution that hung by the thread of his own life, the tradition of the bachelor don (*don* being a British term for *professor*). "Of all the bachelor dons, Paul Fenlon was the best-known," according to one expert. "He lived his role longest and most fully." The Notre Dame dons were unmarried professors, not priests but laymen living in the dorms with the students. There were precedents for such living arrangements at Oxford and Cambridge, and the earliest American colleges imitated them with on-site professors to guide the moral and intellectual development of their students. Even today you can find faculty members in residence halls, most notably at Yale University. Yet the Notre Dame dons were a breed all their own, a colorful array of scholars, hermits, and dandies. Many were popular with the students, counseling and befriending them, and modeling adult civility and learning for them, in ways professors living in town never could. Generally not part of the official disciplinary apparatus of the hall, they were free to skirt the rules or discuss student problems in a way priests in charge of the dorms couldn't. The rectors were great favorites with the students, too, but they were authority figures set apart by a priestly aura and lifestyle.

The Professor grew up in "the age of the bachelor," the period roughly from 1870 to 1930, when life-long bachelorhood was relatively common in the United States, and he joined the faculty when the dons were in their heyday. In the 1920s an entire wing of Sorin was allocated to them and a quarter of Notre Dame's lay faculty lived in student residences. As the modern university became more professionalized, however, this institution faded from the scene. Just as the student-don relationship did not fit neatly into an organizational chart, so the school's paternalistic agreement allowing the Professor to live rent-free harkened to an earlier age.

He was a relic of the past—the last of the dons. Befriending him, I was privileged to witness the end of a campus tradition dating to the 1840s. By a minor miracle of circumstance, I preserved an intimate account of his last years.

When the Professor first arrived at Notre Dame as a student in 1915, it was a small campus surrounded by farmland, and faculty sometimes had to help with the harvest. The president was toiling to change what was essentially a prep school into a real college, and the football team was just making a name for itself by beating Army with the forward pass. The all-male student body barely numbered a thousand. Few faculty members had doctorates and about half were priests.

When I first arrived at Notre Dame in 1976, priests made up a tiny minority of the faculty. The university had seven times the number of undergraduates, and the first class of women had just graduated the previous spring. Now Notre Dame boasted a genuine graduate school and a reputation for academics. The football and basketball teams were experiencing glory days of their own, and I had just missed Daniel "Rudy" Ruettiger's walk-on performance that was to inspire a Hollywood film.

Recent reforms in the Church, the most significant in four hundred years, made it an exhilarating time to be a Catholic at Notre Dame. Yet after Vatican II, the Professor wondered whether the priests, like the students, had lost their way in the relaxed discipline of the age. Even more troubling to him, the freewheeling hedonism and experimentation of the 1960s had not yet burned out. With traditional norms of behavior and belief under attack, he might have regarded Sorin Hall as his refuge, but Sorin had become *Animal House*. As he was fighting a rearguard action to uphold the old ways, a baby-faced freshman walked in the building. He had a curiosity about Sorin only the Professor could satisfy.

[1]

Notre Dame Revisited

ON MOVE-IN DAY I had thought to myself, *Now at last I will discover whether all those stories I've heard about Notre Dame are true.* Until that moment, my knowledge of the school was mostly second-hand. From an age when I could sit on my father's knee, I'd listened to his stories: how in a pick-up game he had once tackled Paul Hornung, a classmate and Heisman Trophy winner, or how at mid-semester half the freshmen received pink slips under their doors saying they had flunked out and would be escorted to the first train out of town. On Saturday afternoons we would do yard work together, listening to Notre Dame games on a small transistor radio. On Sunday mornings we watched the television re-play show hosted by Hornung and Lindsay Nelson. These were the great Ara Parseghian teams that won two national championships.

My father owned some Notre Dame books that gave me the basic story of the school: a handful of French missionaries, led by Father Edward Sorin, had made its way to the northern Indiana prairie and in 1842 settled near South Bend. With just $300 in his cassock, Sorin founded the school on the shore of two snow-covered lakes. From these primitive beginnings, the university grew, guided by Sorin's religious order, the Congregation of Holy Cross (CSC, by its Latin initials). The success of Knute

1

Rockne's football teams helped the school weather the Great Depression and made it famous. In 1952, an ambitious young priest named Theodore M. Hesburgh became president, and the day I became a student he was still in the process of transforming the school into a great national university—what some called the Catholic Princeton.

As much as I had learned about Notre Dame, its actual campus remained unfamiliar to me. I had seen photographs, of course, but my first visit came as a four or five-year-old, and it left me with a handful of fleeting images—the Golden Dome on a lazy afternoon, an ivy-clad dormitory in the shade, the lakes in bright sunshine. My only vivid memory was arriving in South Bend late at night and being hustled by my parents into the LaSalle Hotel downtown. We made our way to a large room with walls that appeared covered in plush red carpeting. There was a night club atmosphere: loud voices, live music, drinks, cigars, and cigarettes. We snaked our way through the crowd to stop at Moose Krause's table for an autograph, which he signed with a green felt-tip pen on a scrap of paper pulled from my mother's purse. Moose was big, relaxed, and spoke through his nose. I was too young to understand he was the Athletic Director and once a basketball All-American in the '30s.

So on that warm Saturday morning at the end of August, each step I took revealed something new to me. My mother accompanied me to check in, while my father stayed with the car and my two brothers. I set out from the Main Circle a half step in front of her, anxious to see the dorm that would be my home for the next four years. I knew Notre Dame had no fraternities and the dorms were the source of identity. Students asked new acquaintances not "What's your major?" but "What hall are you in?"

Over the summer I had received a mimeographed sheet describing the dorms. An intended history major, I narrowed my choice to Sorin or St. Ed's, based on their small size, central location, and antiquity. My father remembered Sorin as a prestigious address, so I marked it as my preference and got in.

As we walked, the Golden Dome disappeared from view, obscured by the large trees dominating this part of campus. We came to the statue of Father Sorin, then broke left along a curving drive. We couldn't see Sorin Hall yet either, because of the dense foliage. Walsh Hall, a four-story building of bright yellow bricks, appeared on our left, then my first glimpse of Sorin came into view. It was a grimy old pile, covered in ivy, three stories high, turreted like a castle.

We climbed a half dozen steps, crossed the porch, passed through two large doors, then stopped at the first room on the right, where a committee of student volunteers greeted us and we met the rector, Father Greg Green.

In those first minutes, I felt as if I was back in summer camp. Everyone was wearing shorts, t-shirts, and flip flops. There was shouting down hallways, doors slamming, fans whirring in windows, people coming and going. After getting my room key, I raced up the long flights of stairs to check out my new digs. The open stairwell echoed with the noise below, and the floors flashed past me like a carnival funhouse, each brightly painted in its own garish color. When I got to room 331, I was thrilled by the view. My room was part of the central block that protruded a few feet from the east side, giving me an extra window looking north—a postcard shot of Sacred Heart Church and the Golden Dome. The room itself was a narrow rectangle with a high ceiling, and I had to scoot sideways to make my way past the bunk bed, desks, chairs, and wardrobes. It was a double, but a connecting door led to an identical-sized room. Because that door was left open, we had what was essentially a four-man suite.

I shared 331 with Tom, who wore Brooks Brothers clothes

and was always hunting down copies of *The New York Times*. Next door was Bart, probably the most level-headed and likable person in the building and a great favorite with the ladies. With him in 329 was Paul from New Jersey, who played Bruce Springsteen every night until lights out. As different as we were from one another, the four of us got along from the start.

We lived in a peaceful district of campus, where the stillness was broken only by the tolling of bells on the quarter hour or the marching band setting off for practice in a spine-tingling rendition of the Victory March. Groups of tourists strolled the pathways admiring the historic buildings, manicured lawns, and abundant flowers.

Standing at the statue of the Sacred Heart, less than a hundred yards south of the sprawling Main Building with its famous dome, and looking left, you saw Sorin Hall. Tracking to the right, you saw Sacred Heart first and then the dome straight ahead. Next came the theatre, Washington Hall, and all the way to the right was La Fortune Student Center. Tucked away just beyond this horseshoe were Corby Hall, the priests' residence, and another dorm, St. Edward's Hall. This suite of buildings was built in the late-nineteenth century using sandy gold bricks, many of them quarried from the marl of campus lakebeds. Architecturally, they shared Gothic, French, and Victorian elements, especially the steeply pitched mansard roofs.

After a few weeks, I had a group of friends who met for dinner at the South Dining Hall, then trouped to the Memorial Library, or in our parlance, "hit the 'brar." Returning to Sorin, we were always welcomed above the second set of doors by a mosaic depicting Father Sorin with outstretched hands. Sorin really came alive between eleven p.m. and two a.m., and it was common to be awakened at four a.m. by firecrackers or prank fire alarms.

Discipline was supposed to be maintained by the rector, the

assistant rector, and the resident assistants (RAs)—upperclassmen assigned to each floor. Yet to a man they insisted they were not a police force. My own RA was never around, and when he was, he appeared just as guilty of violating the rules as any of us.

Marijuana was common in Sorin, not just in the art studios of the crumbling old Fieldhouse we walked past on the way to the library. But the RAs seemed less concerned with drugs than with parietals, the visiting hours prescribed for members of the opposite sex. Even so, "breaking" parietals was commonplace and many couples won the cat-and-mouse game to escape detection.

Dorms were single-sex, and women made up just 20 percent of the undergraduate population. St. Mary's College, an all-women's institution, was only a fifteen-minute walk away, but Notre Dame, with its overwhelmingly male faculty, administration, and student body, had a decidedly masculine ethos.

The first home football weekend was the highlight of my first days on campus. At Friday night's pep rally, there was pushing and shoving and moments of sheer pandemonium as we surged towards the stage and the band plowed into the crowd, horns blazing. At the podium, Paul Hornung promised he would leap from the press box if Tony Dorsett gained another three hundred yards, as he did a year ago. The pep rally atmosphere carried over to the game the next day, until, that is, Dorsett touched the ball for the first time and ran for sixty yards. We lost by three touchdowns.

[2]

The Professor

THE DAY AFTER THE PROFESSOR invited me to visit, I decided
to take him up on his offer. Shortly after returning from dinner, I
headed to his room. I wasn't sure what to expect. I barely knew
the man.

It was the week of fall break, so the hall was unusually quiet
for a Friday evening. Occasionally, I heard a door closing or voices
at the end of the hallway. Outside it was cold, but the radiators
had been activated for the season, so the building was warm.

The four corners of Sorin Hall are made up of three-story
cylinders topped by turrets. Anyone living in such a corner,
whether on the first, second, or third floor, was said to live in
a turret or tower room. The Professor lived in the turret room
closest to Sacred Heart Church.

As you entered Sorin and took a right down the main corridor,
room 141 was about forty feet straight ahead of you. The west
door to the rector's office was on your right, the women's restroom
and north stairway on your left, and just beyond them the chapel.

You didn't enter the Professor's room directly from the hallway. The door of 141 led to a kind of private entrance hall. Later I
learned this was the "vestibule" or "sheet room," where the maid
stored linens, and it functioned mainly as a passageway to the
Professor's room. Along one wall was a green daybed and beyond
it a wooden tower cabinet. On the other wall were bookcases

7

filled with yearbooks. At the far end of the room was the door to the bathroom, what he called the "biffy," and next to it the door to the Professor's room.

I knocked at the outer door, just in case, heard nothing, and pushed it open. The sheet room was dark except for a shaft of light emanating from the inner door, which was ajar. As I approached it, my tennis shoes squeaked on the bare tile and I became aware of a musty fragrance and the sound of television. I stopped at the door, strained my ears, then knocked twice.

"Come in!" shouted the old bachelor professor. "Come in!" Stepping through the doorway, I still couldn't see him. To my left, a tall wardrobe blocked my view. All I could see was a dresser ahead of me. I took a step further, then another, cleared the wardrobe, then turned, and found the Professor seated in the middle of his little kingdom. He smiled. "Well, hello! Hello, Philip. Come in and sit down."

He gestured and I found a spot next to him in front of a small black-and-white television. "I'm watching the debates," he said, before turning back to the TV. And so we watched the presidential debates together, making occasional comments to one another. He seemed to have a mild preference for Ford over Carter, though he never came out and said so. This was the final debate in a close election and it clearly captivated the Professor, but I was less interested in who the next president of the United States would be than in this room. My eyes darted left and right to study it whenever I thought he wasn't looking.

The room was a time capsule from the 1920s, with its faded fabrics and threadbare carpeting. Bric-a-brac filled every available space. The ceiling was eighteen feet, a few feet higher than on the second and third floors of Sorin. Three large windows were covered with monks cloth drapes. One of them afforded a magnificent view of the dome lit up at night, except the shades were drawn.

Entering the room and turning left as I had just done, you saw a narrow bed with a thin cloth bedspread up against the left wall. The headboard and pillows were nearest you and rested against the back of the wardrobe. At the foot of the bed was a black Windsor chair with the university seal, a retirement gift from the school. Straight ahead was a big desk, littered with papers, books, and photographs. A square piece of raw foam served as seat cushion for the desk chair. To the right, between two windows was a mammoth piece of wood furniture, a mantelpiece with built-in bookshelves and a false fireplace made to fit the curve of the wall. It, too, was covered in mementos, and books and papers were piled where the fire ought to have been. On either side of the fireplace were two stuffed chairs, one a rocker, the other paired with an ottoman. There were several magazine racks crammed with newspapers, pamphlets, and booklets, and I counted four bookcases. The books were green and brown and black hardcovers, with little slips of paper and letters secreted between their pages.

Once the debate finished, I abruptly stopped my inventory of the room, and the Professor and I exchanged some pleasantries. Then I thought, *Let's see what I can learn about this old building.* Knute Rockne was the best-known person I could think of in connection with Sorin Hall, so I asked, "Professor, what room did Rockne live in when he was here?"

"Oh, Rockne didn't live in Sorin. Rockne never lived here."

He didn't? Everybody knew that Rockne lived in Sorin. This was a bedrock tradition of the hall.

"Well, then what about the famous photo of Rockne in the rec room?" I asked.

"Why, that only proves he was in the subway when the picture was taken. It doesn't prove that he lived here."

I squirmed in my seat. I didn't want to get into an argument, but this sounded wrong to me. *I'll go along with you for now*, I thought, *but you're going to have to convince me you know what you're talking about.*

"The subway was located in the north wing," he continued, "including under this very room. I remember going down there as a freshman in 1915. It was a dreadful room. It had an awful piano and some straw or maybe rattan chairs. All of the athletes lived in the subways or basements. The cheapest were in Corby and Sorin. Sleepy Crowley and probably Layden both lived in the Corby subway."

Well, at least I've learned something about the Sorin basement, I thought, *and we've got two of the Four Horsemen on the radar.* As every football fan knew, a sportswriter named Grantland Rice had immortalized Rockne's 1924 backfield made up of Elmer Layden, Jim Crowley, Don Miller, and Harry Stuhldreher.

"Okay, then, where *did* Rockne live?"

"He lived in Corby Hall, and the people at Corby have known that all along. Walk over there someday and take a look at it. I think you'll find it interesting."

I nodded politely, but all this was hard to swallow. *You just brought Sorin Hall down a peg in my estimation, without its tie to Rockne. So is it Corby that is the historic building, not Sorin?*

"Did you ever meet Rockne?"

"Oh, my. Heavens, yes! I exchanged a few words with him on various occasions. I remember him as a brilliant chemistry professor. One day I was sitting in Father Eugene Burke's class when we were interrupted by Rockne lecturing across the hallway, so Father Burke had someone shut the door. Rockne's staccato speech was peculiar, not unlike Ara Parseghian's, except it was more penetrating than Ara's.

"But I remember best the time I was waiting out here for a bus. Rockne recognized me as a professor and stopped his car to give me a ride downtown. He made some comment about the car's running boards and how fast cars moved nowadays."

"Was he famous then?"

"No, he wasn't that famous at the time, just 'Mr. Rockne,' our football coach."

This is getting better. I can't believe I'm sitting across from someone who actually knew Rockne.

"What else do you know about him?"

"Well, the football team used to take ten-day train excursions to California for the USC game. They made multiple stops, especially in Arizona. These little vacations were much more popular with the teams than the jet flights today are. It was on one of these business-and-pleasure trips to New York that Rockne went to the Ziegfeld Follies and saw the dance that gave him the idea for a new football formation.

"When Pat Manion lived on the first floor here, he didn't have a radio, just a piano. I was in my tower room one day when he came rushing in to listen to the radio; there was a rumor that Rockne was dead. After listening, we found it to be true. I will never forget that. Rockne died on Tuesday and his funeral was on Holy Saturday. He was a convert to Catholicism, you know, but like any other Catholic he was not given a funeral mass, just a funeral. In those days, funeral masses were not allowed during Holy Week.

"President Charles O'Donnell sent all of the students home early for the Easter holiday, which he later considered to be the greatest mistake of his life, because no students were able to be on campus for the services. They had to settle for listening to O'Donnell's brilliant eulogy on the radio. Throngs turned out. It was a very sentimental and emotional thing." The Professor began reciting the prayer "Hail, Holy Queen" under his breath until he arrived at the part he wanted, then resumed a normal speaking voice, "'… our life, our sweetness, our hope.' That's when O'Donnell broke down."

As the Professor told these stories, I began warming up to him, setting aside my initial doubts. Perhaps I was wrong about Rockne and Sorin, after all.

"Well, what about George Gipp?" I asked. "'Win one for the Gipper.' He stayed here, right?"

"No. Gipp had no hall, or I should say, he lived mainly off campus. He lived in Walsh Hall for the last few months of his life."

Here we go again. Are the history books I've been reading all wrong? Are you telling me you were an eyewitness to all this and no one ever bothered to get your side of the story? Are you just a curmudgeon who wants to debunk everything I know about Sorin Hall?

"Did you ever meet Gipp?"

"Oh, I saw him. I didn't meet him. I just said hello to him three or four times, he going up and down the stairs as I would, or something. He was a very intemperate athlete and didn't train on the weekends. That was partly the cause of his death: he just didn't take care of himself. But it was very common to die of pneumonia then, if that's what he died of.

"Presumably, Gipp was a convert on his deathbed by Bonnie Rockne. His parents were very strong Protestants and dead set against it, but Mrs. Rockne took a great interest in him. And I think she knew he was going to die before he himself did. Maybe he never knew. I don't know, but he became a Catholic—Mass and everything—and he was buried from this church. Pat Manion and I went in the long funeral procession all the way downtown to the train station. If I had to make that long walk again today, I'd never dream of making it. And when they took him up to Iron Mountain or something in the northern peninsula, his people were not happy about that and they had the services from their own church. I don't know whether he was a Lutheran or a Baptist or a Presbyterian or what."

We were a good twenty minutes into the conversation and I still couldn't believe I was speaking to someone who knew these people from so long ago. But without Sorin connections, Rockne and Gipp now became less interesting to me, so I tried to confirm a different piece of local folklore.

"Now the Shea brothers composed the Victory March in Sorin, didn't they?"

"They were here before my time, but, yes, that's the story."

Well, at least the Victory March is safe. What about Cardinal O'Hara? You have to know something about him—a former president of Notre Dame and the first Holy Cross priest to become a cardinal.

"Where did Cardinal O'Hara live?"

"Why, he lived in this very room," the Professor replied proudly.

Right here? Wow. Now we are getting somewhere.

"He was prefect of religion in this room, and in the vestibule he had racks filled with religious literature. Before becoming president, John F. had the door to this room open day and night for spiritually-troubled students. He heard confessions in this room."

"Where, exactly?"

"Right where you are sitting. That's where they would kneel, and lines of boys would extend out of his room into the sheet room. When I moved down to live in this room for the first time, I was told, 'if these walls could talk, you wouldn't be able to sleep.' You know what Frank O'Malley said about these old buildings—'there's blood in the bricks.' But O'Hara made his fame at Dillon Hall. He had a little buzzer outside his door and he asked that you press once for him to come and distribute communion and twice for confession. He introduced daily communion at Notre Dame in the 1930s, and he always had a little clicker in his hand to count communions and confessions. Every time you stood up to leave, you heard a little *click* on his counter. Cardinal O'Hara commercialized religion.

"I remember him as a young man. He graduated in 1911, I think it was. The end of my freshman year I can remember seeing him, before I knew who he was, coming out of Walsh Hall and walking quickly past here, when we would be on the porch or something. He was very thin, ascetic looking—oh, he walked very swiftly, very energetically, and he was thin as a rail. And John F. smoked incessantly. In fact, when they built Dillon Hall, O'Hara had them build a little platform outside of the building, which led to his confessional there. Whenever he needed a cigarette, he'd just flip the light from green to red and step outside for a smoke."

I listened to the Professor with growing excitement as I realized he just might be the genuine article, after all, the grand old man of campus and the guardian of its secret history. Yet as much as I was enjoying his stories, all this historical talk was exhausting me. After a good hour and a half with him, I shifted to a contemporary topic.

"What do you think about Father Hesburgh as president?" I asked.

"Oh, he's done a wonderful job. His greatest little project now is improving the graduate school here."

"Who do you think will succeed him?"

"The rumor is that it will be one of the three Bs—Burtchaell, Burrell, or Bartell—but I don't think it will be the provost, Father Burtchaell. No, Burtchaell is out of the running; he's too brash."

"Is he a liberal like Father Hesburgh?"

"Of course he is. Both of them are too liberal for me. Why, just look at the way they remodeled Sacred Heart Church."

And so my visit ended, and I climbed the stairs back to my

room, thinking, *What a gold mine of history! What an extraordinary human being!*

That night I tossed in my sleep as pieces of conversation kept coming back to me, and his words went round and round in my head: *Rockne never lived here—our life, our sweetness, our hope—Gipp had no hall—if these walls could talk—the three Bs.*

The next time I spoke to my parents on the phone, I told them all about the Professor. "Oh, Fenlon was well-known, very popular with the students," my father told me. "I had him for class." The Professor really *did* know everyone if he had taught my father, a marketing student who chose his major because he could get to all his classes without climbing any stairs in the Commerce building. Even with the receiver to my ear, I sensed a reversal of roles taking place. From now on, I would be telling the Professor's stories to him and he would be the one listening to me.

[3]

Visiting Hours

THE PROFESSOR had invited me to return whenever I wished, so I came back two days later, then a couple days after that, again and again until I was visiting three or four times a week, and eventually almost every day. I usually dropped by on my way to lunch or dinner or late at night after the library closed.

I would always find his door ajar. If I didn't hear voices within, my first thought was that he might be dead, since he always emphasized his days were numbered. I half expected to find him lying motionless in the middle of the floor.

I'd rap the door three times. Then, to be sure I was heard, I'd raise my voice redundantly, "knock, knock!" There was always a pause, never an immediate reply. In that moment, the same morbid fear would cross my mind. As I'd begin to cross the threshold and push open the door, the Professor would cry out, "Come in!" He would be at his desk with his back towards me. Neither of us would say a word until he heard the creak as I landed in the chair at the foot of the bed. At that instant, he'd swing around, get me into focus through his thick lenses, smile, then say emphatically, "Good!" as if I'd just accomplished something important. There would be a folded section of the newspaper propped up on his desk or a magazine opened to a certain page. "Here, I've got something for you," he'd say.

Normally, I'd remain for twenty or thirty minutes, sometimes an hour or more. Our late night visits would break up by 12:30 in most cases. The Professor would give the signal by saying, "Well, I must get to bed." He'd escort me out of his room into the vestibule and we'd continue talking for another minute or two, exchanging several "good nights" in the process. At last I'd turn and walk into the corridor. After a pause of about four beats, I could count on him to call out after me, "Good night, Philip!" or, if I was with friends, "Good night, gentlemen!"

Our conversations ran the gamut—campus gossip, politics, family news, sports. I usually steered the discussion back to historical topics, trying to pin down the tiniest details. This sometimes left him with his hands cupped over his eyes groping for dates and blurting out, "You ask the damnedest questions!" What I liked about our talks was how tolerant and easygoing he was. He didn't tell me what to do or how to think. He didn't give me advice except once: "There's good blood in Cincinnati, a good place to find a wife." He didn't pontificate or deliver monologues either, because that would be impolite. Instead, he valued the give and take of a good conversation.

Visiting him, I never found myself thinking, *When will this end?* or *Can you get to the point?* He liked short stories—his academic specialty—or, shorter still, anecdotes—something just the right length to amuse or entertain his guests. He had a showman's gift for storytelling, too. He didn't exactly mimic the accents of the characters in his stories, but he did imitate their voice inflections and use pantomime to dramatize their actions.

As delightful as he was, our society, or at least the prevailing youth culture, dictated that I shouldn't have liked him, but I did. I should have been put off by the double-generation gap separating us, but we met each other half way, as it were.

Cheerful and tender-hearted though he was, he could also speak in acid tones. When he did make a cutting remark, I found it hilarious because it was so out of character for him, but I never lost sight of what an effervescent personality he really had.

Soon enough, my friends began to tag along on my visits to see him. There was my roommate Tom, *The Times* in hand. Then there was Bill, an accounting major who taught us that parties were better for having delicacies like napkins and food, not just girls and beer. Tim was also part of our set. He lived in Flanner Hall and knew the lyrics to every Gilbert and Sullivan opera, among other feats of memory. Like me, these friends found visiting the Professor a refreshing break from the typical student day. Yet only one of my core group sought out the Professor on his own, a very musical, very Irish young man raised in a large family on a ranch out West. The Professor nicknamed him "Big Boy" on account of his height.

Whenever any of us visited the Professor, we found he had saved up little chores for us to do. In return for prying off juice lids or looking under the bed for him, he heaped praise on us, and it was nice being able to help him out. As entertaining as it was to spend time with him, however, I had one motive for visiting that my friends did not, a compulsion so strange it requires explanation: my interest in history.

Two years earlier, my family had travelled to England for the first time since my father, after ROTC at Notre Dame, had been stationed there with my mother, and I was born outside of Cambridge. To get ready for the trip, I immersed myself in travelogues, histories, and historical novels, and soon became entranced by all things English, especially English history. I even set my watch on English time to keep in sync with what was happening there and to remember a promise to myself to return one day in some great adventure yet to be determined.

As a freshman, some of my historical interest now shifted from England to Notre Dame. Like England, Notre Dame seemed

historic and important to me, more real than the transient tour-
ist destination of my Florida childhood. Campus history books
told me Sorin Hall was significant as the first Catholic residence
hall in the United States to feature private rooms. Before Sorin
opened in 1889, students slept on beds set out in long rows
in the Main Building. Sorin Hall represented the university's
recognition that college students needed more privacy and
independence than the high school and grade school students
sharing campus with them. As interesting as this larger historical
context was, however, it didn't mean much to me yet.

My sense of history wasn't very analytical or academic; it
was vicarious. I simply wanted to touch it with my bare hands,
to see where history happened. Anywhere I stood, I wanted to
know who else had once stood on the same spot and what had
occurred there. As an eleven-year-old visiting Ford's Theatre in
Washington, D.C., I stood before the pock-marked door to the
presidential box and focused intently on the peephole. Seeing
exactly how the wood had been whittled, I felt the full force of
the past. My body actually shuddered, I drew in my breath and,
for an instant, I stood with the assassin as he bored the hole.

At Notre Dame I had yet to experience such a super-charged
sense of time and place, but I did have a desire to piece together
the history of every square inch of Sorin Hall. I was forming an
attachment to the building, not just the inhabitants. So if anyone was living in the past, it was me, not the Professor. Only
occasionally did he pine for the good old days, but I egged him on
because I enjoyed contrasting the past and the present. I was the
one forcing our conversations in a historical direction, the one so
nostalgic for the golden era conjured up by my father. I was the
one complaining about the modern direction of Notre Dame:
the bland new architecture; the abolition of the Founder's Day

celebration; the emphasis, as I saw it, on academics over school tradition and Catholic character; the fair-weather football fans.

Although I didn't air these ideas in public, I recorded them in a journal required for one of my favorite classes. In Humanities Seminar, Professor Dennis Moran had asked us to write about our assigned readings and anything else on our minds. He took a special interest in what I had to say about the Professor and encouraged me to keep an account of my conversations with him, so I started a second journal devoted to this subject.

I had another source of inspiration as well. This past summer I had come under the spell of James Boswell's classic biography of Dr. Samuel Johnson, published in 1791. As a young man Boswell was awestruck by the great man of letters and recorded his table talk. With the *Life of Johnson* fresh in mind, I cast myself in the role of Boswell and the Professor as Johnson.

But there was a catch. I knew the Professor wouldn't stand for someone taking notes in his presence or tape recording him. We both valued the friendly, informal nature of our chats, which would be ruined if he had to worry everything he said was going "on the record." So I decided I would have to keep my journal secret. That meant going straight to my room afterwards to write everything down before I forgot it.

"I don't like to be interviewed with a tape recorder because I don't like the way my voice sounds," he said the first time I raised the issue. "Besides, I'm really not important enough to be interviewed. The only reason everyone wants to interview me is that I am an antique."

"But don't you think that maybe in two hundred years someone will be writing a history of Notre Dame and want to know more about a legend like you?" I asked.

He laughed hard. "I do have a few things that I would like to give to the archives one day. It is true that I was once asked to donate my correspondence to the archives, but I told them that I really didn't save any of it. Most of what I've kept are personal letters from family members that would not be interesting to anyone else."

Regardless of what the Professor thought, I was convinced his personal history, like the campus history, was underexplored, so I set myself the task of writing down everything he did and said. Eventually, as I got to know him better, I hoped to tell him about the journal, but for now I just enjoyed visiting him and writing about it.

[4]

The Sorin Seven

FATHER HESBURGH was making the rounds of the dorms and stopped by Sorin after dinner one day. I had never seen him at close range before, but on this occasion I thought he cut an impressive figure with his crisp blazer and sharp jawline. He spoke for several minutes to us about the importance of the residence halls to the Notre Dame experience, and then he invited our questions. We were more interested in his life and career than in how he was running the university. We learned that when he was training to be a priest all the seminarians spoke Latin to one another. We found out that when he served as chairman of the US Civil Rights Commission, President Nixon fired him, and he took that as a badge of honor. Father Hesburgh had actually held several presidential appointments and later that fall, when there was speculation President-elect Carter would choose him as secretary of Health, Education, and Welfare, everybody wondered whether he would accept. "He wouldn't even consider it," said the Professor, indignant that we would ask such a question.

When I stopped by to report on Father Ted to the Professor, he was complaining about the rough-housing in the hall. The only way to improve matters, he said, was to instill discipline in the newly-arrived freshmen each year. "Because Sorin was the oldest hall, it was always reserved for seniors. But now the whole thing has suffered because they integrated the classes. If they had only left a good thing alone! But when McCarragher, I think it was, came along years ago and they made him prefect of discipline, he thought bringing in the upperclassmen would be good for the freshmen and their studies. But the seniors only teach them how to drink! They drink beer by the gallons and the little freshmen do it, too."

I recalled that Father Charles "Black Mac" McCarragher was prefect in my father's time, and according to him McCarragher or a member of his staff would take off a shoe to chase students down the hallway. The footfalls, sounding at half speed, lulled students into a false sense of security, making it easier to catch them. The Professor laughed. "I can't imagine where you hear such fantastical stories." Undeterred, I told him another, this one about Father Patrick Dolan, who married my parents and had written the letter of recommendation that constituted my father's entire admission application to Notre Dame. At one time Dolan was prefect of discipline, too, and, so the story went, he once had gone to the extreme of punching a student.

"No, that doesn't sound like him," said the Professor, questioning my father's credibility a second time, then continuing: "Before the present regime, years ago, a German priest, Father Schlitzer, was the rector. He was very strict, like most rectors in the old days. Back then there was none of this parietals business. At least, there wasn't so much noise. Students used to be much more polite than they are today. We had study hours in those days."

"We still do, technically," I said.

"Technically, yes, but they meant it. Now a man like Father Farley used to patrol the halls and so did another rector, Pat Haggerty. Of course, those men did nothing but rector. You see, today we're so hard-pressed for priests that they do other things. Now you were speaking of Father Green the other day—I don't know what he does. He's supposed to be attached to something in Campus Ministry. No, but they meant it when you had to be up for morning prayer and things like that.

"To get appointed rector of Sorin was at one time looked upon as something worthwhile, but no longer. There's been a different rector here every year for the past five or six years. One reason for that, though the priests won't admit it, is we are such a fire hazard with our open stairways. In fact, not many years ago, this building was condemned and slated for destruction, but it caused such an outcry among the alumni that they couldn't do that. There has never been a fire here, but I've seen so many fires on this campus over the years that I think it's inevitable. That's why I pray every night this building won't go up in flames. But it's not by my prayers that Sorin stands. It's by the prayers of many old members of the community who love this old hall," he said, pointing to the priests' residence at Corby Hall.

"The students don't respect the building," I said.

"Yes, I agree, not enough students respect or love Sorin Hall."

Soon after this conversation, as if in answer to the Professor's request for something like martial law, the dean of students, James Roemer, exiled seven students for tossing beer bottles and firecrackers from their windows, violating parietals, and running a well-stocked tavern out of their tower room in 315, the "Dew Drop Inn," just down the hall from me.

The corridors were buzzing with the news:

"They had it coming to them."

"No. They never had fair warning."

"Good riddance. They were the only unfriendly people on the whole floor."

"Did Green kick them off?"

"Who turned them in to Roemer?"

"Do you think it was the firecrackers or the bar?"

The "Sorin Seven" were the talk of campus. Many Sorinites saw them as heroes and they were furious with the administration. Attempting to defuse the situation, the rector agreed to discuss the matter during his homily on the feast of All Saints, ironically. On that day, Sorin Chapel was overflowing and tense with anticipation. Father Green explained his decision to hand over the wrongdoers to the dean, but he was immediately challenged by angry voices from the pews. In the stormy debate that followed, no one denied that hall rules had been repeatedly violated or that Father Green had warned the guilty, but what several upperclassmen wanted was what previous rectors had given, a final warning, "next time, you go to Roemer." Without a free pass, they feared being sent to the "Grim Reaper" on the very first infraction. After an ugly few minutes, we somehow got through the rest of Mass. As we filed out, it was clear not everyone thought Father Green was being unreasonable. Most of the freshmen on my floor took his side. We wondered how such behavior could *not* warrant punishment.

I reported all this to the Professor, who was eager to hear the details. "I'm glad something was done about it," he said, before launching into a diatribe about student misbehavior, ending with the words, "Why, if John F. Cardinal O'Hara were here we'd have things nothing like we have them today, but we don't even have the position of prefect of religion anymore."

"But we have the Office of Campus Ministry," I said. "Doesn't that help?"

"No, not to my mind it doesn't," the Professor said, before reminiscing about the room at the center of all the controversy: "Jack Robinson, a big All-American center, lived in room 315 with Eugene O'Brien of the paint and varnish company and with a McGrath boy. I knew Jack quite well. He had four horses, one named 'Lady Edith' and one named after me,

'Professor Paul,' which won a few races at Arlington before retiring early as a stud."

Very soon, room 315 was vacant, and a small sign appeared on the porch, "Apartment for Rent." Bags were packed, the Sorin Seven left, and the furor over one of the most sensational things to happen my freshman year died down. In its immediate aftermath, with the headlines staring me in the face, and the Professor seconding them, I began to wonder whether I had landed in the worst hall on campus. So far, the verdict was still out.

With final exams fast approaching, I was spending less time visiting the Professor. For the holidays, he was flying back to his family in Blairsville, Pennsylvania, a small town forty miles east of Pittsburgh. I told him my hometown could be depressing on account of the retirees sitting alone on park benches, abandoned by their families. "Yes," he said. "I know many friends who have retired to St. Petersburg. It's depressing to return to Blairsville, too. So many of my friends have died, you see. The ones still living haven't adjusted to retirement very well."

"You have, haven't you?"

"Yes, yes, you could say I have."

On that note, in the middle of finals week, the Professor left for Pennsylvania. When I returned to Florida, I was surprised to see *Notre Dame Magazine* had a four-page spread on him. Written by his friend Ed Fischer, it focused on the Professor's lifelong "harvest" of friendships, which peaked in the 1930s and ebbed in the 1950s. The Professor was quoted as saying that as he aged students believed him to be older and less approachable than he actually was. My father thought the Professor was selling himself short, however, telling me, "He was a good teacher, as I recall, and pretty popular even with those of us in Business who really weren't interested in English. He was often in front of class doing dramatic readings of American fiction—Hawthorne, *The*

Glass Menagerie, and, I think, one day someone like O'Neil—
and taught large numbers of non-English majors. He had a little
trick to make sure you were paying attention. Once I was either
sleeping or daydreaming, and Fenlon saw me and called on me.
'Mr. Hicks, could you please tell the class the meaning of the
word being used on such and such a page?' And he accepted
what I had to say. At least I was awake enough to know what was
going on."

Fischer said the Professor was best-known for teaching three
courses: American Fiction, Victorian Novel, and Short Story.
That last one I could easily believe, for what had I spent two
months doing but listening to the Professor's own short stories
about life at Notre Dame? It was as if I had been taking an extra
class last semester. There was Hum. Sem. with Moran, Western
Civ. with Burns—and Short Story with Fenlon.

After break, I flew back to South Bend, and as the taxi
dropped me off at the Circle, I noticed the flag on the South
Quad was at half-mast. George Shuster had died the previous
day. *This will be a terrible blow to the Professor*, I thought, *and he'll
never make it back for the funeral with this storm brewing*. The Professor's conversations with me frequently mentioned "George,"
but all I could remember distinctly was, "George is now inactive
and trying to write his memoirs, but I doubt he will live long
enough to complete them." As Ed Fischer had explained, Shuster was one of the Professor's closest faculty friends. Like Pat
Manion, he had left Sorin Hall decades ago to make a name for
himself in the wider world while the Professor remained at his
post. Shuster became managing editor of *Commonweal* magazine
and later Land Commissioner for Bavaria during the reconstruc-
tion of Germany after World War II. As chair of a historical
commission, he personally interviewed several top Nazi leaders,
including Goering and Ribbentrop. He was president of Hunter

College for twenty years and then returned to Notre Dame to serve as special adviser to Father Hesburgh.

The funeral for Shuster went on as planned, despite a blizzard that closed the school. A large crowd filled Sacred Heart, and the big men of the university concelebrated the Mass— Hesburgh, Burtchaell, Joyce, Wilson, and Egan.

A week later, the Professor was back on campus, and I found him in his room when I came in from the library. "My good friend George Shuster died," he announced, explaining he had been in constant contact with Mrs. Shuster and other friends, who told him not to come to the funeral. He insisted on coming anyway but couldn't get a flight in time.

"I am not the same man as I once was," he sighed, describing a recent bout of bronchitis and complaining about his hands. The weather in Pennsylvania was awful, he said. He missed Mass two consecutive Sundays and his niece Betty Casey was stingy with the heat. "She believes in the strict conservation of natural gas. We were afraid the entire area might run out of gas completely. I thought I might never see this warm room again."

The Professor worried he should have stayed in Blairsville to straighten out the family finances. In that small town, Betty's husband Tom was overqualified for the few jobs available and he had to take work selling furniture. "He's unhappy to be making $180 a week, but I am overjoyed that it is at least something. He is forty-five and my niece is forty-nine. They have a little red-headed seven-year-old—Danny. They've been living in my house for free these last three years. As I say, it is my house. I pay the taxes; all they worry about is the heating and utilities." I had heard almost nothing about his niece's family before. To be honest, I wasn't particularly interested in that double life away from us. It was hard to imagine him living anywhere but Notre Dame.

A few days later, the Professor was still going through the

mail that had accumulated in his absence. He was sitting in a chair, sorting envelopes into piles on his bedspread. Many former students had written in response to the article in *Notre Dame Magazine*. "I made some enemies," he joked. Telling Ed Fischer the class of 1931 was his favorite got him into hot water with all the other classes. The Professor had me count all fifty-one letters, then he stacked them on his desk. These fresh letters were in addition to the ones responding to a longer version of the same story Fischer had published over the summer in the *South Bend Tribune*. All told, there were over two hundred letters. The Professor did not remember several of the correspondents, but many of his former students were now doctors, lawyers, and congressmen, he said, adding there was no way to tell how a student would turn out later in life. A particularly awful student, he said, was a very respected surgeon today.

The Professor read Johnny Lujack's letter aloud to me. The Heisman Trophy winner said he and his friends always believed the Professor had been around as long as Father Sorin, but years later he discovered the Professor was only fifty-two at the time, just as young, in other words, as Lujack was today. He complimented the Professor on the "remarkable" job he had done aging so gracefully.

There were Christmas cards, too. Father Green's was a view of Sorin Hall based on the same woodcut the Professor had hanging on his wall. "Thank you for being with us and for your patience," the rector wrote. The Professor laughed and put it on the mantle next to Father Hesburgh's card.

[5]

A Day in the Life

THE PROFESSOR has an unbreakable routine that brings him great joy. I never witness the early morning part of it firsthand, because he begins his day slowly and keeps to himself. He gets up at seven thirty or eight, he tells me, and Eddie the janitor drops by to say hello and hand him the newspaper. Sometimes Eddie reports wiping snow or leaves off his car, a brown Dodge Dart parked in the courtyard out back.

The Professor puts together a light breakfast, relying on a hot plate, toaster, and small refrigerator, or he walks to the South Dining Hall, where he enters the Pay Caf, the public cafeteria situated between the two student dining rooms. This is his favorite spot for breakfast or lunch. Mornings are the only time of day he isn't very social: "I was at the Pay Caf today, reading my *Chicago Tribune*, when a lady came up to me. 'Hello! I'm your neighbor.' I didn't know who she was. 'I'm the rectress of Walsh Hall,' she said. 'Oh, how nice,' I said, and then I went to one table and she to another. No one disturbs me while I'm reading the *Tribune*—that's an old rule that Pat Manion and I established."

After breakfast, the Professor runs his errands to the cashier's office in the Main Building or the dry cleaners. Returning to Sorin, he tackles his correspondence. At his desk, he stares intently at the keyboard of his portable typewriter and raises both index fingers high in the air before pounding the keys in rapid succession, elbows out, forearms churning like pistons. If he de-cides to write by hand, he uses a red ballpoint pen, as if he were still grading student papers. Though he blames the grading of so much hand-written work for ruining his eyes, he won't let go of his red pen.

The Professor spends the better part of the day reading the *Chicago Tribune*, the *South Bend Tribune*, the student paper the *Observer*, *Time* magazine, and *The New Yorker*. He works his way through magazines from back to front, then tears out several pages at a time and rearranges them in order of priority. "That's a trick that Mr. T. Bowyer Campbell taught me," he explains. "He would go through the magazine quickly selecting what he wanted to read so that later he could get right to it. My niece was infuriated trying to make sense of a *Time* I had gone through." The Professor is reading a new bestseller now. "I love fiction," he says, "but the critics agree this has been a bad year for fiction."

At midday, he drops everything he's doing for Mass. On Sun-days, he stays clear of the big church and all its hoopla, opting instead for the basement crypt, where he takes his place on the right side of the aisle next to his friend Dick Sullivan. Otherwise, he is content to worship on the main level of Sacred Heart at the eleven-thirty daily mass. Anticipating that event, he waits in his room until he hears the church bells ring twice on the half hour—his cue to get ready. He puts on his overcoat, steps into the sheet room, and grabs his fedora from the side table. Then he puts on his scarf, gloves, and clip-on sunglasses, and takes the short walk next door. If he is lucky, he finds his pew—two-thirds of the way back, right side—at 11:40, just in time to miss the homily. "They're too long," he says, "and I usually don't like what they say." As for the period of silent meditation after the sermon, he says, "This always reminds me of a Quaker meeting." But from that point in the

Mass until the closing prayer, the Professor is all business, his bony fingers in constant motion massaging his rosary beads.

After Mass, his best friend, Father Daniel O'Neil, checks on him. With his severe black glasses and neatly pressed black trousers and jacket, he seems out of place on campus and more like a business executive (except for the Roman collar). "You know, Ara Parseghian used to take O'Neil with him as the chaplain for away football games," the Professor says. "Early in his career, he served the freshmen in a religious capacity, and they liked him very much. Today he is in charge of the international students. He was so naïve that in his first years he made the mistake of assuming his foreign students would not be allowed to leave campus over the holidays, so he made a point of staying on campus over Christmas to be with them. They left, of course—the students today are dying to get away—and he was left stranded here."

If Father O'Neil drops by and no one's home, he leaves his "calling card" for the Professor, a triangular block of wood jammed between the door and the frame, placed just below the lock.

At three o'clock, the Professor takes his tea. His cup and spoon are on permanent loan from the Dining Hall. "In fact," he chuckles, "I have a few spoons marked 'USN' from when the Navy was here back in the '40s. They're just behind you in the drawer there. Take a look."

While I scrape the bottom of the drawer, the Professor stretches to the window sill behind his refrigerator to get the tin of Mrs. Busby's cookies. He has to be careful, he says, because they stick to the roof of his mouth, but he eats four of them anyway, smacking loudly. He squirts a long stream of artificial lemon juice into his sugary brew.

In the early evening, the Professor watches some television and has dinner around seven o'clock, always preceded by cocktails. If my friends and I are there, he says, "I'd offer you boys something to drink, but you're not of age." As he sits in bed with his ankles crossed reading the paper, a shot glass rests on a little nightstand. Behind him on his desk is the bottle of Scotch next to an empty glass. In one surprisingly fluid motion, using his left hand, he swings the shot glass over his shoulder and into the glass.

The Professor eats on campus at the Morris Inn or the University Club or goes into town with friends. His most frequent dinner partners are alumni like Myron Busby and Paul Boehm and their spouses, or Tom Stritch, a former bachelor don still teaching in American Studies, or an assortment of faculty widows.

Dressing for a dinner party, he has me button up his vest. "Now be sure to leave the bottom one unbuttoned," he says. He checks to make sure he doesn't have "a baggy seat," then moves closer to the mirror and laughs at the gap between his neck and shirt collar, which reminds him of a character in Dickens, one of his favorite authors. "My neck must be getting smaller. I hear that happens with older people. The rest of my body must be shrinking, too, because I used to be six feet tall, but not anymore."

Before going out, he always places three objects in his pockets: a relic of Saint Elizabeth Seton that a Setonite nun gave him years ago, his rosary, and a statuette of the Infant of Prague discovered among his father's possessions after his death.

If the weather is bad, the Professor takes his cane. He doesn't like to use it but knows someday he will have to rely on it. His favorite cane has a metal tip and a handle carved like a bird of prey, an inheritance of his friend Charlie Phillips. He also has a spare cane that he's loaned out to a freshman with a broken ankle and to his friend Miss Murphy, who had been using a yardstick for her injured leg. A third, purely ornamental cane is part of a set he bought in Ireland. He gave the matching one to Father

Hesburgh's predecessor, President Cavanaugh, who still makes good use of it now.

After dinner, the Professor settles down with a novel or magazine. Rather than sit spotlighted under a reading lamp, he leaves every light in the room on. This is also the time of night for his hand exercises, when he squeezes a billiard-sized green rubber ball in one hand, then the other.

Later, he rolls up his sleeve and labors to remove his wristwatch. He also has a thin metal wristband for arthritis. "It's the first thing they give you when you arrive in Arizona for health reasons," he explains. Both he and Father Hesburgh have the bracelets and believe in their healing powers. Hesburgh's is so embedded in his wrist that it appears surgically implanted.

Once I wind his watch, the Professor places it upside down on his right knee, then puts his wrist over the watch, palm up. He uses his left hand to join the bands together. Unless it takes him more than a few minutes, he refuses help. "It's good therapy for my hands," he says. This watch was a gift from Father O'Neil, who bought it in Switzerland.

Next, the gold pocket watch comes out, a high school graduation gift from his father, dated 1915. It keeps good time but needs winding and has numerous small indentations, which are actually teeth marks. "I used to be rather fidgety or nervous, I guess, in class, and would bite my watch." On the front side are his initials—PIF. "I was given my middle name because my mother could not think of another name not already used in the extended family. So she simply chose Ignatius because his feast day coincided with my birthday. I hate the name!"

Once a week, at nine or ten at night, the Professor takes his shower. His skin is so dry he can't bathe more frequently, on doctor's orders. His own bathroom lacks a shower, so he has to walk the length of the building to use one of the student stalls. This makes the process a dreaded, hour-long ordeal. He begins by placing his valuables—both watches, a ring, and his bracelet—in his eyeglass case, which he hides in his room for safekeeping. Then he says three or four Hail Marys. Next, he sets out in his gold robe, with his rubber mat in one hand and his cane in the other. Once inside the public restroom, he puts his belongings on a chair he leaves there permanently for that purpose. In the shower, he places towels on every side to cushion a potential fall. He puts on his shower cap and keeps his glasses on—"I try not to get them wet, but I can't see without them." Finally, he turns on the water and hangs on for dear life.

The Professor ends his day by going just around the corner to the chapel. Here, in his pajamas and robe, he shuffles up the aisle saying his rosary. When he reaches the altar, he reverses course and walks backwards so as not to turn his back on the tabernacle. Near the last pew, he catches sight of two columns on either side of the aisle—his prompt to start forward again. "Chic Sheedy was a prefect on the third floor," he says. "It was he who taught me to pray this way." Back and forth he goes in near total darkness until his rosary is finished. Then he says a final prayer kneeling before the statue of Mary. "Tonight I found a couple in there lovemaking in the second to the last pew, but that did not stop me. I still went straight to the Blessed Mother."

Before drifting off to sleep, he listens to the radio. Treating it like a new technology, he doesn't understand that if the AM/FM switch is in the wrong position, he can't get his favorite station.

[6]

Tradition

"OF COURSE, the stairways you people use going up and down the Main Building were forbidden in our day," the Professor was telling me. "We used the two back stairways. We were never allowed to go up the front steps."

"Well, that's still the tradition," I said. "You're not allowed to until after you've graduated."

"You people use the front steps all of the time."

"Not all of us!"

"Well, most of you."

"You're not forbidden, but if you want to follow the tradition—"

"If you want to follow the tradition, but tradition is out the window now."

Notre Dame was known for its traditions, but these days even here traditions were falling by the wayside.

One Sunday afternoon, I came to visit the Professor, only to find myself interrupting a serious discussion. He invited me to take a seat, and Father O'Neil, sitting on the bed, greeted me warmly in his strong Boston accent, then turned back to the Professor, who was rocking his big chair, clutching the armrests.

"Now right here, this is just what I'm talking about," the Professor said, picking up a wrinkled leaflet and waving it in Father O'Neil's direction. "And I want you to explain it all to me, every bit. This is the missal for the Mass you said a few days

37

ago in memory of George Shuster. This thing calls it a 'memorial *liturgy*.' Now just what is that, Dan, this 'liturgy' thing?"

"It's simply another name for the Mass, Paul. The liturgy is our coming together as a community to pray, to celebrate the sacrifice of the Mass."

"Yes," said the Professor, sensing he was finally making headway. "It's Mass. But why don't they just call it that? Now I've gone to Mass my entire life, Dan, but just within these past few years they've started calling it the 'liturgy,' and I don't like it. And while we are at it, there's something else I've noticed: what's happened to the Seven Deadly Sins? Why, these people today never even talk about the fear of God!"

"That's because the Church has taken a new slant on such things," Father O'Neil said, shifting on the bed as if to leave. "Today we think of a compassionate, loving God, loving one's neighbor as oneself. Oh, Paul, but don't you see? Love: that's where it's all at. That's the whole message of the Gospel. Love is why Christ came here. Love!"

"Well, we should just be thankful God forgives all our sins and allows us to pray to Him. 'Love this' and 'love that.' People nowadays use the word so often they don't even know what it means."

Father O'Neil rose, shook my hand, and said to the Professor: "I should probably be leaving now, Paul. I'll give you some time to talk to this young man. Goodbye."

"See you later, Dan," said the Professor. We listened as Father O'Neil's footsteps receded and the front door of the building squeaked open and then shut. The Professor sighed, smiled, shook his head. "Poor Father O'Neil. He's a very dear friend of mine, but sometimes we don't quite see eye to eye. We didn't agree today. That argument you came in the middle of is a common one between us, because we have such different views.

"And I think today Father O'Neil was tired. Did you see the way he was lying down on my bed? He's the only one I allow to do that. It's funny: Father Dan comes in here to visit, which is fine, and I'm getting ready to go someplace, but he says he just wants to lie down to take a rest. The next thing I know he's sound asleep for an hour or more. Now today he left earlier than usual. I don't know why. Maybe it's that 10:45 Mass he was in today, the 'liturgy' he enjoys so much. I suppose it's tiring marching around in all those processions they have, the incense, the length of the whole affair, but O'Neil loves it. I go to the 12:30 in the crypt, as you know."

"Have you ever gone to the daily masses here in Sorin?"

"No," said the Professor, lowering his voice to a whisper. "You see, they have *private* masses here. They have their own special group and they meet in secret in the rector's office. They sit on the floor in a circle, right on the floor! And there's our lovely chapel, empty always. I just don't understand it."

I suppressed my laughter and tried setting him straight: "Anyone can go to those masses, Professor. The only reason the masses are held in the rector's office is because so few go to daily mass that the chapel is just too big, too overwhelming. They prefer an informal little mass."

"I still wouldn't dream of going in there. I know one thing they do. With this 'informal' business they change the words of the Canon and make up things as they go along. That man tries to improve on what God said, what the Lord said, and that's not right."

Improvised prayers were one new aspect of worship ushered in by the Second Vatican Council (1962-65) a decade earlier. Whether or not the rector had the backing of Vatican II when he invited students to give sermons at Mass, the Professor didn't like that innovation either. Even so, he was adapting to change surprisingly well, I thought, considering his love of routine and advanced age. I never heard him rail against Vatican II or express an interest in going back to the old Latin Mass, as I'd heard a number of conservatives do. Granted, he did have to make adjustments to avoid what he regarded as the worst excesses of the reformers. This meant choosing his masses carefully and sometimes skipping one third of Mass to avoid the homily. It also meant blowing off some steam with friends. But so long as he could keep his private devotions—his rosaries, relics, and statues—he was happy.

Clerical dress was another sore point for him. He admired the oldest priest living in Corby for still wearing the entire panoply of the old clerical garb—the biretta hat, cape, and cassock. "Every morning he takes a walk from Corby to the South Dining Hall. In fact, we had an argument about birettas last night. Tom Stritch doesn't like the birettas, but I was arguing for them. And I said I think there are some boys at Notre Dame right now that have never even seen a biretta. Pop Farley used to put his on the back of his head."

By way of contrast, the Professor showed me the directory photo of a priest wearing a sport shirt unbuttoned to expose his chest. He had a mop of unkempt hair and appeared for all the world high on drugs. Another priest, the provost no less, wore stylish layman's clothing and drove a Mercedes around campus.

"What about their vows of poverty?" I asked.

The Professor smiled and leaned back in his chair. "We used to say the priests took the oath and the professors observed it. I once knew a very ambitious student who wanted to be a professor, and he asked me, 'Mr. Fenlon, how do I get a job at Notre Dame?' I told him, 'Work hard, get your degree, and be willing to live in poverty.'"

Church decoration was also a touchy subject. Leaving Sacred Heart one day, the Professor was asked by a visitor where the Stations of the Cross were. The Professor pointed to the gold crosses painted on the walls, then explained that the original Stations were large oil paintings that were removed in a recent renovation and distributed across campus. "They say the fourth floor of the Main Building is stacked with the beautiful Stations, one of which is in our hall, in our chapel. Taken from Sacred Heart!" Getting rid of the old pews and the cherubim and seraphim on the pillars was also a mistake, the Professor thought, though he did approve removing the old communion rail, pulpit, and high-backed chairs from the main altar.

This wave of modernization was spreading to our very doorstep, we learned one day. The Professor and I were getting ready for Mass when we heard voices in Sorin Chapel. There we found Father Jerry Wilson, the university's vice president for business affairs, Professor Robert Leader, an artist specializing in stained glass, and a third man talking among themselves. The Professor asked, "What are you doing to our chapel?" Leader seemed amused and stepped back to let the priest take the question. "We're going to replace the broken stained glass windows, Paul," said Father Wilson. The windows didn't look broken to the Professor, and he said so. Then he turned away, starting for Sacred Heart. "They think nothing of destroying it," he muttered.

Once the Professor had a chance to reflect, he decided the chapel would never be gutted so long as Father Wilson was in charge. But after what they had done to Sacred Heart, we were prepared to believe the wildest rumors about campus renovations, no matter how insensitive they might be. Father Green denied it, but could I really be so sure Cardinal O'Hara's famous confessional was not being used to store hymnals in Dillon? The very idea was "a disgrace," said the Professor. "But I have heard Father Hesburgh wants to take down Father Sorin's altar from Sacred Heart. He wouldn't fight for that but he would allow it to happen. Thankfully, George Shuster and Ned Joyce kept it there."

I didn't realize what was at stake in an overhaul of Sorin Chapel until the Professor gave me a tour of it one day. We started with what was familiar to us both. In the back corner was an ornate communion rail with kneelers and behind it a statue of the Virgin Mary on a pedestal, her eyes downcast. Next to it, on the back wall, was a painting of Veronica wiping the face of Jesus. This was the Sixth Station of the Cross, one of the Stations missing from Sacred Heart Church.

Turning up the main aisle, we walked past two posts that went floor to ceiling. "These big beams mark, I think, the end of the old chapel. This whole area in back I think just used to be part of a student's room at one time. My own room used to be bigger, I think, about the size of Charlie Phillips's room above me, but Cardinal O'Hara put in a wall by my bed so that he could make a little bathroom for himself between my room and the chapel. That also created my little vestibule. O'Hara set up a confessional in a doorway between this room and the back of the chapel. That's been filled in now for some years, but I remember coming in many nights when confessions would be going on right here in my vestibule. I would have to sneak in by tiptoe so that I wouldn't overhear what was being said."

We walked past a dozen shiny pews that creaked when you sat in them, echoing through the room. On one wall were wooden Stations of the Cross and on the other were the red stained glass windows.

"We have a beautiful chapel: these wonderful pews, the altar. They've changed other chapels into psychedelic lounges. Why, you can't even find the tabernacle. There aren't even any pews! We've got real Stations in our chapel, a real altar, too. We used to have two dreary little white altars up here," the Professor said as he approached the altar and turned around to look back at me in the middle of the pews. "One was where the one is now and the other was over to the left up front here, where our piano is now. Long ago, Sorin Hall had at least three priests and each needed an altar for daily mass—no concelebrated masses then. The altar we have today was donated by a man who built altars for a living. He had a son who lived here and died in the 1930s. So the father gave us all these beautiful things in memory of the son. You can read all about it on the plaque behind you."

The altar consisted of a wood table trimmed in gold and above it a matching canopy suspended from the ceiling. On the altar sat a tabernacle draped in white cloth and above it a crucifix. Behind the cross, dominating the entire altarpiece, was red drapery. In concession to Vatican II reforms, the actual altar used for Mass was a table set out from the original altar. It was covered by a white tablecloth with a vase of artificial flowers. On either side of the altar were doors leading to storage in the northwest turret. They were hung with matching drapery. The Professor pointed to one of them. "At one time there was a confessional through there. Now it's the sacristy. I hear they're turning it back into a confessional again—a good thing!"

Using both hands to brace himself, he held onto the top of the front pew to genuflect, then turned to leave, and I followed. Making his way back down the aisle, he glanced for a moment at the statue of Mary. At the back door, he dipped his hand in the stoup, crossed himself, and swatted the light switches, leaving me in the dark. "The boys never turn off our lights."

[7]

Starting Out (1896-1916)

FOR ALL THAT WENT ON during my visits to see the Professor, I remained focused on his stories. Visit after visit, he was taking me through a personal portrait gallery of Notre Dame history. It wasn't a continuous history or a comprehensive narrative, just a series of anecdotes in roughly chronological order. These chapters of memory weren't easy to date since they centered on people, not events, and he was prone to digress. As I say, he wasn't an historian; he didn't describe changes to campus in a systematic way. Instead, he did something more valuable: he introduced me to the colorful personalities who made Notre Dame the beloved place it was—the presidents, professors, priests, and students. Some of these men enjoyed national reputations but many were simply endearing local figures who gave the school its unique spirit.

Initially, I was more curious about them than the Professor's own experience as a student here, and I had no great interest in his life before Notre Dame. Yet as time passed he began volunteering more and more about those early years, and I came to appreciate the gentle Victorian world that gave birth to him. So this is where his series of formal reminiscences begins:

"My home address is 234 South Walnut, Blairsville, Pennsylvania. Father O'Neil says every small town has a Walnut Street, and we're no exception. I was born in the very same house. Dan

45

Fenlon was born in '59 and my mother, Rose McManus, was born in the last year of the war, '64. My mother was a big woman: six feet, 220 pounds. My father joked that he would have to grow taller or stand up straight to catch up with her. He was the same height as I. When I was rejected for World War I, they said I was 5 feet 11½ inches tall. I had two older brothers, twins. One died at six months, the other at a year. Then a sister was stillborn. I think this was the cause of my mother's gray hair. Then I was born, followed by my sisters, Mercedes and Sarah.

"I was born on a hot night on the very last day of July. I was not expected to live, of course. They said I looked like a withered prune. My father spoke to our wonderful family doctor, who, I suppose, brought half of Blairsville into the world. Father said, 'I'm Dan Fenlon and my wife just delivered.' The doctor said, 'Your wife needs to be with her mother now,' so he suggested that the two of us be sent off to see mother's mother. He told my father, 'Don't be surprised if you never see Paul again.' But I went with my mother to Woodstock, Illinois, and even at that age—I suppose I was three months old—the change in the air did me good, and I survived, though I was a frail little boy. They thought I wouldn't make it, just like the Army didn't in 1917. And now look! I am the oldest of our clan. I am the very last of the line, the end of the Fenlon blood.

"My first memory was as a six-year-old. We went to visit Aunt Pauline, my mother's sister, in Woodstock. I was playing on a steep slope at the back of the house and I fell. Later, I noticed a pain and a limp in my right leg. I was taken to a specialist in Chicago who was from Austria or Switzerland. They took me in, took off all my clothes, and strapped me down to a table. The doctor kept moving parts of my body all over the place as I was there screaming. He said I had tuberculosis of the bone. I had dislocated my leg because all of the lubricating fluid had drained out of the socket. Without fluid, my joint was just grinding itself up. I either had to submit to an operation or stay in bed for three months back home.

"So I was put in bed with my leg extended and connected by a string and pulley to the ceiling. The wraps were put on from my toe to my waist and connected at the end to the winch. Every three days or so, father added a pound of BB shot to a bag, which further extended the leg, allowing the fluid to get back in. I was so small that I kept slipping, so they had to strap me in under the armpits to stay upright. I remember my father carrying me to the bathroom all of the time.

"As I grew up, I had no real trouble walking, but now sometimes I have stiffness in my shins. Lolita Armour, the Armour meatpacking heiress, had the same condition as I did. She chose the operation and had a limp until her dying day.

"Because of my leg, I never went to school until I was nine. I couldn't get to school because it was a long walk and we didn't have a horse and buggy or, of course, a car. For my first three years, my mother tutored me. I could never kick a football or use my leg for much in sports, but my father built the famous Fenlon tennis court for me in our backyard. People used to come from everywhere to play on that court. My mother had fits the way it used to dig up the lawn, but I know that I survived and healed so well due to her prayers.

"There were sixteen in my high school class, and I can still name every one of them. I was the valedictorian. My valedictory address was one of the few speeches I ever gave in my life. It caused something of stir, because it was delivered by a Catholic in a very Protestant little town.

"After high school, a good friend and I wanted to go to Princeton. He attended the same high school with me and came from a wealthy family. But unlike that boy, we didn't have enough money to attend an expensive university. I don't know how my father got by with so little money, though of course he had stock in US Steel and I still receive the dividends to this day.

"I had never heard of Notre Dame until a cousin graduated in the class of 1910, Paul did, and Rupert graduated in the class of 1907 or '08, and that's the reason I'm here. I had no choice about coming to Notre Dame, you know. My father said, 'No. You went to a public high school, so now you must go to a Catholic college.' My father was a very pious man, a very good man. I had to get religion, so he sent me here, even though my mother didn't want me to come. She thought the only boys at Notre Dame were spoiled ruffians from Chicago sent here to be reformed. She knew such students well, because before she was married she taught for ten years in the Chicago public-school system.

"We didn't have any entrance exams to take, of course, before coming here. It wasn't very hard at all to get admitted. My sister Sarah, who later went to St. Mary's, never even completed high school. She played basketball there and then flunked out after a year.

"I remember my very first day here. My father and I had spent the night in South Bend at the old Oliver Hotel. The next morning we got on the street car, then walked the length of campus on a beautiful day. Standing on the porch of the Main Building—I didn't know who he was—was a priest who welcomed us and said, 'I'm Father John Cavanaugh.' The president of the university was just standing there in those days, apparently welcoming the students.

"I spent the night in the Main Building, but only one night. Since I've never had any brothers, I've never slept in the same bed with anyone in my entire life. I only ever shared a roommate my first night here as a freshman, then I moved into a single. I told my father I didn't want a roommate, so I went to see Father

Cavanaugh and told him, 'I don't like this room.' The president said, 'You'll have to tell me more about that.' And I said, 'No. No, I won't tell you!' For a little extra money, I signed up for Corby Hall.

"Father Cavanaugh was in the presidency here from 1905 until the year I graduated. He was a charming man. He bought the school's first car, a red Cadillac. He wanted to drive it himself, but first he had to learn. Before 'Cadillac Hall' was built for the car, it used to sit on the dirt floor of the old gym, which is now the art gallery. One famous day he backed out and went right through the wall. His beautiful sister frequently came to act as hostess for events like commencement, and she was alarmed whenever her brother was driving and would turn to talk to her without minding the road. Cavvy had many accidents because he was always letting go of the steering wheel.

"He always spoke about the dangers of Je-su-it-i-cal influence. Another time he was asked what the population of South Bend was. He replied, '30,000 whites and 30,000 Poles.'

"Yes, he was a very unusual man. After they made him, they threw away the mold.

"He gave flowery orations, which would not be as popular today as they were at the time. There is a story, which I can't authenticate, that he was giving the eulogy at the funeral of a sister of a student friend of his. At one moment, he tossed a rose from the pulpit and it landed perfectly on top of the coffin in the center aisle. He was much criticized at the time for it.

"Long ago, they had the Dante Collection all in one room, and that's where Father Cavanaugh used to store his liquor. I remember Paul Boehm used to work down there. One night, a reception was taking place at the same time as Cavanaugh was making a pick-up. He grabbed one of the bottles and put it under his arm, thinking he would walk away with it, but as he was walking, it dropped and smashed to pieces all over the floor. Boehm had been watching all this. Cavanaugh pretended that nothing had happened and calmly walked up to him and said, Mr. Boehm, I believe I dropped something back there. Would you please go pick it up?' He picked it up, but the liquor stank there for days.

"If there was a distinguished visitor or bishop or someone like that here, Father Cavanaugh would ring the bell and announce: 'My dear students, I have today the honor of breaking the bread with Right Reverend so and so or such and such a man. And he will lecture or he will talk to the student body in Washington Hall at two o'clock. All classes are dismissed for the afternoon.' We would clap and give him a big cheer. He would dismiss classes at the drop of a hat or even without the drop of a hat sometimes.

"On my first day of class, I went to see Father Schumacher, who handed me a card with my schedule on it: 'Breakfast— seven a.m. sharp. At 7:50-8:20 Christian Doctrine with Father Burke.' Burke always started class with something like, 'Last week I was in Gary …' and he would describe a confession he had heard: 'A little boy said to me, "Father, I have committed adultery." I said, "You couldn't have done that. What did you actually do?" The boy said, "I pissed on the side of a church."' I thought this was very funny at the time, and Father Burke repeated the story over and over again.

"The rest of my classes were an hour long: 8:20-9:20, 9:20-10:20, and so on. Bells were ringing all the time for classes.

"I had Professor Hines for Ancient History at 1:20. He was one of the very few laymen who taught here—the rest were priests. On the first day of class, I sat next to my great friend 'Stretch' O'Connor, since we weren't sitting in alphabetical order. Hines walked into the classroom without saying a word, scribbled a few words on the board and accidentally, it seemed, dropped his chalk. He picked it up, wrote a few more words, and dropped the chalk again. At this point, Stretch whispered to me, 'I think we've made a mistake.' We thought he had palsy or something. Hines picked up his chalk, wrote some more, and dropped it a third time. He then turned around to face the class for the first time and said, 'Just so does history repeat itself, gentlemen.' I was so impressed—as were the others—that I remember it very well and fondly to this day.

"You know, Stretch was really my best friend from the class. I used to visit him every year in Erie before he died not long ago. He lived on the first floor of Walsh looking out at Badin. Of course, Walsh was a part of the Gold Coast then. It had just been built in 1909 and had suites and built-in closets. On the north end of the basement they had a real bowling alley. They charged—what, twenty-five cents?—to play.

"Stretch had come to Notre Dame as a prep. The preps and minims kept the school going for a while, because they brought in so much more money than the college did. The minims were sixth to eighth grade. The preps were four years and then the four years in college, and if they succeeded in living through all that, they were called 'lifers.' We had rich young boys here then.

"I had English with Father Crumley at 2:20. Crumley lived on the first floor of the Main Building and always walked into class with wrinkles on the side of his face. That's when I first learned that you could never find a CSC in the afternoon, because they all had their naps. Crumley walked around the corner straight into our classroom, right from his bed. He came in and very carefully reached into a little pocket at the belt level of his cassock. He'd get out a very small pencil and take roll so slowly, so carefully, '... Mr. Fenlon, Mr. Fitzpatrick ....' It took him fifteen minutes just to call roll.

"Then John McGinn taught me my philosophy. One day I

remember a boy in the front row sneezing. McGinn stopped his lecture immediately and pointed at the poor boy and, with that whiskey tenor voice of his, said, 'You're never nearer death than when you sneeze. Remember that!' Then back to logic he went. We enjoyed McGinn. I remember him approaching me after class one day and asking if I would be his corrector. I said, 'Father, how could I? I've never even been able to understand *your* logic in this class!' And he said all I'd have to do was look at his answer key and go down the list, and he'd tell the people in the Main Building to knock fifty dollars off my tuition.

"In those days, we had each class four hours a week. We met Monday, Tuesday, Wednesday, Friday. Twice a week we had to go to the big church for Mass, on Thursdays and Saturdays. Thursdays were our free days, but we also had 'military' every Thursday morning. We marched around with our guns on our shoulders with the officers yelling out, 'Squad, right!' and other things that I never knew. The seniors acted as student captains. We also drilled on Friday in the early afternoon, so on Fridays our classes ran late, almost until five o'clock.

"I used to go into town on Thursdays. It was before Prohibition, and we would go down to the bar of the plush Oliver Hotel. Some of my friends were real drinkers, but I hadn't had a thing in my life. I was going to try and learn to drink beer, but I never have liked it. We also went to the bar to see the nude behind the bar, a thing none of us had ever seen before. All the bars in those days had a nude lady behind the bar. It was the style, until nudes were later replaced by mirrors in such establishments. Of course, you have to remember, it was all a different age then.

"We went to classes on Saturday until three p.m., unless there was a football game or something, then we got off, though there were very few home games. Football was not a big thing in those days—as it is today—before Rockne. I remember one

Saturday I was in South Bend at the Orpheum—it's no longer there—watching the vaudeville when the public address system announced that we had just beaten Creighton in a home game. And we really didn't care, even though Creighton was one of our big rivals then.

"In the spring of that year the Easter Rebellion took place. We were taken out of class—all that had to be done in those days to get everyone together was to ring a bell—and we assembled near the statue of the Sacred Heart. Con Hagerty was furious about news of the whole affair. He planted a little tree there, which of course died soon afterwards. Then he said some prayers and gave a little talk, but I didn't attend, because I didn't like Con for such Irish favoritism. I don't like the Irish and I've never kept it a secret. I guess that's why I took so little interest in William Butler Yeats when he came to Notre Dame. I didn't meet him or even go to any of his lectures."

[8]

Wheat from Chaff

ONE DAY I WALKED in on the Professor during a conversation he was having with a young man who seemed too old and well-dressed to be a student. "Oh, I'm sorry, Professor," I said. "I'll come back another time."

"No, Phil," he said. "We were just saying goodbye." The visitor rose from his chair and shook the Professor's hand, but the Professor didn't want to let go. Finally, he released his grip and raised himself from his seat to escort the man out. The Professor had tears in his eyes. I stepped aside to make way for them. The Professor then called out to him in the vestibule, just as he had done so often to me. They chatted another minute, then the Professor returned to his room and sat down with me.

He spoke softly, his eyes still glistening. His friend, he explained, graduated five years ago. He worked at the university for a time, then went to graduate school, but had just flunked out. He was leaving in the morning for Chicago to look for a job, hoping to capitalize on his Notre Dame connections.

Until this moment, I had considered myself the surest friend the Professor had in Sorin, but now came along another student who was clearly much closer to him. It got me to wondering just where everyone stood in relation to the Professor. If I had to guess, a solid half dozen of us visited him regularly and knew him best. Another five or ten students visited him in special circumstances.

55

Another ten were quite friendly with him and he called them by name. Perhaps twenty-five were just polite acquaintances. You could count on them to say "Hey, Professor" in the hallway or stop to ask how he was doing. Then there were eighty or so—half the hall—who were aware of him but indifferent. Twenty probably disliked him but didn't go out of their way to show it. That left a gang of a half dozen hardliners who wanted him out of Sorin and would act up in order to provoke him.

That he had these enemies was a surprise to me. When I first arrived in Sorin, I had assumed the Professor was a revered figure on campus and universally loved, but after a few months here I understood that some students couldn't stand him because he put a crimp in their style. For his part, the Professor thought they hadn't been raised properly: "I think we should go back to being a prep school," he said, "and teach some things like manners." When my friends and I admitted we weren't very pleased with the state of discipline either, he asked, "Why don't you band together to put a stop to it?" None of us was ready to go that far, we told him. It would mean social death for us.

The geography of the hall favored the Professor, shielding him from some of the misbehavior. His room had buffers on all sides—the chapel, the vestibule, the rector's room. However, he had no protection above or below his room. "The second floor has always been the worst, *always!*" he said. To prevent a troublemaker from ever living above him, he had the rector agree to restrict room 241 to RAs only, in the belief that staff could be trusted to behave. Yet the new RA dropped a wall bed into position every night at one a.m., resulting in a tremendous crash. One evening the Professor investigated some commotion and found three students, including this same second-floor RA, yelling in delight as they bounced a rubber ball against the foot of the stairway. The Professor calmly asked the main culprit, "What are you doing?" The student looked embarrassed. "Playing with a ball," he replied. The Professor put out his hand: "Give me the ball or leave." They left.

Over time, the Professor had worked out an uneasy truce with the basement. Whenever the noise rose to an unacceptable level, he pulled out his weighty letter opener to bang on a set of pipes that ran the height of the building from 341, down through his room, and into the basement. This usually brought "those obstreperous boys" to heel. At other times they gave *him* warning. "The boys just below in room 41 informed me they were having a Wapatula party tonight. I said, 'Alright, until two a.m., but if I see my pipes rattling, I'm phoning Security to quiet you.'"

So long as the Professor insisted that his watches keep good time, he had two choices: either wait for us to help him or search the hall for "someone who at least looks civilized." One evening, he tired of waiting on us, left his room, and screened several students. "There was an uncivilized bunch at the end of the hall that I wouldn't even let near this room," he said. At last an unfamiliar student greeted him, the Professor took a chance, and the watches got wound. Another night, the only person he could find was someone he had nicknamed "the Gangster," who told him the rest of us were at the library. The Professor refused to say another word to him, much less ask for help.

These skirmishes might not seem like much, but they wore on the Professor's nerves. It was plain to see that he savored his orderly life, and until the last decade or so, he had had his way— the place had been run like a boot camp. But now he had to live with a cohort of students brazen in pursuit of their freedoms and pleasures, while the university exercised minimal supervision over them. He was the only thing standing in their way, and he refused to be a prisoner in his own room.

In his defense, the Professor could actually be very reasonable, even tolerant. He didn't particularly care what went on behind closed doors so long as the building was quiet, his own room and its contents were safe, and the public spaces weren't vandalized. The sex and the drugs didn't seem to bother him; it was the rock 'n' roll—the noise.

One day he caught my friends snickering at one of his highly colored accounts of Sorinites behaving badly. "Don't be so sure that you have passed my test!" he said, before bursting into laughter. Yes, "the test": we had passed it alright. We were all aware that in the months we had known him, the Professor was busy separating the wheat from the chaff, and now he had put us at the front of the class—teacher's pets. "These days I don't know too many of the boys, except you fellows," he told us. "I like talking to you because you always have interesting things to say. They say they get the cream of the crop here now, but I don't think so. Some of you men are good, but the others don't belong here."

In many ways, we didn't have to do much to impress the Professor. I remember he offered me some chocolates one evening, and I declined, saying I had given up sweets for Lent. Now I'm sure half the campus was observing Lent in a similar way, but he gushed, "I haven't seen boys like you or your friends for quite a while. You're amazing."

We were certainly a contrast to rougher elements in the hall, but we weren't saints either. The day Notre Dame upset an undefeated University of San Francisco basketball team, we tried explaining what a food fight was to him, describing how after any great sports victory, students threw food at each other in the Dining Hall, ducking for cover under the tables. This happened after the Alabama football and UCLA basketball games last fall, and now the USF game. This evening one brave soul donned a pith helmet in the middle of the free-for-all, then stood on a table and spread his arms calling for a cease-fire. Instantly, he was splattered by food hurled from a hundred directions.

The Professor was horrified. I showed him evidence of cottage cheese on my sweater and jeans, and he was disappointed we could get caught up in something like that. "I'm surprised," he said solemnly.

[9]

Grand Tour

ON A VISIT ONE DAY I was startled to find the Professor struggling to put on his sweater. His arms were waving in the air and I cold just see the top of his head trapped under his cardigan.

"Need some help with that, Professor?"

"Oh! Who is that? Phil, is that you? Yes, just pull this thing over my head. It's been buttoned, but it's easier to get on that way. Just slip it over my head. That's it, *there*. Whew! Thanks. How's my hair?"

He looked like a mad professor with long white strands standing on end.

"It's a little messed up."

The Professor pressed his hair flat, then asked for his glasses. I grabbed them from the couch in the sheet room. He smiled.

"Are you going somewhere?" I asked.

"Yes. I am going for a walk around the hall. My walks are good for me. Besides, today is special. Once a year I make it a point to get back up to my old rooms on the third floor, once a year, no more and no less. At my age, I'm afraid this might be my last visit up there. Say, would you like to come along?"

"Of course I would. We could have tea in my room. We've talked about doing that all semester, right?"

And so we met up again in the afternoon, setting out from the sheet room, then climbing the stairs, side by side. We stopped on the first landing for a breather, just halfway to the second floor. "A man by the name of Vurpillat succeeded Colonel Hoynes as law dean," the Professor said, "and there was a man by the name of Howard, Judge Howard, a very distinguished-looking man. The pictures of all those people used to line the walls, then they threw them all out or stored them someplace. They used to be up and down both stairwells." We climbed another flight, then stopped on the second floor. "Well, this floor hasn't changed much in a year. It still looks like a common tenement house," he said, standing beneath a bare light bulb, all that remained of the exit sign. The Professor pointed his cane to the right, towards the 215 turret room. "That room was always where the floor prefect lived, but for many years my dear friend Mr. Byrne, our librarian, lived there." The south wing was "a good neighborhood," but the Professor headed in the opposite direction until he stopped at the room directly above his own. "This alley," he said, "was the 'Professors' Alley,' though I never lived here." We strolled down the corridor, the Professor tapping on each door with his cane as he named the bachelor don who once lived there.

Then we trudged up the stairway again. The Professor stopped and fingered his ear, grimacing. "It's the altitude. This height is stuffing my ears up. The popping—ohh, ohh! Let's have tea now in your room. Is that alright?"

All three of my roommates were at home. They were surprised to see the Professor and just as excited as I was by his visit. After greeting him, Paul went back to the connecting room, Bart stayed in the doorway to watch, and Tom joined us for tea.

"Now where do you want me to sit? I want some of your tea," the Professor said.

"Why don't you take this chair," I said, offering a chair in the spot created by removing the trash can between my desk and the sink. I sat on the lower bunk. Several students gathering outside the doorway peeked in, not bothering to whisper.

"The Professor's up here!"

"Look in there. Is that him?"

"How'd he get up here?"

"What are they *doing*?"

The stereo next door began to play. With the Professor distracted by something else, Tom asked me, "Do you recognize the tune? The '1812 Overture'—Paul's perverse idea of humor." I told the Professor the music was a reference to his age. "You're not that Victorian are you?" I asked.

"No," he laughed. "No, I'm not."

"Napoleonic, actually," Tom said under his breath.

I asked about a story in Francis Wallace's book, *Notre Dame: People and Legends*. "Was there actually someone who stood on the Golden Dome playing a coronet on St. Patrick's Day?"

"I never got inside of the dome, though I had a chance when it was being re-gilded. I like and know Wallace quite well, but not all of his book is truthful. I'd apply one of my favorite sayings to him: he won't let the facts get in the way of a good story."

Tea lasted forty-five minutes, and then the Professor said, "It's getting late and I want to see my rooms. I've enjoyed your hospitality very much. My ears have popped open, too." With that, he gave a loud clap of the hands, and we got up to leave.

He led me a few doors down, then stopped. "Of course, here is my first room in Sorin Hall. I enjoyed living in the front of the house, too. Say, is anybody home? Oh, yes, well hello there."

"How're ya doin', Professor," said the incumbent of room 327.

"Fine, thank you. You know this is where I lived when I was a student, the room you're in right now."

"You're kiddin'! You were a student here? How long ago was that?"

"Oh, a hundred years ago. You have a nice room here, a good view. Now I want you to take good care of that room. Alright?"

"Sure, Professor, anything you say."

"Good! Well, I've got to be going. I'm giving this gentleman a tour of our hall."

"See you later, Professor. Come back up here again some time."

We made our way past the broken water fountain and around the corner to the Professor's old tower room.

The door to 355 was swung wide open, either that or removed from its hinges altogether. The Professor found a spot on the doorframe to knock. Three students stretching out on couches looked up from the television.

"Excuse me," said the Professor. "I hope I'm not interrupting you. This was once my room. I come up here every so often just to see how it looks. Say, don't you have any beds in here?" The three jumped up to welcome him and explain they were using the turret room as their lounge and had their bedroom next door. The Professor approved of this setup, which was identical to his own decades ago, but he was mortified by the condition of the room. Invited to sit down, he said, "Oh, no. I don't need to do that. I wouldn't want to disturb you boys and it's getting late."

Back in the hallway, looking out at the fire escape, he said, "I remember many nights dangling my feet off this fire escape, relaxing. It hasn't changed since my day, except we didn't have the ladder part to it. I don't know how they expected us to get down."

The Professor did well getting back to the first floor, refusing my arm so that he could test his own mobility. Later, in the evening, I encouraged him to come upstairs for another visit this year. "Not this week," he said. "I doubt if I can this semester." I persisted. "We'll see," he said. "Now go to bed. You must get your sleep. Good night. Be gone, be gone!"

The Professor never gave me a formal tour of his current room; he didn't need to—I knew all its quirks by now. There was the false fireplace he'd inherited from his old friend Charlie Phillips. Near it was a room divider that gave him privacy whenever he was at the medicine cabinet with his back to guests. This curtained partition doubled as a tie rack, and was another legacy of Phillips. "Charlie put it on one side of the fireplace. I'm not sure why he put it in such an odd place, except that once I think I heard him say the artificial firelight bothered his eyes."

Some strange things turned up in that room. Once, I found a shot put and a baseball bat in a dusty spot behind the door. "They've been here for a hundred years," the Professor said. "I'm always meaning to get rid of them but keep them in case I have to fight off any intruders." The idea of the Professor defending himself, especially with the shot put, which he couldn't even lift, was far-fetched, if not preposterous, yet he was always concerned with security. After a dog wandered into his room one day and he had to yell for help, he vowed to keep one of his two doors, and both chapel doors, closed at all times.

More than once, he said, "Why, we could all be murdered in our beds! We're the only hall on campus with the doors wide open twenty-four hours a day." One blustery evening, he left his room to shut them six times.

That phantom intruder of the Professor's imagination wouldn't find much worth taking. An oversized pipe might catch his attention. "This was a recent gift from Father Burtchaell. He's threatened to come over here and smoke it sometime." With the exception of his books and personal effects, the Professor's most prized possessions are of sentimental value only. There are framed drawings, poems, and photographs on the walls, and pictures of his parents, sisters, and grandnephew on his desk and fireplace. Elsewhere, including his dressers and window sills, I recognize photos of John Towner Frederick, Charlie Phillips, both president Cavanaughs, Father O'Neil, Father Kerndt Healy, and a score of former students and their families. His mother's photograph is the largest in the room, in the center of his desk, behind the blotter, a black-and-white oval with red matting in a gold frame. She is posing in profile, her head bowed demurely.

These pictures aren't the only way the Professor remembers those dear to him. On a notepad, he's scribbled the death date of one friend, "29 April 1976—T. Bowyer Campbell," and funeral cards are strewn across his desk. Pointing to one, he says, "Four days past his eightieth birthday, Father Charles Miltner was at a dinner party speaking about how life begins at eighty, and Miltner dropped dead right there in the middle of the talk." The Professor is so conscientious about observing anniversaries like Miltner's that he has what amounts to a shadow church calendar. At daily mass he prays for the friend of the day in addition to the official saint of the day. In this sense, he works just as hard keeping up with his friends after their deaths as he does during their lifetimes. For him, friends may die, but friendships never do.

There was more to learn about his friends, I thought, if only I could do a proper interview with him. I approached him again on this prickly subject, knowing well his aversion not just to interviews but to microphones of all kinds, including the small, toy-like cassette recorder I once showed him. He looked upon this device like a prisoner might regard an instrument of torture laid out to terrorize him into a confession. At first he was evasive about an interview and spoke only in parables. He reminded me that Father Matthew Walsh, Notre Dame's president from 1922 to 1928, also disliked being recorded. Walsh was famous for his powers of memory, the Professor told me. "One night Moose

Krause decided to put a tape recorder under the dinner table, but Walsh spotted it right away. He didn't like the idea of being double-crossed, so he got up from the table and walked right out of the house."

For several days, as the semester drew to a close, we negotiated. "What exactly are you going to do with this?" he asked.

"I want to write a history of the hall. Every hall on campus ought to have its history written up, right, especially ours?" This finally satisfied him, so we met in his room one evening. He was nervous and gave the impression he was consenting to this imposition only as a great personal favor to me. I set down my tape recorder in front of him and snapped the *record* key into position.

Sure enough, he counted the minutes until the ordeal was over, but I judged the interview a success, pulling in a trove of new details. However, the most revealing thing he said to me before I left for the summer came during one of our regular visits, not while the tape was rolling. I certainly didn't feel I knew him well enough, or it was any of my business, to ask a question like, Why have you remained a bachelor all your life? Yet I did have the impudence to say, "You're 'Professor Fenlon' but not 'Dr. Fenlon,' isn't that right?"

"No, I am not a doctor, don't want to be one, and never will be. In my day one didn't need a PhD to teach here. I was here for four years, then I earned my master's degree here in '22, I think—I've forgotten."

"Have you done much writing or research?"

"No, I haven't. I haven't published a thing in my life," he said triumphantly.

"What about 'publish or perish?'"

"Well, I haven't perished, have I?"

$\left[10\right]$

Wartime (1916-19)

IN THE NEXT INSTALLMENT of his reminiscences, the Professor continued with his early life—his student days in the shadow of World War I:

"Colonel Hoynes was one of the first professors-in-residence at Sorin. He was here long before I was a freshman; he taught my cousins, both of whom graduated in law. He lived in the rooms across from the rector, on your left as you enter the building. We used to look straight into his room through the window on the porch, while we waited for the night watchman to lock up the building at ten o'clock or to let late students in after being out at a play. We used to see the Colonel sitting in that room at night, with that cord light down from the ceiling, and he'd sit in the middle of the room. He did nothing but read the dictionary with a big magnifying glass.

"I don't suppose I would have liked the Colonel if I had made a point of meeting him when I was a student. I never entered his quarters, of course. He was an old man to us; we would never think of approaching him; we had no cause to say a word to him. We thought he was much older than he actually was, and he was treated with much more respect than these boys today give. You people, you see, are much bolder than we were. We were raised differently.

"It was said of him, 'few knew him, but all loved him.' Hoynes

never lowered his dignity. He was just a little drummer boy in
the war, you know, but he played the role of 'colonel' to the nth
degree. He wasn't actually a real colonel, but he just earned the
title out of respect and love.

"The students got a real kick out of Colonel Hoynes. He
was sort of a legend, a character. He dressed rather shabbily and
he had a funny little walk and then he'd always say, shaking his
head, 'Gentlemen, gentlemen, good afternoon. Gentlemen, gentlemen, good afternoon.' And he'd come out on the porch and
everyone would say, 'Yeahhh, the Colonel!' 'Good afternoon,
good afternoon.' They used to show movies in Washington Hall,
and Hoynes would stand up, doff his cap, and take a bow. But I
remember one day before class the boys put butter on his seat.
Colonel Hoynes sat on it and from that day on, every time he sat
at the head table for a meal, he would pull the chair out all the
way and brush it off clean. Poor old Colonel Hoynes.

"The law school where he taught was just a few steps from his
own room. The law classroom was one large room that stretched
from the tower room all the way down to practically where your
post office is now, and then that room there, with the room next
to it, was the law library. That was all they had. And it was most
distracting when classes were going on. A boy would come in
and would have to walk the full length of that room to find an
area to study in the law library or to get the books that had the
cases he had to read. I have a law degree as well as an AB degree,
remember, so I sat in there and took some law.

"Later, the law school was moved out of Sorin over there to
the law building that was named after Hoynes, what is now called
the Crowley School of Music. I think they were attempting here
what was done at Oxford, where they have their rooms, kitchen,
dining hall, library, and classrooms all in a single building. They
tried that at Sorin with the law rooms and had planned to do the

same thing with an English classroom, but it did not work out at all. The experiment with single rooms succeeded, but after a few years with the law classroom, that whole idea failed, I think. They found out you just couldn't do that here.

"Maurice Francis Egan was a lot like the Colonel, very polite and, oh, so courteous. 'Oh, yes, sir! Yes, sir!' Freshman year I used to visit some friends who lived at Maurice Francis Egan's old house on Notre Dame Avenue called 'the Lilacs.' The loveliest row of lilacs stood in front of that house. For really the first time in Notre Dame's history, there wasn't enough room on campus for everybody, so President Cavanaugh chose a dozen or so students to rent Professor Egan's old house. 'The Lilacs' they were called. A grander bunch of guys never existed.

"Egan was a very short, undistinguished-looking man, but he knew TR. He got an appointment from Teddy Roosevelt as ambassador to Denmark. Then someone died in Europe and Egan became the dean of US ambassadors, which amazed everyone, of course. He was the oldest one over there, so he headed all of the ceremonies, all of the line-ups. He came back here in the spring of my freshman year and they honored him with a ceremony over in Washington Hall. He always wore a frock coat, and I remember him walking across the stage holding a silken hat. He talked in a very low voice and had a moustache or a beard. I really didn't know anything about him, so wasn't terribly impressed by the whole thing.

"The story I remember was one that Father Eugene Burke was fond of telling about him. You see, Father Burke had Egan as a professor in an English class, I think it was. Of course, from the front Egan was meticulously dressed with his frock coat and he greeted all the students very formally. Then one day he turned his back to the class to write on the blackboard. When he stretched to write, you saw the vent in the back of his Prince

Albert expose his back trouser pocket. It had a hole half the size of New York. You saw all the way to his underwear.

"Because I lived in Corby, we were all assigned to Father Scherer the Latin teacher to hear our confessions. No matter what sin you confessed, halfway through your Act of Contrition he would slide the door, saying, 'Say one Hail Mary, one Our Father, and one Act of Contrition.' We always thought about going to him and saying, 'Father, I killed a man and a woman.' Today Father Carey is my only confessor. I've outlived all of the others like Pop Steiner and for years Father Scherer.

"All of us in Corby were waiting until we were juniors so we could move into Sorin Hall, but we got there early. Once the war broke out in April, President Cavanaugh announced that seniors who enlisted before commencement would be exempt from exams and graduate immediately. About a third of Sorin vacated to the officer training camp at Fort Benjamin Harrison in Indianapolis. I lived in 327 Sorin for just over two years—my junior, senior, and part of my sophomore year. It was the room of Matt Trudelle, a nice enough fellow in architecture who ended up surviving the war. I was never so shocked as when I first went into my new room to find a man I recognized as a Brother cleaning it. Men used to work as the maids or janitors here. 'Aren't you a Brother?' I asked. 'Yes, I am, but I'm not wearing my cassock. It can't stand the dust,' he said. 'Neither can I,' I said. 'This is ridiculous!' This Brother died that same year of tuberculosis.

"After the war broke out, I was sent to Allentown, Pennsylvania for military duty and I was classified 4F. At the physical, the doctors simply told me to leave—bad eyes, bad feet, bad heart, and bad everything else.

"When I first lived in Sorin, Father Gene Burke had his famous song, 'The Ten o'clock Walk.' After our showers, we walked down at ten o'clock to fill up the pitchers and put them on the radiators so the water would be warm in the morning for shaving. That went on until we got our own sinks. The song was part of a musical comedy that the boys put on, in which Charlie Macaulay played the role of a girl and so did Tom Beacom.

"When I was a sophomore or junior, I went into South Bend to see one of the most famous actresses of our day, Sarah Bernhardt. I forget the name of the play but know it was French, because she always was in French plays. She never said a word of English, and we didn't understand French, but she was wonderful. She had one leg amputated at the knee, so she never moved on stage. She always stood to the side with the half leg on a crate and the good one standing. That's how she said her lines.

"Father Crumley would always dismiss us from class for something like Sarah Bernhardt or Shakespeare, providing we would show the stub of the ticket the next day. But we went to some play during Lent, and we were not allowed to go to the theatre in Lent, and we were discovered. So the rector gathered all of us together in the law classroom and we had to write out so many lines so many hundred times.

"After my junior year, we came back in September to find that the Army had taken us over. The military took over this hall and Corby for the ROTC, which was very poorly managed. Those of us who couldn't stay in either one of these halls—like me—were moved into Walsh Hall, which was almost vacant because the enrollment was cut down terrifically. I lived on the fourth floor of Walsh from September to Armistice Day, or rather until December, 1918. I was only away from Sorin for those few months. The war, you know, had scarcely begun before it was over.

"I remember Armistice Day. The bells were all ringing at 'the eleventh hour of the eleventh day of the eleventh month.' We had a false alarm a few days earlier, so this time we weren't sure it was for real. We had no idea the war was really coming to an end. We went to bed and the next morning—bells! We all went downtown to go drinking and dancing. I was old enough legally. That day we all raised hell at the Oliver Hotel and nobody could stop us. I remember Father Farley arrived at the Oliver and joined in the fun.

"That was undoubtedly one of the most wasteful semesters I ever put in. It must have been awful for the teachers. In the middle of class a bugle would blow and anyone in uniform—and most of us were, except those of us like me who could not pass the tests—would have to get up and leave, no matter what. We had Father John McGinn in Logic, and I can still see him waving, 'Go on, get out. And the rest of you, follow!'

"One day in early December, we all crowded around President Cavanaugh as he posted the announcement that Notre Dame was shutting down within forty-eight hours. Classes would start up again the first week of January, 1919, and I could move back from Walsh to my old room in Sorin. Father Cavanaugh assured us that despite all the missed class time and the fact the war class was so small—less than a hundred of us—we would all still graduate. I think we were the only class not to have our own yearbook.

"I remember one of my last classes. We used to have to take psychology, which I disliked, but all the seniors waited for Professor Z's last class lecture, when he explained the facts of life. He taught before the mandatory retirement law was in effect, but later he was asked to retire, which made him quite angry, so he left to teach at St. Mary's, then went out West. He came back to South Bend when he was well in his eighties. He was not liked by his family, but he came to stay with a daughter here. When he got off the plane, he said, 'I've come to die.' The next day, he was found dead. Because of his knowledge of medicine, some people imagined he had not died of natural causes."

$\left[\,11\,\right]$

Father O'Neil

AFTER MY FRESHMAN YEAR finished up and I was back in Florida, I wrote the Professor. His reply was typed on a five-by-eight sheet of note paper, single-spaced, and mailed in an envelope with the stamp upside down. On every page, the *es*, *rs*, and *os* fell out of alignment, almost touching the next row of type, and words were cut off on the right margin because he typed off the paper onto the typewriter roller. He used lots of abbreviations and ended sentences with ellipses.

His correspondence was one of a kind and conveyed his light-hearted charm as nothing else could. The letters were the man.

"Dear Phil: What a nice surprise! Delighted with your letter and I shall try a reply today—but it is so damned cold here the old fingers refuse to type too much ... The reunion was most enjoyable although by this time you know I didn't see your respected father." Dropping off an alum at the Amtrak station, he slipped on the curb, fell, and "shook for hrs. afterward as that was the ONE thing I feared all this past yr. ... but the Lord was good ... just a bit of a bruise on delicate part of my anatomy ...

"Now for a few notes: O'Neil went up to Mayos last Fri ... as yet nothing too definite but no surgery as he feared since the M. D. from S. B. had thought necessary. Dan O'N. may be back tomorrow ...

75

"Thanks so much for the pictures, one good other too much of my scrawny neck, but they're nestled away with other two you gave me.

"I was all ALONE in this cold hall for five days, locked in. ... Janitor here every day so he winds the watches every morn when he comes in to see if I am still alive. ...

"Graduation came off splendidly here—such mobs to see that Jimmy C. ..." The Professor was listening to President Carter's commencement address when he received a call "telling me that my good friend Harry Conley (knew him since 1914) had died in Green Bay, Wis. ... which sent me into an emotional upset... But I am going with the Dunns of Morris, Ill. next Thurs. to Minn. for long week-end with friends there. Then back here for about a wk. getting rested and off to Pennsy around 23-25 June."

He continued typing on another sheet of paper: "Will start this page (I vow never to write more than ONE page so see what you do to me). ... One last thing: yesterday I did, as you suggested, see Father Blantz." Rev. Thomas E. Blantz, CSC, I should explain, taught in the History Department and had held a number of administrative posts at the university, including his present one as university archivist. He was my academic adviser and I saw quite a bit of him when I poked around in the archives researching Sorin Hall. Father Blantz was writing a book about George Shuster and encouraging the Professor to share his Shuster correspondence.

As the Professor closed his letter to me, he added, "Father B. likes your idea of a history on each hall. Don't check this for mistakes ... you're damned lucky to get a reply so soon but you're a good fellow, did much for me this past term and I'm eternally grateful ... Bestus always." The letter was signed "Paul" in a bold hand, underlined. "Bestus" was not a typographical error but a made-up Latin word he used to match the Latinized form of his name. "For years," he once said, "men like Stritch have called me 'Paulus.'" I didn't know what to make of his use of his first name; I would never dream of addressing him as "Paul" and he knew that.

The real news in the letter was Father O'Neil's failing health. In the spring, I had heard he was sick, never imagining it was anything more than the flu. In his next letter to me, the Professor noted an ominous silence: "Not a single word as yet from Father O'Neil—he told me when he left he doesn't write much, true as I've found so I sent off a line to his faithful sec. to see if she has any word." He quoted Mr. Stritch as saying, "no one in or around campus has heard from O'Neil."

For now, Father O'Neil's illness was just a speck on the horizon. None of us realized that one day it would grow into a storm powerful enough to blow the Professor away. Who could have imagined?

Unaware of just how serious that illness would later become, the Professor continued blithely with this second letter, commending my work on a "hall lecture tour," a room-by-room account of the history of Sorin. "I told Father Greg that I thought you had a great idea and should be encouraged to go on with it," he wrote, before commenting on two newspaper clippings he'd enclosed. One was Red Smith's *New York Times* column reporting on last month's reunion. "'Red' Smith as you probably know is one of best sports writers in US. He was back for his 50th. I didn't have him as a Fresh but he's friend of mine and we had drinks together." The other clipping described halfback Al Hunter taking Notre Dame to court for suspending him from the team. "Silly to think he can sue the 'U' … Father Ted is sticking to his guns." The letter ended by asking me to "keep the faith as well as your English time on watch … did I tell you my digital still on SB time … my niece winds my watches for me … Regards to your Dad … I shall be charmed to meet more Hicks."

The Professor would have his chance to meet more of my family soon enough, because my brother Andy had just been accepted to Notre Dame and would be living in Howard Hall. I'd remain in Sorin, of course, and had done well enough in the room lottery to get the southwest turret in 301, the former home of Four Horseman Don Miller.

I returned to campus in August before the Professor got back from Pennsylvania, and who should I run into but Father O'Neil, the subject of so much concern. He didn't look ill; in fact, he seemed his usual upbeat self. When we spoke, he was disarmingly frank considering I had never spent any time alone with him before. "I know Paul the best of anyone," he said. "We travel together, you know. I used to laugh at all his fears; he was always prepared for death. Now he sees me, a man in the best of health, full of disease, so that has been hard for him to accept. I think my illness disturbs him so much, because I had never been sick a day in my life and now this."

I nodded politely. It was clear he had more to say, and I was all ears as he then addressed the Professor's health: "He is too frail to be living on this campus, you know. I doubt he'll be back this year—he *shouldn't* come back. When he finally does leave Sorin for good, I don't know who is going to move all of his things out of his room. I don't want to have to do it."

All this surprised and confused me. Was I being asked to clear out the Professor's room? I knew the Professor had fallen in his bathroom over the summer and this would delay his return, but this wasn't supposed to be anything serious. Was he hiding something from me? And what kind of friend was Father O'Neil if he didn't want the Professor to stay in Sorin?

My encounter with Father O'Neil left me feeling very young, as if I had just been schooled in the hard facts of adult life. I just hoped he was wrong. For the time being, he *was* wrong. Shortly afterwards, the Professor returned to campus and he was in fine mettle. When he and Tom Casey stopped at the Security booth to enter campus, the guard pointed at the parking sticker. "Yes, I know my sticker has expired," the Professor said, "but *I* haven't expired!"

"You've been around here for a pretty long time," the guard observed.

"Yes, I *have*."

That evening several of us kept him company and helped unpack. "I want to stay incognito this week," he said. "I'll take it easy so that I can rest and get settled. I've had an extended vacation due to my foolishness. I've gone from running on eight cylinders to six, and I was born with seven." He noticed some unwelcome changes had taken place in his absence. Father Green was no longer the rector, and the new rector had staked out a parking space next to the rear stairs. That would have to go, the Professor told us; he needed that spot for his own car. Some vacuum cleaners and cleaning supplies had gathered in the vestibule, blocking the path to his room. They would have to go, too.

News of the Professor's return soon spread through the building. I was waiting on a pizza at food sales in the basement, when some students started talking about him.

"Man, all he ever does is bitch," said one. "He's a bastard."

"Come on," I said. "He's an old man. Give him a break."

"The Professor's immortal," said someone else. "He can't die."

"If he ever does die," said another, "they'll cart him out to the back and dump him in the trash dumpster. He'll go in shaking his cane and yelling, 'you bastards, you bastards....'" Here some explanation is in order. "Bastard" was the Professor's all-purpose term of abuse, and it went way back: "One day the new obediences were announced," he had told me, "and all the priests were excited to learn where they would be assigned. Charlie Phillips asked our friend Father Crumley about his, and he said, 'The bastards sent me to Anderson,'" a remote Indiana posting tantamount to exile. "Charlie and I were so amused that we began using the word."

Just three days after returning to the hall, the Professor had recourse to this word in a battle with some old adversaries. A party was planned for the room below him and he asked the new rector how long it would last. "Until two a.m.," came the reply. "I simply turned around, without saying a single word," said the Professor, "and went straight back to my room. With that damnable party, I didn't get to bed until three. It wouldn't have been so bad, except they were playing the same old records from last year." The Professor hummed a few bars for me.

"Mack the Knife?"

"That's right. Then they had that other silly movie music on. You've heard it before."

"Yes," I said. "You mean *The Wizard of Oz* and the little munchkins all singing? That's absolutely bizarre."

"That's absolutely bizarre, yes. I phoned down there and told them to stop it. A girl answered the phone and started singing to me."

"Did she have a nice voice?"

"No, as a matter of fact, she actually had a rather *beautiful* voice. And after the singing I asked a boy I know down there if they were going to do as the reverend promised.

"Now the other day I was talking to Father Riehle and he asked, 'How are things at Sorin?' I told him they couldn't be worse. The new rector is too young. He's just been ordained. It used to be that a rector was a rector and in the house all the time. Now today they take them inexperienced, freshly ordained, right from the cradle. It's just dreadful. Half the freshmen don't even know he's a priest."

"I've never seen him in a Roman collar," I said. "The story I heard was that he tried to break up a fight over at Dillon the other day and they just pushed him away because they didn't know he was a priest."

"No!" the Professor gasped.

That very morning, we noticed the fire hoses had been removed from their glass cabinet and laid out on the floor in the entrance foyer next to the rector's office. The second-floor RA blamed someone outside the hall, but the Professor told me, "Don't be so naïve. You know someone from this hall did it."

$\left[12\right]$

Teaching (1920-24)

AFTER RETURNING to Notre Dame to teach in 1920, the Professor was back on the third floor of Sorin, eventually landing in his favorite room, 355. In these years, he met his two greatest faculty friends, George Shuster and Pat Manion, shortly before their ascent to high-profile careers that would one day put them on the national stage. Here's the story he told me:

"After graduation, my father set me up working in Chicago for my uncle, my mother's brother, who was one of the many vice presidents of the First National Bank. In 1919, the soldiers were coming back from the war and jobs were not easy to get, and I wanted to stay on and teach here. Right at graduation time Father Joseph Burke, the director of studies, offered me a job, but I said I didn't know. That summer I had several discussions with my father. He said to me, 'What teacher has ever amounted to anything?' 'What about Woodrow Wilson?' I said. Now father was an ardent Democrat, so he couldn't answer me.

"I was at the bank from August, 1919 to May, 1920, but I hated it. I worked in the bank that one year, but I just didn't understand how banks make money. For the same reason, I still to this day do not understand the question Professor Bolger used to ask in the economics class I took as a sophomore: 'What is more absurd than last year's Easter bonnet?' Economics was boring to me; I didn't understand it.

"I remember that awful year when I worked in the Loop and used to live near Hyde Park. A great train full of Pullmans passed by and the announcement was made, 'the President of the United States.' I never actually saw Woodrow Wilson, but I saw his train, which was going to change tracks in Chicago that afternoon. He was sick and on his way back to Washington. I also remember being at the famous old Congress Hotel in Chicago at the bar, bringing my sisters, Sarah and Mercedes, to St. Mary's. There we sat. Prohibition had been passed but was not yet in effect. We saw men at the bar trying to sell cases and cases of liquor, but neither my father nor I, of course, bought any of it. My only pleasure that year at the bank was taking the South Shore on the weekends to visit Notre Dame and my sisters. On one of those visits, I finally signed a secret contract with Father Burke without my father's knowledge.

"At that time, we were still, as Father Morrissey once called us, 'just a little boys school.' President Morrissey was Irish, and he said in his brogue, 'This is just a *byes* boarding school.' But I came in under the innovative Father Burns, who changed the place so much that they forced him out after only three years. One of the first things he did after I began teaching was to switch us from a quarter-system of nine weeks each to the present semester-system of seventeen weeks each. Burns—and I agreed—thought we were just coddling the students on quarters: 'Why, you can't do any serious study or research in just nine weeks,' Burns said.

"There was too great of a change from having a nice agreeable man like John W. Cavanaugh to having James Burns as president. Father Cavanaugh had grown a little lax in the discipline of the priests and the students; he was just too nice a man. But then Burns came in, with his nose glasses and severe manner. And he was so unpopular with his strictness and his new ideas that he was our shortest-term president. Just three years and then they fired him!

"They tell a story on Burns that I heard from my friend Pete Hebert. Father Hebert needed a hat, so he asked Father Burns and got permission to trade at Max Adler's. Pete bought a black felt hat, but two weeks later he was summoned to Father Burns's office. 'Father Burns would like to see you,' he was told, and Burns said to Pete, 'You received permission from me, yes, but my God, man, what did you buy last week, a stovepipe?' Burns had found the bill for ten dollars, which he thought was the height of extravagance, and ordered the hat sent back, which it was. In those days, special permission was needed from the president himself to go off campus. Even today, the CSCs must obtain permission from the head of the order to go off campus for any length of time or buy much of anything. Episodes such as this one did not endear Burns to the community.

"There was a famous scandal during the Burns administration, when Father Lange posed with a football player we had here, Buck Shaw, one of the few athletes that I knew well. Lange had photographs taken of Buck and himself practically naked, showing off their muscles and Lange's fat, and the photos were sent in to a physical specimen magazine. A few weeks later, they were published on the cover with the caption 'Rev. Bernard Lange, CSC.' Oh, was Father Burns angry! He sent for Lange to come to his office and chewed out poor Bernie Lange: 'My God, man! Have you no better sense than to have *photographs* of a prominent athlete from a Catholic university and of you yourself, a Roman Catholic priest, sent off to some physical culture magazine?' Oh, poor Father Lange, did he get it from President Burns that day.

"When I was a student, I remember Lange as the fourth-floor prefect at Walsh Hall. And he made the mistake of trying to imitate King Farley. He'd come up to you from behind and give you a big slap on the back and maybe call out your name. But, boy, we used to fear him he was so strong. He hit me once and I remember it took four days to recover from it. Lange, though he was supposed to have his PhD, knew only enough Latin to say his Mass. That was the only way in which he was like Farley. And it was very poor form for Lange even to try modeling himself after Farley. Nobody could do that. No one could get away with the things Farley got away with. Lange's problem was that he had nothing between the ears.

"During my first semester teaching here in 1920, my father died at age sixty, and I tasted my first hard liquor. Marr, my cousin, was a courtly gentleman, quite portly, with gray hair combed straight back and a moustache. He did not wear the full tails, just the tails Prince Albert had popularized. He said, 'Paul, I think you need a drink. Where does your father keep the liquor?' 'I don't know that he has any liquor.' 'Oh, yes, he does. Go look in your father's dressing cabinet in the bedroom.' And sure enough, my cousin knew where it was. My father had a few bottles of brandy, and I brought some down. Later, I drank Manhattans, before my drinking evolved to a minimum of one Scotch or a maximum of two per night.

"My first year here I taught senior high school English. Those preps were awful! I taught them English and Manion taught them history. In the middle of the next semester, George Shuster called me up and told me I was to teach Freshman College English. I didn't want to, but I did it. 'Twinkle toe' Maher was seventy years old and got sick, and I had to replace him. I taught a two o'clock class of seventy students and then another with sixty-five.

"When I started teaching, we had none of this 'tenure' or 'promotion.' We didn't think anything about it. We just taught. And each year we would be hired back again. We didn't have to worry about publishing to keep our jobs: we just taught.

"In those days, the straight AB courses included four years

Latin and four years Greek. There was a boy from my early teaching by the name of F. X. Disney, who graduated in the class of '23, a big, long, tall drink of water who was a track man and got his monogram. Rockne used to single out Disney and say, 'Well, there's one fellow I don't have to worry about being academically eligible. Any man who can take four years Latin and four years Greek, he's eligible.' F. X. just loves to tell that story.

"I remember another boy who lived in Sorin in 1920 or '22 who never graduated with ceremonies, because he was fired a week before graduation. He was hanged with six others. They went to the LaSalle Hotel after a big senior dance or something and had a private party with their own dates and some other girls, I guess. And at the party a girl named Blonde Mama took every piece of clothing off while she danced. And they were all discovered—'the Seven who were hanged.'

"At that time, I roomed on the third floor of Sorin at the south end, across from the tower. My one window was facing the old library, and that's where I started, in room 302, and Pat Manion lived in 304. The first place I met Pat was at the table for scrub faculty. I had never realized he was living right next door to me until I walked back from a meal with him. We both walked to Sorin, then went up the flights of stairs together, until we finally asked where the other one lived and discovered we were neighbors.

"Pat Manion had been a pudgy boy from Kentucky attending a Catholic prep school where, as at Notre Dame, there was mail call. He was 'Clarence' until the priest looked at a letter and yelled out 'Pat Manion.' He had misread the envelope, which was addressed 'Fat Manion.' Pat wrote an American history textbook that was used by high school boys. Father Matt Walsh handed his notes over to Pat and asked him to write it. President Walsh was a very good American historian but too lazy to write his own book.

"At that time morning prayer was still mandatory for the students, mainly as a means of getting everyone out of bed, and the boys had to check their names off a list. If they missed morning prayer, they were denied permission to go into town that day, and so on. But eventually morning prayer degenerated into the boys just signing in or checking off while wearing their bathrobes. Morning prayer only lasted for five minutes or so. It wasn't really 'chapel.' At morning prayer we had some funny rectors like the Rev. Marr. He used to rattle off: 'Our Father, who art in heaven, hallowed be thy name—will the boy who dropped the shoe above me last night drop the other tonight? I'm still waiting—thy kingdom come, thy will be done. ...'

"And Pat Haggerty rang a bell as he strode down the hall. Pat had been a coal miner in Pennsylvania. The boys used to say that when the new mules got too smart for him he left to become a priest. He used to have a dickens of a time getting up little Jimmy Murtaugh in 306. Murtaugh disliked Haggerty, and Haggerty came early in the morning unannounced. Pat Manion and I would be listening down the hallway and we would hear, 'Murtaugh, get up! Murtaugh, get up!' We'd hear a door slamming, then, 'Get out of the cupboard, Murtaugh! Get out of the cupboard!' Murtaugh was small enough to hide in the dressing locker, you see.

"I lived next to Pat Manion for three or four years, then Lyons Hall was built and they planned for the piece above the arch and everything to the right of it to be reserved for the bachelor professors, and I would have moved from Sorin to Lyons. But by the time the thing was built, thank goodness, there was no room for us, and I stayed. George Shuster was living in room 255 at the time and a Father Zacharias—some big old German professor who made too much noise—lived up above him. I don't know what he did up there, but it bothered George to no end. Somehow George got him to move and put me up above him to keep things quiet. Initially, I just had the one tower room in 355, but once the Depression came, many rooms became vacant, including the one across the hall, so they let me have it and I then had two rooms. And when students started filling in rooms again, they still let me keep my bedroom in 356.

"By the time I got my tower room, Pat Manion got the tower in 115. Pat was always a great politician, a great Democrat. Paul McNutt, a man who was elected governor of Indiana, formed a great friendship with Pat. And he and Pat went up and down the state campaigning, and McNutt was elected—he was a very popular man. Pat then was going to run for office, so they told him, if you're going to, you can't live on the Notre Dame campus. So he moved to South Bend. He got an apartment on Washington Street, right up by the courthouse there, by the old Oliver estate, about a block and a half from it. And then of course he was married in 1936, and I was best man. Pat was chums with LaGuardia and supported Al Smith, but after marrying Gina, he became a Republican—very conservative.

"But as I say, Father Burns was very good. I agreed with his improvement of the school academically, but after three years they threw him out—a bad thing. George Shuster got wind of it, learning that the replacement was to be Father Matt Walsh, who would be returning us back to a 'byes' school, as Morrissey would call it. George disliked Walsh greatly and that's why he left Notre Dame and why he never received the Laetare Medal, because Walsh prevented George from getting it. He didn't come back for the next thirty-five years until Walsh was dead. George went to New York and wanted me to come along to teach at a new prep school and be the head of the English department there. But the one thing about it was that I don't like New York. It's too big. I'm just a country boy at heart and I was happy at Notre Dame.

"George later became editor at *Commonweal* magazine, which was more highly respected then than it is today. He thought it was so refreshing because it was written by laymen for laymen and showed that Catholics could be cultured also. John Conley had once been prominent at the magazine, and he came to George one night, had a long talk, and a few days later it was discovered that he had converted to Episcopalianism. Everybody was very shocked. We all thought a conversion from Catholicism to Protestantism could hardly be sincere because one had to give up so much of what one previously held so dear. Soon afterwards, he died an Episcopalian, and George sent a very nice note to his wife. Doris said, 'George never hurt a soul in his entire life,' and I suppose she's right. The widow wrote a nice note back. When George died, she and Doris exchanged notes.

"George's original name was George P. Schuster. He was so German and wanted to hide it after World War I. He changed the spelling to S*h*uster and since he hated the middle name Peter he changed that to Nauman, his mother's maiden name. He knew German, French, and English so well and was such an accomplished journalist that he became an intelligence officer. After the war, he stayed a year to write his master's thesis in French. There was no best man at his wedding because we disapproved of his marrying Doris. But Doris was a major reason for George doing as well as he did. Without her he would not have been so active. George was too modest and it took Doris to push him on, to give him ambition to do great things.

"George tells the famous story of visiting Eisenhower, as one university president to another, when Ike was at Columbia and he was at Hunter College. That austere English butler presented George, using his full name and his titles, which George had supplied at their request. And Ike said, 'Dr. Shuster, I don't know what I'm doing here. I wish someone would tell me.' George did not want to tell him that he was put there to be polished up for the presidency, but it was true, of course, that Ike did not know then whether he wanted to be a Republican or a Democrat."

[13]

Cheer, Cheer

ONE DAY THE PROFESSOR was complaining about having to walk an admissions application over to the Main Building. He couldn't remember how many times he'd done the same favor for friends or relatives.

"Do people ask you for football tickets, too?" I asked.

"Oh! Countless times. And you don't know how frustrating that can be. Why, I think it was in 1947 that I bought a ticket for the Army game for someone. He never showed up and I never have heard from him since. But I still have the ticket. If you look, it's in my dresser drawer."

We were now in the midst of the football season, as if anyone needed being told, and Big Boy's sister had come out for a game. After being introduced to the Professor, she kept referring to him as "the headmaster" the rest of the day. The Professor laughed at the mistake, striking his chest three times, saying "*mea culpa, mea culpa.* I would have invited her into my museum, but the bed was not made. You know, a couple of years ago, a friend of mine from New York brought someone to campus for the first time. They had been drinking and after the game my friend said, 'Let's go to Sorin.' When they got here, his friend said to me, 'I'm glad to know you, Father Sorin.'"

On Thursday of the USC weekend, an alumnus who ran a famous men's clothing company stopped to visit. The Professor

93

pointed at his own black leisure suit and asked, "Do you recognize it?"

"Yes," Mr. Haggar replied. "It's one of ours."

The Professor gave his measurements and requested another color. "He laughed, but I was serious. His money is responsible for Haggar Hall, you know."

"Did he live in Sorin?"

"No, he was quite vehement in denying it, and I thought of you. I told him I know a man—your father—who told his son to go to Sorin. He said, 'How foolish! I would never send my son into a fire trap like that.'"

Speaking of fathers, I mentioned that a father visiting his son this weekend had been cursed out by several students. No one told him you have to shout, "Watch the water!" when you flush the toilet or you'll scald people in the showers. This reminded the Professor of an incident involving Elmer Layden, one of the Four Horsemen and later the head coach at Notre Dame and Commissioner of the National Football League: "Elmer Layden's father was visiting his son once, unbeknownst to the rector of Corby Hall. The rectors always went through the rooms waking up those who had slept too late. The rector came in and pulled the mattress from under Mike Layden, who was a very dignified man, with a gray beard and hair, and so on. Everyone was quite embarrassed. I can't recall who the rector was, but it was either Tuffy Ryan or Pat Haggerty. Both men were very bad rectors."

That evening Sorin had its pep rally, a day before the main one in Stepan Center. While I was in front of the building with hundreds of others cheering, the Professor was in his room reading the paper, when he was startled by a crash. In his bathroom he found that a large piece of plaster had fallen with such force that it knocked over his chair. The dust was still suspended in the air as he walked through the debris. "I guess those are the problems you have with a mid-Victorian bathroom. That was the straw that broke the old ceiling's back," he said, referring to the jumping up and down in the RA's room overhead during the rally.

"Pep rallies used to be held in the Fieldhouse," said the Professor. "For a time, they also alternated between Sorin and Corby. I'll never forget one of the pep rallies when Pat Manion spoke about our opponent. Pat's line was: 'Just as it's raining tonight, they will be weeping tomorrow.' We ended up losing!"

On Friday, excitement continued to build for the game and for fall break. I was preparing to visit relatives in Watertown, Wisconsin. "Our only saint was from Watertown, you know, Father Thomas Irving, Saint Thomas. I knew him well. He was a little boy when he enrolled in the seminary, what we called the 'little sem.' Later he ran the seminary."

"What made everyone think he was a saint?"

"Because he was. That's the simplest answer to that. He was a saint. He trained all of those men over there. He was one of the most wonderful men in the order. 'Saintly Irving,' they called him. I say a prayer every night to Father Irving that he'll let me be his altar boy in heaven.

"But I know many people in Watertown, including one of my eleven godsons, Dick Conley, who teaches high school there. His father Harry, who just died, was my oldest friend. I knew him since 1913. My family and his kinfolk both come from Woodstock, Illinois.

"If you see Dick Conley in Watertown, introduce yourself by relaying this message to him: 'I am a good friend of your godfather, Paul Fenlon, and have made many visits to the museum. My incessant questions have picked his brain apart and I am driving him crazy.'" *Fair enough,* I thought. *"Good friend" is nice, but am I really asking that many questions? Or is this just your teasing way of saying we spend a lot of time talking about campus history?*

The weekend was special for me because my parents and youngest brother Doug came up from Florida for the game. Andy joined us, of course, as did my Grandma Grace, who made the trip from Texas. My grandmother had been divorced from E. A. "Boy" Hicks for several years now. She was just four years the Professor's junior but seemed a generation younger. A tall, green-eyed brunette with clanking jewelry, overpowering perfume, and the clothes of someone half her age, she made an impression wherever she went. On the day of the game, she was deferential and flirtatious: "Why, Professor, what a pleasure it is to meet you."

"I am so delighted, Mrs. Hicks," he replied. Each was charmed by the other.

That Saturday morning the Professor was wearing a pristine pair of black-and-white shoes. A friend was convinced Notre Dame won whenever he wore them, and they did the trick this time, too. At the game, students chanted, "We are the Green Machine," just as basketball coach Digger Phelps instructed at the pep rally. A Trojan Horse was rolled onto the field and the team wore green jerseys. We beat USC by four touchdowns, clearing a major obstacle on our way to a national championship.

After my week in Wisconsin and following up with Dick Conley, I returned to campus for the Navy game. "I saw Father Theodore over the vacation," said the Professor. "We talked about George Shuster and he boasted about his graduate school's latest accomplishments and his hope for improvement. You know, the graduate school has always been his little avocation. I thanked him for the little card he sent me while I was ill. I also left a note with his amazing secretary, Helen Hosinski. I don't think Father Ted could function without her."

The Professor was bracing for another football weekend. "I dread it. Everywhere I'm recognized. Even in the Pay Caf four or five came up to me. I don't know how many thousands of

times I've been approached. 'You're Paul Fenlon, aren't you?'"
On Friday a steady stream of visitors made its way to 141 Sorin,
including Ziggy Czarbosky, a burly football star who played for
Frank Leahy in the '40s. "Ziggy's just a bouncer at some saloon.
He does a good job, and looking at him it's no wonder."

The next day the Professor began receiving guests around ten
o'clock. After a full morning, he went to the game, arriving early
in the second quarter and leaving at the start of the fourth. Ziggy
Czarboski was honored with a special presentation at halftime.

Late that night, the Professor was free from the last of the
day's guests, when exhaustion set in. We talked as he got ready
for bed. "Throughout the day, people kept coming up to me and
saying how good I looked," he said. "When I arrived at the Dining Hall, five or six people got up from their seats to greet me. I
told them, 'To tell you the truth, I'm so tired I could fall asleep
on the nearest couch.'"

There was a knock at the outer door. The Professor called,
"Come in, come in!" I went to see who it was. A girl my age was
standing there. "Is this where Father Fenlon lives?" she asked. I
went back to get the Professor, who came out in his orange pajamas. "What do you want?" he asked. She relayed a message from
a former student. "That's very nice of you," he said. "Thank you,
but I'm not dressed and can't see anybody tonight. Goodbye!"
Back under his covers, he chuckled at being called "Father."

The Professor had a few days respite before the next influx
of football fans. I accompanied him on an errand before Mass,
the farthest afield from Sorin I had ever walked with him—just
a few steps beyond our usual orbit. At the personnel office in
the Main Building he dropped off some hospital bills, then we
strolled out the back door to the courtyard between the Geology
building and Brownson Hall. "There used to be a convent here
and a beautiful garden," the Professor said, before pointing to

two windows left of the doorway. "That's where Joe Ryan would have been put if he had returned. He was the second to the last of the professors-in-residence, but he went for Easter vacation to Chicago and never came back. He died in the apartment house of a relative there. I heard they wanted to put me in Brownson, too, where the visiting priests now live, but they never asked me. If they had told me to live here, I would have said, 'bye bye.' If I can't live in Sorin, I won't live on campus at all."

We turned around to face the rear of the Main Building, and he pointed to a ramshackle roof overhanging some parked cars. "I once taught a class on the second floor there," he said. "That roof used to extend further. Once I remember turning around from the blackboard and seeing Paul Romweber—the furniture store people—climbing out the window onto that roof. Romweber Furniture made the tables and chairs for the Dining Hall and they made my dresser and bed. The man saved the matching twin bed in the warehouse for my wife. That was years ago. Now it's an antique."

Just then someone shouted, "Paul!" We spotted Father O'Neil coming from the Student Center towards church. The Professor rushed to greet him. I waved, then left them to talk by themselves as I continued to Mass.

Later that night, I expected the Professor to be full of news about Father O'Neil, who had just returned from his medical treatment in Boston, but instead he told me about hearing a tremendous bang overhead that sounded like the rest of his bathroom ceiling had collapsed. "And I went up to the second floor," the Professor boasted.

"You went up there?"

"Yes, I went *up*!" he said, with a twinkle in his eyes. "I ignored my own personal safety. I was propelled by anger and said to myself, 'I'll do my duty or die!' I got up there and asked if they knew what they were doing to my ceiling. 'If I hear more noise or there's more damage, I'll report you to Dean Roemer. Do you have barbells?' They said no, but I saw them kicking it under their bed, even as they muttered their denials. How I would love to be rector for a day, if that were possible. A few of these boys would get kicked out. The current rector is simply not fit to be rector. We'll probably have a new rector next year, and I just dread to think of the possible replacements."

Next on the football schedule was Georgia Tech, and the Professor attended this game, too. "It even got me excited," he said. "It was one of the best games I've seen in my hundred years." The next day, the Professor bumped into a student who was saying goodbye to his parents returning to New Jersey. "Then," said the Professor, "I heard a voice, 'Paul! Paul!' I'll be damned if I didn't turn around to see the reverend president. There was Ted, very excited, with his raincoat over his arm and that white hanky of his. He was hurrying away to Dillon or Badin, I guess. I had never seen him in that spot behind Sorin before. He apologized for not telling me about the Mass for George that he said. I told him it was fine, because I told Doris I couldn't go. While the boy stood there looking on as Ted and I spoke, a thought flashed through my mind. Years ago, I was going to benediction with three boys and Father Ted stopped me outside of church to ask about Father Kerndt Healy. Afterwards, the boys were surprised that I knew Ted. They said they had never seen him before. I told this to Ted and he told me if I was ever with a student to be sure to introduce him. So on this occasion, I introduced the New Jersey boy to Father Hesburgh. Later, the boy said, '*You* know Father Hesburgh?' I said, 'Oh, yes, quite well.'"

$[14]$

Distinguished Guests

CHET GRANT'S name came up occasionally in my discussions with the Professor, and once I heard he had a memory for the sports side of things, I wanted to meet him. The Professor made the arrangements and I went to visit the International Sports and Games Research Collection on the first floor of the library, where Grant was a curator.

Four years older than the Professor, he could have passed for a man in his sixties. He had a slight stoop, a few wrinkles, white hair, and a pair of black-framed glasses, but he still retained the spidery build of his student days, when he quarterbacked Knute Rockne's teams in 1920 and 1921. Listed as five foot seven, 138 pounds, he had lost perhaps an inch in the intervening years. At one time, at age eighteen, he had been the sports editor of the *South Bend Tribune*. Later, he was Elmer Layden's backfield coach in the '30s and wrote a book on Notre Dame football.

The Professor first met him in class when they were both students his freshman year, since "Grant" and "Fenlon" were so close alphabetically. Grant was a day student living at home his first two years at Notre Dame, then went off to war for three years. Only after he came back to Notre Dame in 1920, did he really get to know the Professor. After World War I, the school had toughened up its graduation requirements and Grant learned he was short an English class. He went to the Professor, who gave him a stack of books to read. Instead of reading them, Grant wrote a ten-page essay on the most beautiful sunsets he had seen on his European travels. The Professor accepted the paper for credit on the condition Grant never write another paper for him again.

After the war, Grant lived in the Sorin subway, which he described as a separate hall unto itself. In 1920-21, he roomed with freshman quarterback Frank Reese. In 1921-22, his roommate was a future Four Horseman, Harry Stuhldreher. "Reese survived living with me, so Rock figured Stuhlie could, too," Grant told me. "Rock decided who roomed where. It might be inferred that Rock put Harry with me so my skill might rub off on him, but it was just expedient to put us together." They lived in the smallest room in the basement, which, he joked, is probably a storage room today that "should be dedicated to our memory." So far as Grant knew, Stuhldreher was the first freshman ever to live in Sorin, a hall reserved for juniors and seniors. I remembered the Professor once telling me, "The most famous athlete I ever knew—knew well, I mean—was Harry Stuhldreher. He was about the only athlete with any brains. I knew him as a freshman until the day he died."

After Grant and I finished up, I mentioned the Professor thought the three of us could have tea together sometime. Several days later, we convened in the Professor's room at one o'clock. After some small talk, the Professor asked, "Alright, now what do you want to do, Philip?"

"We'll go downstairs and look at the old haunts of Grant and Stuhlie."

"It was a resort, not a haunt," said Grant.

As we left the sheet room, we were greeted by the sound of shrieking electric guitar. I led the way down the steps, with the Professor taking up the rear.

"The last time I was down here was probably 1922," said Grant.

The first person we encountered was Eddie Kostanty. The Professor said, "This is our nice janitor. Edward, this is Mr. Chet Grant." They exchanged greetings. "Alphonse was our man," said Grant. "Did you ever hear of Alphonse? No? Well, you are in distinguished company."

Soft rock was playing down the corridor, as Grant homed in on his old room. Its current occupant, Jerry, introduced himself and welcomed us, and Grant began to describe where his bunk and other furniture used to be located. But then he suddenly admitted he was all turned around, lost in fact. He didn't re-member living in a tower room like this one but a narrow room with a view of the church. So we tried knocking on other doors. "Oh, wait a minute," the Professor said, peering through a door-way, "They're all sleeping." Soon four or five others were up and about, eager to help us find the room. The Professor seemed to know and like them. "I tried to call you last night," he said to one, before introducing "my friend, Mr. Chet Grant."

"Nice to meet you, sir."

"This is Kevin," said the Professor.

"I'm Tim," said another.

The students were impressed by Grant, once they learned his history, and they knew who Stuhldreher was, too.

"So you roomed with Stuhldreher, huh?"

"No, he roomed with me! He was nineteen and I was twenty-nine. Now who do you think was boss? *He* was, even at that age!"

The Professor apologized for rousting them from their naps.

"No problem, Professor. No problem."

"I was down here yesterday."

"Well, you should come down here more often, Professor," said one of them. Before shoving off, he turned to Grant. "Nice seeing you, sir. Bye now."

"Nice to have met you. Delighted to see your quarters."

Grant could not get over the material abundance of these students compared with the austerity of his own time.

"Well, you see, they have all sorts of things now, Chet. They have televisions," the Professor said, as if describing a new invention Grant had never seen before, adding, "What beautiful carpet they have on this floor."

Grant remembered his own room was just wide enough for a table on one side, a bunk and a table on the other, and maybe a wastebasket. "Where were your clothes?" the Professor asked.

"We didn't have any clothes in those days!"

"How did you like it back then?" a student asked. "Alright?"

"Well, sure, sure," Grant replied.

All this time I was going up and down the corridor trying to find rooms that fit Grant's description. Rooms 43 and 47 were early candidates, but then he decided on 55, before giving up and wandering to the other side of the basement. "Well, thanks a lot, gentlemen," said the Professor to the remaining students.

"You're truly welcome, Professor. Have a nice walk."

The three of us then marched upstairs all the way to the third floor and sat down in my room for tea. Grant had never heard the story of the famous author G. K. Chesterton visiting Sorin Hall, so the Professor began a leisurely version of it. Whenever one of us would interrupt, the Professor would patiently pick up the thread of the story, just where he'd left off, determined to finish it. Occasionally, he got so badly sidetracked I had to provide cues: "So, Professor, Mrs. Chesterton was pretty angry?"

Inevitably, the talk turned to football. The Professor said, "Now, when I was over in the art gallery last year, they had some of these pictures blown up. And they had George Gipp there, and Father Conyers met me after coming out with Brother somebody, and he said, 'Paul, have you seen this? There's a sentence under

Gipp's picture. Did you ever think he was a womanizer? And I said, 'Well, Father, frankly, I don't know. I know that he dated a good many girls. I do know that; he dated girls in South Bend, but I wouldn't necessarily call him a womanizer." Grant agreed "womanizer" was too strong a word but he did remember, "Gipp had a thwarted romance with a woman down in Indianapolis."

Grant had a keener interest in Gipp's spiritual life than his love life. He mentioned a letter he'd discovered describing Gipp being given the last rites by Father Pat Haggerty. I'd always thought Cardinal O'Hara converted Gipp, but Grant was adamant that I was wrong. The Professor was just as convinced that Grant was wrong, and he tried pinning him down: "Did Gipp ever submit to any of the sacraments? Did he go to confession?" Chet admitted Gipp was not actually converted but had only expressed an intention to convert. The Professor persisted: "I can't picture Pat Haggerty being in that hospital. I've never been able to get Pat Haggerty into the picture that way."

The Professor had to leave it there because he needed a bathroom break. After two and a half hours, our visit with Chet Grant ended. A week later the Professor was amused to receive a note from Grant addressed in care of the "Sorin Subway."

It wasn't every day that someone like Chet Grant was our guest, but the most exotic visitor we ever had came in the guise of a short, pigeon-chested woman with dyed hair swept up in back, tied with a scarf, and mounted on her head like an overturned pail. She had a pair of large trifocals and wore an orange floral dress. With her angular features and swarthy complexion, she bore a passing resemblance to her famous ancestor, Rev. Edward Sorin, CSC.

One of my roommates had received a call from a hometown acquaintance, Marguerite, whose husband, the Professor's friend from the class of 1937, worked in the alumni office. She was arranging a campus tour for Madame Sorin and wanted to include Sorin Hall on her itinerary. She warned us her charge did not speak a word of English and she would have to do the translating.

We met in room 141. The Professor was dressed up in a tie and vest and at his most animated, just like football weekends. He told Marguerite how much he had heard about her, then he rehearsed some biographical details about her, just to confirm he had his facts straight. When it came time to be introduced to Madame Sorin, he appeared startled and irritated he couldn't communicate without a translator. A moment later, when she was speaking to the rector, this fact still hadn't registered with him. "I don't understand her," he whispered to me.

The Professor now played host, directing each of us to take a seat. Madame Sorin sat in the retirement chair, I sat on the bed to her right, Tim sat next to me, Bill was on the floor below Tim, Tom stood next to the wardrobe with the rector, the Professor sat in the red chair on one side of the TV, and Marguerite sat on the other side. We learned that Madame Sorin was not only the granddaughter of Father Sorin's older brother, but also the wife of one of his distant cousins, which is why she retained the Sorin name. This was her first trip to the United States and she came for the sole purpose of visiting Notre Dame, a lifelong dream come true. When she first stepped on campus, she was moved by the sight of Father Sorin's statue, because the face bore such a resemblance to her father's.

I told her the hall used to have a miniature version of the statue, but it disappeared many years ago. Sorinites would taunt authorities with postcards from around the world: "With Father Sorin. Having a great time. Wish you were here."

"Once it was found floating in a boat in the lake," said the Professor. "It was holding a fishing rod and was mistaken for Frenchie Doremus, a priest who taught French here. After

Father Steiner saw that, he ordered it put away over in the archives someplace. It was a metal statue on a sort of imitation marble pedestal. He stood there in the corner as you came in. The Colonel Hoynes room was opposite the rector's office, and it was in that niche, that square over there. It was revolving, and one of the things that the boys enjoyed doing when they came in late at night was to turn Father Sorin to the wall, so he couldn't see them breaking curfew."

"When I pray to the Blessed Virgin and she doesn't answer my prayers, I turn her statue to the wall," said Madame Sorin.

"Father Steiner was provincial," the Professor went on. "And he just simply said, 'Now, they've done enough with that. We're not going to have it turned around anymore. Treat it with respect.'"

According to rumor, Father Burtchaell had the statue stashed away in Dillon Hall. Marguerite said she'd try to get permission to see it later in the week.

Madame Sorin knew this was a football school but admitted, "My favorite sport is not football, not basketball, not baseball"—here her face lit up as we waited for the translation—"but boxing!" And with that, she delivered a stinging right jab to my shoulder.

She was astounded to learn the Professor had lived on campus for sixty-two years, even longer than Father Sorin's fifty-one years. "Do students like these visit you often?" she asked.

"Yes, they do," said the Professor.

"Do all the students at Notre Dame get along with their professors this way?"

He smiled broadly. "Yes."

As they spoke, I was trying to think of all the Father Sorin stories I knew. "Professor, do you want to tell about the time you were mistaken for Father Sorin?" He fell back in his chair with delight, exclaiming, "Oh!" He started out by saying how many scores of people came through his door on football weekends.

"Do you dread it?" Madame Sorin asked.

"I do sometimes dread it," he replied, before relating the tale of the inebriated campus visitor: "He was told he was going back to see Sorin. ..." Madame Sorin listened, waiting for the punch line in French, and when it came—"Well, hello, Father Sorin!"—she exploded in laughter. Then she studied him, cocked her head, and said, "And you have no beard!"

"No!" he cried.

"What sort of man was my ancestor? I've heard he was very stubborn. Was he?"

"Oh my, yes," he said, as if he were once on close terms with a man who died three years before he was born: "They tell the story. ..." And he proceeded to describe how Father Sorin sent his men to a neighboring property to destroy a dam responsible for exposing the campus to diseased swamp water. "I'm the same way," Madame Sorin said. "It's the Sorin way."

As our visit wound down, we took some photographs, and the Professor kissed Marguerite goodbye. Madame Sorin thanked us, then paused to find the right words for a benediction: "You are all most worthy of Father Sorin's school."

"Very well said," the Professor responded. In the corridor, outside the rector's office, she made her final farewell, waving to us, regretting she had to leave, fighting back tears.

After she left, the Professor, Tom, and I compared notes. So what did the Professor think of her visit? "It pleased me to no end. And if George were here, oh, would he have loved it. You know, once he traveled over to France just to see Sorin's chateau. To think that someone, no matter how distantly related, was actually a descendant of our Father Sorin! And they thought enough of it to come visit our school."

[15]

Professors' Alley (1925-29)

IN THE 1920S, the bachelor dons were in their prime, and the Professor was one of them. Some of his fondest memories dated to this period, and he recounted them to me:

"George Shuster invited me to teach Freshman English in the summer school. That was when we had an avalanche of Sisters. One of the reasons I enjoyed summers here so much was because of the Sisters living in Walsh Hall. The state made them all work to get their degrees. Before that, you could be a religious and teach without much formal education at all aside from your seminary or convent training. But then things changed. And for some of those poor old nuns it was almost a crime. They would do their work and graduate and then two years later you would hear they had died. They were just so old when they finally got their degrees.

"During the summertime, there would be five hundred, six hundred, seven hundred nuns out here and they would all stay on the Gold Coast—Walsh, Lyons, Morrissey, Howard. It was so peculiar seeing all those nuns, all those women occupying our halls, but I loved them and made many friends with those dear nuns, Sisters I still keep in touch with today. I had not been living in my third-floor tower room very long, but I could see them from my window. I used to watch them with their various habits go in and out of church and I could listen to their beautiful singing in Sacred Heart. It sounded as if I were in heaven.

"They ate over at Badin's old dining hall. Before the new dining hall in 1927, remember, Badin Hall was where the off-campus boys or anyone else could get a la carte. I remember eating in that dining hall with a Sister I knew. When I walked in the door, there was quite a funny scene. Here all these nuns would be eating their 'brown cows'—some brown stuff over ice cream—while a nearby phonograph would be playing music. What a contrast! Seven hundred nuns gorging themselves on 'cows' while the music played 'Heaven Can Wait.'

"You know, the best view in this hall isn't from Charlie Phillips's old room. I think I had the best view from my own tower room on the third floor, especially in the summers, when the nuns were here and summer school had just been established. That was the most enjoyable time here. I loved the summers here in the 1920s. I loved them. It was so peaceful with the students away. I used to look out at the Corby porch and there would be Father Eugene Burke. After the community breakfast, he would be there with his little coterie telling wonderful stories, one after the other, laughing and laughing, with his arms shooting up in the air, shouting. The priests were so happy; there was such harmony among them then.

"And in the evening after their dinner, President Walsh, who had been head of all the World War I chaplains, would have cigars passed out to everyone on the porch of the Main Building, and they would take their walks with their stogies. We called them 'ropos'—the smelliest things ever.

"Yes, of all our rectors the man I enjoyed most was the Rev. Eugene Burke, CSC—Father *Burke*, whom I had known in my sophomore year as a prefect in Corby. He became rector of this hall about the beginning of my teaching in the early '20s. He and his brother Tom Burke were two of the most popular Holy Cross Fathers on campus. One was the rector—Gene—who was also a teacher of English, and Father Tom Burke was the assistant editor of the *Ave Maria*, and he was a punster and a writer of limericks. He signed everything 'TEB'—Thomas E. Burke. He published a column in the *Chicago Tribune* called 'A Linotype or Two.' Frequently, you would find 'TEB' contributing a little limerick or something. I remember *Ave Maria* magazine was doing a special issue on the Blessed Virgin Mary [BVM], and one of them asked Father Thomas Burke to contribute. 'I need a poem,' they said. So he delivered one. I used to remember it but now I only know the last line: 'Oh where, oh where, have my BVDs gone?' The next time I saw TEB, I asked, 'What did you lose? Your mind?' He was quite a marvelous man to be with—quite an imagination.

"But Eugene Burke and Arthur J. Hope and 'Dopey Dan' Lahey used to take a walk every day and tell stories. You could set your clock by it. A great bunch of storytellers they were. Father Thomas Lahey taught in the school of commerce, I think. I believe it was Lahey who invented those strips of paper that you see put over toilet seats in hotels so you know they're sanitary. He was a very imaginative fellow, one who could make up stories, as I think he did about Colonel Hoynes in the little book he wrote about him.

"Of course, by this time Colonel Hoynes wasn't teaching anymore. He lived here, a bachelor resident like I am, and he served Mass every day of his life, morning after morning after morning in our chapel. We all worried that when he turned the page of the lectionary he might fall, or fall as he came down the two steps from the pulpit. He was blind in one eye, you see. He liked to be photographed in profile, but it wasn't so much because of his deformed eye as it was his bulbous nose. The Colonel got that nose from all that drinking he did. When the alumni came back to visit him, they flocked to his room to drink.

"He was very pathetic at the end, just an old man and, as I have said, he didn't fraternize with the students. You should have seen how poor Colonel Hoynes deteriorated. That's why I would never want to stay here in Sorin another twenty years. I don't want to live to a hundred! We thought the Colonel would die right in Sorin Hall, but they bundled him away to the infirmary, where he died, not the present infirmary but the old one. I don't remember whether they had a state funeral for him or not.

"He was a sly little old boy though. He received dividend checks from his quite valuable property in Chicago, but he allowed the checks to accumulate. And the rector would say, 'Colonel, let me fix those up for you. I'll take those to be cashed.' He died without ever endorsing them. And after he died, Colonel Hoynes left money and they built a new front to what is now Holy Cross Hall and a new rear to it. It was 'the little sem,' and that's where men like Tom Burke and Gene Burke and John McGinn and Charlie O'Donnell went—the high school for seminarians. Then when they finished their studies, they went over to the *old* Moreau, which is still standing. Someone said it's that house where they go when they're 'betwixt and between' whether they are going to be a priest or not.

"The first several years I was teaching, we had all sorts of bachelor professors besides Hoynes. Most lived in the 'L' of the second floor of Sorin, the rooms running above my room, what we called the 'Professors' Alley.' Later they all moved out. A Professor Caparo lived in the room above me. He lived in 241 and Hiney Morris was above him in 341. This would be the mid-1920s. These two were bachelor professors who both married late in life. Morris was fifty-five years old when he left to marry a girl in her teens. Awful! He didn't fraternize with the students much; they feared him. Then the Confrey brothers, Augustine and Burton, lived together in room 241 and a connecting room.

They were fine teachers, although not Notre Dame men. They were very strange boys. Burton was the older of the two; Gus was the more human. As brothers they were very distant towards one another.

"Somewhere around room 246 lived 'Big Mac' McCarthy, a commerce professor who later became dean and moved to Hoynes's old room. In 248 was little Father Catapang. He was a secular priest. In 251 was Dan Waters, 'Chappy' Waters we called him. He was an Englishman, or at least had an English accent, though I think he was really an American. Quite an odd fellow. His idea of changing clothes was changing his socks. He always taught in a gown, the same one he had at Oxford. All that was in his locker were one pair of trousers, one Oxford gown, and thirty-six pairs of socks!

"In 254 were Gene Payton and Dave Weir—a good friend of mine, one of the few here with a real PhD—and they took over the Confrey suite after those brothers left. I knew Vincent Fagan the architect. He designed some campus buildings and lived in Professors' Alley. He has a sister living on Angela who married the band director Joseph Casasanta. And then, of course, George lived in the tower room at the end. I've told you something about George Shuster.

"Cardinal O'Hara slept in room 250. That was his sleeping place in Professors' Alley, but his office was in what is my room today. You know, Cardinal O'Hara did not like the philosopher Maritain. After O'Hara became president, Maritain visited here and O'Hara never met him. For his lecture, he was supposed to be publicly greeted, welcomed, and introduced by John F., but when the lights went down in Washington Hall, there was no introduction. The Cardinal simply sat there in the first row to watch the lecture.

"O'Hara turned out his famous *Religious Bulletin* in room

141. That was one of his favorite bits of work. At first, he personally typed it up, but then you see he had two boys working for him that would run it off on the mimeograph machine. We hadn't any such thing as Xerox in those days. Every hall, every room, under the door at night. You would find it when you'd come back from your late afternoon class, but mostly when you were back from your evening meal. Father John Cavanaugh, I think, succeeded this man as prefect of religion and *he* got Ned Joyce to be his student secretary and he used to go around distributing the *Bulletin*. I had Father Joyce in my class when he was a sophomore. He always wore a blue sweater.

"I never lived on the second floor in 'Professors' Row' because I didn't want to be there. I had a chance at 355 and jumped at it. That's where I was living when I saw something I'll never forget—the night the barn caught fire. I was in my tower room one night when someone yelled, 'Mr. Fenlon, Mr. Fenlon!' We went over to look from the fire escape of the opposite tower and from there we heard all the poor horses screaming. At first I thought Badin was on fire—remember, back where Fisher Hall is today used to be farmland. I'll never forget seeing Jack Chevigny with hoses around his neck, soaking wet, wearing nothing but his pajama bottoms. He'd been putting out the fire. Poor Jack, God rest his soul, as Mr. Stritch would say, died in World War II. When they wheeled Rockne out to the game in his last year of coaching, it was Jack who helped him. He was Rockne's valet or butler. He did everything for Rockne and played football a couple of years, too."

[16]

Out and About

THE LITTLE WORLD the Professor made for himself consisted of several concentric circles. In one was the first floor of Sorin Hall—the porch, public restroom, lounge, back door, and chapel. In a larger ring were the Main and South Quads, including Sacred Heart, the Main Building, the Pay Caf, and the Morris Inn. A much larger circle was made up of South Bend, where he visited friends, ran errands, or went out to eat. But no matter how often I heard him describe his comings and goings, our visits were concentrated in the innermost of these circles, the tower room itself. Here we sat and talked like characters in a play. The set was so crowded we couldn't get up at the same time without some choreography. Occasionally a minor character, in the form of one of my friends, made a stage entrance to deliver a few lines, but this was essentially a two-man show, a dialogue between an old man and a young man.

More than a year passed before I broke into the outermost ring. On an unusually beautiful autumn day the Professor asked if I would like to accompany him into town, and he handed me the keys to his car. We drove to the dry cleaners, stopped for gas, then dropped off a football program for Doris. The Shuster home was so modest that "George used to call himself the last of the proletarians," the Professor said. The next stop was Bill Knapp's restaurant on Highway 31 for tea and cinnamon toast.

115

Afterwards, he pointed out Chet Grant's house at 122 Pokagon and we pulled over at 210 Pokagon so I could take a picture of G. K. Chesterton's old place, even though he hadn't yet told me the full story of Chesterton's visit to South Bend.

On another outing, we went to a movie at the mall, then out to eat. I offered to pay, but he insisted on treating me. In fact, whenever he would take me to dinner, I don't ever remember him letting me reciprocate. On this particular sojourn, we drove back down Vincent Street, and he pointed out the Rockne honeymoon cottage where Ed Fischer lives. "On the wooden floor, you can see dents where the Four Horsemen used to practice plays. They ate him out of house and home." On Notre Dame Avenue, we noticed the Golden Dome was dark on account of the coal shortage. We turned onto campus, and the guard waved us through. "He knows 'the Dodge with the Pennsylvania plate' and I gave him my pontifical blessing."

We drove behind the Dining Hall past a jogger. "I'm always so afraid that I'm going to hit one of those boys. I'm too old to drive at night, you know. I can only drive during the daytime with *my* eyes." We pulled up behind the hall and Sorin was quiet. Getting out of the car, he said, "I try to trick them by locking only the passenger side. Sometimes they put snow all over my roof."

I didn't understand the mind games he was playing with his student antagonists. I wasn't even convinced they all actually existed. I just said, "They're really not that vicious to you, are they?"

"Of course they are. You're being much too charitable. I've got real enemies, you know."

Then I recalled how three hours earlier he'd said, "I've had some mysterious phone calls lately. I think the boys upstairs are calling to see if I'm in." Apparently, a lot of things went on when I wasn't around, though I had trouble believing students would play pranks on him.

With the weather turning colder, excursions into town were becoming rarer, so the Professor had taken to walking back and forth between his vestibule and the back door. "Father Kerndt Healy always exercised here," he said. "That was in the days when priests were real priests. Every day, they used to read their Offices, but today I don't think any do anymore. They had four books about the size of the one behind you. Every day they used to have to read them in Latin. It took about an hour, but longer during some parts of the year. I remember Father Healy would look at his watch and say, 'I must get back to my Offices.' Each day, it had to be read before midnight. You could read it for twenty minutes or so, then after a certain amount of time you had to go back to read a little bit more. That's why I was so surprised to hear that King Farley actually read his Offices, because we all knew he didn't understand a word he read.

"Father Healy was a dear, dear friend of mine. He succeeded Father Hudson as editor of the *Ave Maria* magazine. Hudson was a little saintly man with a pointed goatee. He had the longest tenure as editor of any magazine in the United States. He didn't drive; he only took the train. One day I had to drive him to the hospital to see Father Healy. I asked, 'When was the last time you were downtown, Father Hudson?' 'Five years,' he answered. I laughed all the way there."

One evening, my roommate Tom and I visited the Professor and stayed until 1:45 in the morning. I didn't imagine many eighty-one-year-olds were up at this hour talking to a couple of teenagers, but though the Professor sometimes complained we visited him too late, he didn't object this time. He'd been out to a play downtown with Doris Shuster. "I've never been so embarrassed in my entire life as tonight," he said. "I thought I had lost my ghost." To get to his seat in the front row, he faced a daunting descent down a steep aisle without a railing. "A nice man came up and said, 'You're Professor Fenlon,' like they all do, 'aren't you?'" The usher had seen the write-up in the *South Bend Tribune.* "'Oh, you saw my obituary?' I said. The man helped me to my seat, holding my arm. It was the first time someone had ever assisted me in public that way. I was red as a proverbial beet."

"How was Mass last night?" I asked, knowing the bad weather had forced him to go to the ten-thirty hall mass.

"It started ten minutes late," he said. "It looked like the rector forgot to come, because Greg Green quickly had to throw on an alb and say Mass. He gave a very nice little talk. We had a pretty big crowd; there were even five girls there. They sent a collection basket around and I was petrified to find I only had one dollar in my pocket. I had not wanted to drive in the snow, so Friday I walked to the cashier's office, but they were closed."

The Professor was so frustrated by the weather that he wondered if he should leave Notre Dame and go back to Pennsylvania for good. These days he got winded just putting on his coat and galoshes to go out. "But if I went back to Blairsville," he said, "I wouldn't be able to go to daily mass, because there's only a six-something and a seven, and I can't make it. I could only get to First Fridays." *Good Lord!* I thought. *The only thing keeping you here is the mass schedule?*

Despite the snow and ice, the Professor did get to celebrate Father O'Neil's birthday and visit him in Corby. Though he complained the washbasin looked feminine, he admired Father O'Neil's room: "How I would love to live in the peace and quiet of Corby Hall. But the top man recently said that to make it a truly religious community, the community has to live together, so only priests live at Corby. You know, when they get sick they have Holy Cross House. President Cavanaugh improved so much when he was moved out of the student infirmary into Holy Cross House, where he was around people and not isolated anymore.

How I'd love to live for free as those priests do over there and be taken care of."

With Christmas approaching, holiday cards had begun to pile up. Someone sent him a clipping about former NBA President Walter Kennedy, who came to Notre Dame in 1930 and worked as a student for Rockne. "I didn't have him in class, but somehow I remember knowing him quite well and having liked him. I remember how busy he was." The Professor was typing a note to Paul Byrne. "Mr. Byrne is sick. He will turn ninety if he lives to the feast of the Epiphany. I can't believe he's an old man, just like I can't believe that I'm an old man."

The Professor often referred to this friend by his initials. PRB had come to Notre Dame in 1907 as a prep school student for two years, then entered the university and graduated in 1913. He lived in room 215 and became the university's head librarian in 1922, replacing pudgy little Father Paul "Pal" Foik, whose cassock, by the Professor's account, was always encrusted with food. "The Burke brothers, after seeing him, used to remark, 'Well, at least we know what's for dinner tonight.'" Once O'Shaughnessy Hall was built, Mr. Byrne resigned as librarian to become curator of the art gallery there and live in that building.

Father O'Neil phoned to remind the Professor not to go out to lunch in this weather. The Professor said his banana, toast, and tea would sustain him. "I had just been writing to T. Bowyer Campbell," he continued, before pausing, catching his mistake and laughing. At the other end of the line, Father O'Neil said, "Where are you going to send the letter to? It's going to be hard to get it there anytime soon" (Campbell had died eighteen months earlier).

In the evening, I swung by to take the Professor to a debate on religious belief featuring the provost and a member of the Philosophy Department. He was eating some crackers after drinking on an empty stomach at a party an hour earlier. When we pulled up to the Memorial Library, he struggled getting out of the car. "I'm a little unstable," he said. "I've just had two Scotches." We found some seats in the back of the auditorium. Before the event began, I pointed out the philosopher on stage to say I was taking his class: "He's the one next to Burtchaell."

"You mean the one next to the lady?"

"No, he *is* the lady, the one with the long hair."

"That's terrible!" he said. The philosopher began by discussing the dilemmas facing Christian believers. After fifteen minutes, the Professor said in a loud voice, perhaps audible to the stage, "When is he going to stop talking?" Then he dozed off and on for ten minutes, waking up with the comment, "Burtchaell is bored stiff." Some graduate students looked over their shoulders to scowl at us. After the event finished, the Professor said, "I wish he wouldn't use the word 'okay' so often. That's wrong! All he said was, 'okay, okay, uh huh, okay.' And the way he dressed!" The philosopher wore a checked shirt and a sweater with red, white, and blue horizontal stripes. "I remember that we were ordered under Dean McCarthy to wear shirts with collars, ties, and coats for class every day. If you say he's one of your best professors, this school really has gone downhill."

The subject of the debate reminded him of a joke about the president's frequent absences from campus: "We know where God is, but we don't know where Hesburgh is."

The next day, the Professor was not himself—perhaps still suffering from the ill effects of the previous evening. He admitted being confused about time. "I could swear that right now we're just at spring vacation," he said. "And last night I had trouble getting to sleep and I got up at ten this morning, which is very rare for me."

This was the first time I had ever noticed him being seriously disoriented or not himself, and I hoped it was nothing more than a passing phase. But I got to thinking: if Father O'Neil's illness was the first sign that trouble might lie ahead, this was the second.

A day later, my friends and I ran into the Professor and he was ghost white. "They've broken my window," he said. He trembled as he took us to the bathroom to show us. "I was in another room when it happened," he said, "but I've already called Security." We tried to tell him it was just an errant snowball, but he believed a group of students was out to get him. Checking on him later that night, we found he had thrown up he was still so upset. Now he vowed to leave the bathroom light off at all times so he would never be such an easy target again.

I still couldn't believe a snowball hurled through the biffy window was part of a campaign to drive him out of the building. But whether he was being paranoid or I was being naïve, I was beginning to worry about his emotional well-being. With the shattered window, collapsed ceiling, and constant barrage of student noise, the Professor was justified in feeling under attack from all sides.

Not long after this incident, we heard a disturbance in the vestibule, but this time it was perfectly innocuous. "Oh, that's just Elmo," the Professor said, referring to the maid. He still mispronounced the name of someone he saw every day and did so much for him, including making his bed. Recently, I broke it to him that her name was Elma, not Elmo, but to no effect.

Elma had stopped by with a Christmas gift. From her meager earnings, she had scraped together the money for a psychedelic tie and matching handkerchief. I was sure he would never wear them, but we were both touched by her thoughtfulness. The Professor thanked her profusely, but afterwards we had to laugh at how badly she had misjudged his fashion sense.

On that note, the semester ended. Late Sunday morning,

Paul Boehm and his wife came to take the Professor to the airport. Without much fanfare, his bags were carted away, and he offered me and my friends the use of his room in his absence. He handed me two keys tied to a shamrock-shaped stone, then put on his black hat and overcoat, said goodbye, shook hands, and walked away. Standing there, keys in hand, I found myself in sole possession of the room for the first time. It was like I had never seen it before: tick-tock still, the lights off, everything reduced to monochrome. I paused for a moment or two, then locked up for the holidays.

[17]

G. K. and Pop (1930)

DURING THE PROFESSOR'S long residence, the most memorable visitor Sorin Hall ever had was G. K. Chesterton. One of the Professor's favorite stories was his encounter with the renowned English writer, not least because it gave him a chance to reminisce about Sorin's most famous rector. Like Chesterton, Rev. John Francis Farley, CSC was larger than life.

"One winter, when the days were very short, 'Pop' Farley awoke and went through his morning routine. He pressed his buzzer to summon the students to chapel, then walked into the dark chapel and was surprised to find nobody there. He waited and waited, but still no students showed up. He went ahead and celebrated Mass all by himself anyway. Afterwards, he took his walk through the dark to the South Dining Hall. Something seemed strange to him, but still he continued on his way. In the dining room, he took his usual place at the head table where the priests sat to look out over the students. He placed his order with one of the ladies for fried eggs and bacon. 'Why, Father, it's not time for breakfast,' she said. It was actually late afternoon! Farley had just awakened from his nap.

"This was one of his most famous stories. He used to tell it on himself with a great deal of enjoyment and laugh at his absentmindedness. You see, this was the only place in the world where men got up twice a day: five a.m. and five p.m. During their naps, even the administration could not be found.

"Pop Farley added atmosphere to the place. They called him 'the King.' In the dining hall of the Main Building, he threw your mail to you and would just as soon it fell in your soup. He used to play football, remember, and was very strong. When I got my first Ford in '31, he didn't like me to park it in the courtyard, and I came around one night real quick and there was Farley attempting to push it out of its place. I'd caught him right in the act.

"He had no education to speak of. He barely knew enough Latin to get by and really wasn't much of a priest. With very few exceptions, Farley never said Mass or heard confessions, and he never preached from a pulpit in his life.

"Father Farley was probably the longest-term rector Sorin ever had, and he had plenty of experience because he'd been rector with those preps that were so undisciplined and so wild, those rich boys who lived in Walsh. Farley used to have his little snake whip and he'd *weeeshhh* give them a little tap on their little fannies and they'd bounce up the stairs and scream. He would stand at the bottom of the stairs there in Walsh as they'd come in at night, and if they were feeling a little too happy, he would say, 'Hi, boy! Yes, boy! Get up there, boy!' *Weeesshhhh* and that would be the end of it. He used to pick 'em up by the collar and take them by their little butts and *peeesshhhh* shove them along. He was used to doing this with the preps, but he rarely tried it on the college men. The strict discipline he instilled in the younger boys carried over to the older students and the whole campus, and this discipline only disappeared after World War II.

"There was a story of Manion's about King Farley and two football players. Some one of the football players was campused, but he had a friend call up King Farley and say, 'I'm in town just for the night and I'd like to have my son and his friend down for dinner.' And Farley said, 'Alright, they can get off campus for the night. They'll be down.' So they went out and they didn't get back until pretty close to midnight. And the next morning he walked in their room when they were sleeping—I think one was supposed to be Moose Krause—and with one jerk he just pulled them out of bed, the mattress and everything. He said, 'Now you two get upstairs and write something for ten minutes, then go over to the prefect of discipline's office and tell him what you did.' He said, 'That wasn't your father. I knew all about it and let you go.' He wasn't fooled one single bit, but they were jerked out of bed the next morning like that at five thirty or so.

"He was a wonderful rector. He was a great disciplinarian but he was fair and likable and got results. He would have a stroke if he were alive today to find girls in the hall named after him.

"He met what I thought was a tragic end. His legs had to be amputated and he spent his last years in a wheelchair. I think it was the same disease Rockne had. But even in that condition, he was still the same Farley; he still cried out to his acquaintances and snapped them on their rumps. It was a pathetic end, but luckily there wasn't much suffering.

"Farley was the rector the famous time G. K. Chesterton came to this campus. Chesterton taught for nine weeks. Monday, Wednesday, and Friday, he taught Victorian literature and on Tuesday, Thursday, and Friday afternoon Victorian history. There was just a final exam, which some other English professors and I made up and graded. He made money when he was here, although we've never found out who the benefactor was that guaranteed his $5,000—that's what he got. After he left here, President O'Donnell tried to get Hilaire Belloc, and Belloc—'Just $5,000?'—he wouldn't think of doing it for that, but Chesterton did. He was also given a house on Pokagon Street to use—modest, though not particularly small. He left every Saturday to go somewhere to give another lecture at $500 apiece—Detroit, Chicago, etc. He and Belloc were considered the most famous writers at that time.

"I like his essays much better than his Detective Brown stories or other writings, but he was a wonderful lecturer. He dressed somewhat sloppily but was always dignified. His Inverness cape just covered his shoulders. He was always drawing or doodling. When he lectured at Washington Hall he sat in a chair all alone on stage without notes. He fiddled with his hands and folded a blank piece of paper as he spoke. Whenever he said something that he thought was funny, he would lift up his feet, click his heels together, and laugh. The students then laughed with him and at him.

"President Charlie O'Donnell wanted as many of the faculty as possible to get to meet Chesterton personally, so he held a dinner honoring him, to which all the faculty members and their wives were invited. He had been here a few weeks already. It was set up in our brand new, beautiful Dining Hall, of which they were very proud, upstairs in the faculty dining room. There was a sort of receiving line before the dinner. O'Donnell was right next to Chesterton, of course, but he didn't know the names of all the faculty members. So he selected me to stand next to him and make the introductions. 'Mr. Fenlon, come and stand beside me here and please tell me who these people are. You are about the only one around who can still name every professor on campus.' 'Oh, no, I don't, Father—' 'Oh, yes, you do, Paul; you know better than I do.' So I had to pontificate that evening: 'Mr. Chesterton, this is Professor so and so and Mrs. so and so. ...'

"At the dedication of the new stadium, I sat on the fifty-yard line. As poor as we were, I had donated to the stadium fund along with Manion. Later I moved down to my current seat on the fourth row so I wouldn't have so many steps. The rumor was that the old, venerated sod of Cartier Field had been transplanted to the stadium. I didn't think anything special about the new stadium; it was just a stadium. We were playing Navy, but that's all of the game that I can recall.

"It was a hot day, hot, windy, and cloudy. I remember especially how the flag was flapping the entire time. Chesterton wrote a famous poem and read it on a little platform where the flagpole is today. Everyone was so appalled because his voice could not carry the length of this room. It went right up into the clouds. With the wind, all we could hear were the indistinct tones of that high, squeaky voice. But President Charlie O'Donnell spoke next in a clear, booming voice.

"I never really talked with Chesterton alone. Even Charlie Phillips didn't know him that well. You see, they couldn't carry on much of a conversation. Chesterton's squeaky little voice couldn't penetrate Charlie's deaf ears. It was always such a disappointment: such a big impressive man with such a high-pitched, funny voice.

"One day a colleague and I were summoned to President O'Donnell's office. While waiting to be shown in, we asked his secretary, a small young man, if he knew why we had been called in. The man behind the desk said, 'no.' Remember, at this time and for many years, with the exception of a few nuns, men occupied all positions in the university. But once we finally got to see O'Donnell, we asked him if there was a problem. O'Donnell replied in the negative, smiled, and assured us it was not a matter of great importance but that Mr. Chesterton had expressed a desire to go to an American speakeasy.

"We took him to Mike Alby's on Western Avenue. It was a bad district. We had to go around to the side door, you know, to be identified. They flashed a light on us, and then they knew who we were, and we got in. What a sight! Here was this big man with this big cape and that big funny hat that he wore and those pince-nez glasses with the little string on them, and everybody thought the place was being raided. So they all got up to leave. But he did enjoy it.

"The other thing: Chesterton expressed a wish—well, not exactly to have a party, but we dreamed it up for him. I mean by that it was Charlie Phillips's idea with Steve Ronay and Dan O'Grady. Towards the end of his stay, we set a certain night after his evening lecture. The night before, Pat Manion and I had to go out and get a tub full of ice. It was late, and we spirited it in. We put it under Charlie's bed for a full twenty-four hours before the party started.

"I suspect old King Farley knew what was going on, because you didn't fool Pop Farley about many things. But the biggest problem was getting Chesterton to Charlie's room in 341, because he was at least six foot three and a couple hundred pounds. Somehow we carried him up.

"Once the party began, it was the most interesting conversation I ever remember having. He sat up there in Charlie's room, and as Pat Manion often said, all you needed to do was, 'Mr. Chesterton, what about this situation?' and he was off and running. And you would listen to him. Pat said, 'If only I'd had my little secretary, Eddie O'Malley, who could take shorthand just like that.' But he entertained us until well after midnight. Chesterton drank most of the beer, while Ronay and I've always drunk Scotch, and Manion his Kentucky bourbon. Charlie drank the hard stuff, too, and would say every once in a while, 'Mr. Chesterton, would you like to go to the little boys' room?' And he never had to.

"He had been smoking all the time and tried to reach the ashtray but never got over. So when he finally got up to leave at about two in the morning, the ashes were like Vesuvius: they just fell from out of every little crease on his vest.

"I don't know to this day how we ever got him down those flights of stairs. Steve Ronay had an old-fashioned car of some sort at that time, and you should have seen us trying to get that man in and out of that car. Ronay was an English professor like me, but he was disliked by the boys, probably because of his lisp. When *Lady Chatterley's Lover* first came out, paperback copies were available throughout Europe, especially in England, but they were outlawed in the United States. Ronay returned from England with a copy and somehow got past US Customs, but once be brought it to Notre Dame it went missing within two weeks!

"We got Chesterton in Ronay's car by pushing his rear end in. When we got him home—you see, he had a furnished house—Mrs. Chesterton met us at the door. Chesterton's wife and his secretary came with him from England. I remember be-cause Johnny Conway dated the secretary and took her either to the sophomore formal or cotillion. But Mrs. Chesterton was very disagreeable, you know. We got him up the steps of the house and she said, 'Gilll-*berrrrt!*' She said, 'Gilbert, how late? I told you not to stay out so late!' And I never did hear his reply. She was very much annoyed."

[18]

Blizzard

WHEN WE RETURNED to campus in January of my sophomore year, the Professor seemed to be more agile than before, but he had the same case of bronchitis he used to get every winter as a teacher. "My students would be quite happy because I could not speak and they got a free day," he said.

The Professor rested while Big Boy and I helped unpack. Then, in what was a first, he offered us a drink and took us to eat at the Morris Inn.

After getting settled at our table, the Professor offered his favorite toast, smiling as we tapped our glasses, "To our noble selves." He recalled being at dinner once with his friend Sister Jean Lenz, the rectress of Farley Hall, and making this toast, sitting back, rubbing his hands in anticipation, then asking, "Now what are we going to have for dessert?" forgetting they hadn't had dinner yet.

"If I am going to keep living," he said, "I'm going to have to make a decision soon about where I'll live. I think they may try and kick me out next semester."

"Who would do that?"

"Well, I believe the president of the university has the power to execute that order."

I gave a long list of reasons why Father Hesburgh would never do that. Worn down by my logic, the Professor said I reminded

131

him of what Pat Manion used to say about someone always dis-
agreeing with him: "He was born in the objective case."

A week after our return to Sorin, just as the Professor was
getting re-established, a tremendous blizzard hit South Bend.
Temperatures were in the single digits, the wind blew thirty-five
to forty-five miles per hour, and the wind-chill factor was twenty
to thirty below. Over three feet of snow fell, and the drifts
reached ten or fifteen feet on the backside of Sorin. The snow
was plowed waist- or shoulder-high, so you had the sensation
of walking through tunnels across campus. For the first time in
history, Notre Dame had to close for five consecutive days.

When I visited late in the morning of the first day, a Thursday,
I found the Professor reading the *Chicago Tribune* and eating grape
jelly on toast with a banana. He was snug in his room, happy he had
gone grocery shopping earlier in the week but thinking we ought
to bring him back some ice cream for dinner. I returned at three
o'clock for tea. It was a long, leisurely occasion, as I had no classes
or studying to do and we remained socked in by the weather. We
looked out the window and couldn't even see the Main Building.
"This is the worst blizzard I've seen in my hundred years here," he
said. "But T. Bowyer Campbell would be proud of us having tea. In
the group we had Byrne, Campbell, Madden, and me. Originally
we met in the fourth-floor tower of Morrissey Hall."

On day two of the blizzard, the rector relayed a message of
concern from Father John Gerber, the religious superior for the
Holy Cross community at Corby Hall, whom he affectionately
called "Little Gerber" on account of his size. Gerber sent along
two oranges, two apples, two bananas. Big Boy brought back some
bread, ice cream, and cookies from the Dining Hall. "Someone
told me the day of George's funeral was the first time the university ever closed," said the Professor, "but I disagreed. I remember
as a student getting a day off. It was easier for professors to get to

campus then; most were priests or lived on campus." Later in the afternoon, Paul Byrne phoned from New York to see how the Professor was holding up, and they swapped stories about the snow.

That evening I found the Professor praying in the chapel, but he had abandoned the habit of walking backwards there because it made him dizzy. The stained glass windows had been removed for "restoration"—or so we had been told. The chapel now looked as it did before colored glass was first installed in 1902. "I feel naked now, when I walk into that chapel," said the Professor. Through the clear windows, he saw Father Gerber's light on in Corby, so he phoned to thank him for checking on him. At the end of the call, Gerber told him it had finally been decided Father O'Neil would have an operation in the next few days. The Professor was shaken by this news and immediately returned to the chapel. When he finished there, he phoned Doris Shuster to tell her, but he told me not to share the news with anyone.

On day three, a snowball sailed through the rector's window, convincing the Professor of a conspiracy to knock out every window in the building. This was another day cars couldn't travel on campus, but Ed Fischer managed to walk all the way from his home to Sorin Hall just to visit the Professor. That evening, Father Gerber sent more food via the rector: a bottle of red wine, green beans, spaghetti, and cornbread. "And it's still hot, too!" the Professor enthused. He gave the bottle to Big Boy, Tom, and me, while he picked at his food and I ate the beans and spaghetti.

We were interrupted by a phone call from Mrs. Shuster, who was upset the only plane to get into South Bend was the flight bringing the Maryland basketball team for tomorrow's nationally televised game. She complained Notre Dame was "driven by that money" and thought Moose Krause was neglecting the lesson of the Evansville tragedy last December, when its basketball team was killed in a plane crash.

Day four was the Maryland game. Students were about the only ones able to attend, because neither driving nor parking on campus was permitted or possible. The Professor enjoyed watching the big victory on TV, but he remained frustrated by his "incarceration." The weather was still too dangerous for him—but not me—to get to Sunday Mass at Sacred Heart, so he had to settle for the 10:30 in Sorin Chapel that evening. During Mass, the power dimmed to one-third strength before blacking out completely, and a student had to use a flashlight to get the Professor back to his room. When I dropped by later that night, the electricity was back on, but he was still rattled by the experience. His room was filled with every candle he owned, in all shapes and sizes, just in case we were plunged into darkness again.

The next day, the fifth and final day of the shutdown, a Mass was planned at Dillon Hall for Father O'Neil's recovery. There was no way in this weather the Professor could make the trek all the way to Dillon, but he was able to get over to Sacred Heart using his steel-tipped cane for traction. This was his first time out of the building since the blizzard began. Later in the day, he complained, "I never want to look at another sandwich again!" That evening he got his wish—an invitation from the rector and Father Green to eat at Corby. They formed a procession to walk him there, with one priest in front and one in back. The Professor walked between them concentrating on each thrust of his cane into the frozen trail.

Inside Corby, his hosts unwittingly seated him next to an old nemesis, a former member of the English Department, but the Professor was not about to let this ruin his evening. "They were all drinking at Corby because it was a soirée night. This is their traditional French event on the eve of feast days and other special occasions. And because the school had been closed for so many days, they had one this time. Whenever they want to have a party, they call it a 'soirée' to legitimize it.

"Father Green gave me a good Scotch. While I was dining, I looked up and saw a man in a tweed jacket and brown shirt looking very tired. If it wasn't the Reverend Ted Hesburgh! He said, 'My, Paul, if I'd known you were here, I'd have come to sit with you.' I had no idea whether he'd already eaten or not, but he sat down and chatted for a few minutes. He'd missed the storm but had also missed a connection somewhere. And this night he was off to Belgium."

The next evening the Professor was looking forward to another dinner out, but Mr. Stritch phoned at the last minute to say the roads were still too bad. Tom, Big Boy, and I showed him the *Observer*, which quoted him on the great snow storms of 1918 and 1967. Then the rector came by to check on him. "The food situation is favorable," the Professor told him, before asking, "Did you hear the explosion?" He certainly had: a bottle rocket was slipped under the rector's door and exploded during a staff meeting. "We're after whoever did it," he said. "If they're caught, they're out of the hall."

"Good!" exclaimed the Professor. "If one is given one's trunk, it will do wonders for the others."

The next day, the thaw came and the Professor was at last freed from captivity. Mr. Stritch escorted him to the Pay Caf for lunch. Later, Myron Busby took him shopping and Mr. Stritch returned to take him to dinner. They were having cocktails, when I stopped by to tell them about spending the afternoon in the attic.

I'd always been curious about Sorin's attic, which was supposed to be haunted. With the rector's permission that day, I'd gained access through the maid's closet on the third floor, I told them. Once I passed through the trap door, I had to crouch to avoid low-hanging wires, then crawl across the partial floor on my hands to avoid putting my foot through the ceiling of the rooms below (as someone last year had done to my ceiling).

The dormer windows and bare light bulbs didn't provide much light, but with a flashlight I made out an old water cistern, some television antennas, and a few dead birds. I noted the seam between the original building and the wings added in 1897 and looked up inside the hollow turrets, which were beautiful feats of carpentry. But what really caught my eye was the graffiti that had been carved, painted, chalked, and penciled on the beams and rafters. I counted over a hundred specimens.

"Until you spoke of it," said Mr. Stritch, "I never knew we had an attic." Then he backtracked to say that when the lights were shut off at ten every evening, students who wanted to keep studying and had some electrical know-how would hook up their lights to the twenty-four-hour grid in the attic. "I'll bet you a nickel, that's when they got up there to scribble their graffiti."

The Professor encouraged my idea of writing a story about the attic for *Scholastic* magazine. "I am not a scholar," he said. "*You* are. I have never *been* a scholar, but I enjoy seeing it in others."

The little piece of scholarship that meant the most to me was my history of the hall, I told him when it was just the two of us. My "Historical Guide" was posted at the front entrance to the building and highlighted individual rooms and their inhabitants. After the wild goose chase to find the room belonging to Chet Grant and Harry Stuhldreher, I'd settled on room 56 as the likeliest candidate.

The Professor had already helped me with earlier drafts, but now I presented him with his own copy of the final product. He teased me: "Now are you sure that you can spare this? Are you sure that you want to give me one?"

"Not giving you a copy would be like not giving an author a copy of his own book."

"Yessss," he agreed, laughing. "Say, Phil, you know sometime

I want to get back up to the third floor again."

"We've rigged pulleys to hoist you all the way up to the attic now."

"No, you won't."

"We'll gag and bind you, then carry you up there."

"I won't let you!"

The Professor thought about it and agreed he wouldn't mind at least looking up into the attic. A little later, before I left, he turned to me. "Phil, when did we first meet each other? What vacation period was it?"

"It was in the lounge over fall break last year, when you needed your watches wound. Then I started asking you questions about Knute Rockne. I haven't changed much, have I?"

"Oh, yes you have."

He didn't elaborate. I wondered: *Had* I changed? If so, I wasn't aware of it. After sixteen months, I still had a burning curiosity about Sorin Hall. I still asked endless questions. Neither of us had really changed, except that we were friends now. Is that what he meant?

[19]

The Ghost of Washington Hall

FOR SEVERAL MONTHS, Pat Manion had been complaining about the *South Bend Tribune*'s recent account of the ghost of Washington Hall. The Professor had brought up the subject to Chet Grant weeks earlier: "Manion simply said the other night to me when I was out there, he said, 'I wish someone would write an authentic thing—they've stretched it and not maintained the facts.' And Chet said, 'Well, it sounds like it was a hoax all the way through.' 'Well, that's it,' I said, 'but Pat doesn't like it, because he swears, honest to God, that it wasn't a hoax.'"

Another day the Professor told me, "Last night I was at the Manions, and Pat was disturbed by all of the false stories circulating about the ghost of Washington Hall. He said we must have Joe Corona over sometime to talk. I said, 'But Pat, Joe's been dead for six months.' And Pat said, 'No, he can't be dead. He's the only other one who knows the story. I need him to get the story straight.' And I told him, 'I'll have to check with Margaret in the alumni office to see if Joe Corona is still alive.' Corona was a great fellow, a Spanish teacher here for years, very polite. He always used to bow"—the Professor bowed at the waist—"and he spoke very slowly. As a student he worked in the dining hall and was in charge of all the waiters. He needed the money be-cause his father had lost everything in the Mexican uprising."

Then one evening, at about 10:30, I knocked on the

139

Professor's door, heard him talking on the phone, and poked my head in. He motioned for me to enter and I began paging through *Time*. The next thing I know, he thrusts the phone in my hand. "Mrs. Manion wants to talk to you," he said. On the line, a well-spoken woman informed me that Brad Steiger, a writer on paranormal activities, had published an article in a national magazine claiming there were no ghosts in Washington Hall. "Now Pat, my husband, was there once and there *were* ghosts," she said. "He lived there with Johnny Mangan, the chauffeur, Casasanta, and even Father Cavanaugh was involved. Pat had always wanted to get the survivors together to tell the true story, but he never got around to it." She asked if I would help record his version of the story, and I agreed.

The Professor filled me in: "Yes, they lived in Washington Hall the year before I taught. Pat was teaching history to the preps. The university chauffeur was a little Irishman named Johnny Mangan. Everybody knew Johnny. He lived on the top floor of 'Cadillac Hall,' but also lived in Washington Hall for a few years. I knew him pretty well and talked with him often. He's buried in the CSC cemetery. Johnny with his brogue always called the students 'kids'—so improper. They're 'college men' or 'boys.' The minims were more like 'kids.'

"I always remember the story Pat Manion told on himself in regards to the ghost, how he would return to his residence late at night by cab. At that time, the school's entrance was at the statue of Father Sorin. There was a great horseshoe driveway there that brought you to within just fifty yards of Pat's room, which was on the top floor, above the band building in the back of Washington Hall. Pat was genuinely afraid to go up to it alone in the dark, so he devised a ruse: he told the cabbie he had for-gotten his money, which meant the cabbie had to escort Pat to his room for the fare."

Over the ensuing days, the Professor made arrangements for our session with the Manions. "I told them you had your own car but might have trouble finding them on your own, so I would drive you out there. The Manions, you, and I will meet at seven on Thursday night for a little something to eat and drink. I told them you liked beer. And Pat and I will have a couple of drinks. You know he talks much better with a few drinks in him. He seems anxious to get this done as soon as possible or he's afraid it will never get done. Frankly, he and I both know that in a sense we are living on borrowed time. We could both die suddenly any day now, but I'm just more frank about it."

I went to the library to dig up everything I could on the ghost of Washington Hall. I also went to see Father Blantz for advice on how to record an oral history. Whether or not the ghost story was of historical value, he told me, getting the voice of a famous Notre Dame orator on tape surely was. As for the Professor, Father Blantz said, "Paul has the clearest, most remarkable memory of anyone I have encountered. He's disgusted with himself when he can't recall the fifth person of a group when he's already named four. It's a memory that he works at. He keeps in touch with everyone, of course. When he meets someone, he becomes part of the family and he must know all about your family." I recalled my own first meeting with the Professor, when he asked for my hometown and particulars about my family. Now he always introduces me by saying, "This is a young man from St. Petersburg, Florida. He has a father in the class of '57."

As Thursday approached, I asked the Professor about the dress code, and he told me we would all be in coats and ties. I didn't know quite what to expect that evening. I did know Mrs. Manion had a national reputation as a breeder of Arabian horses. I wondered how someone of her husband's stature could believe in ghosts.

Clarence Manion taught constitutional law at Notre Dame for a quarter century and was dean of the Law School from 1941 to 1952. He ran unsuccessfully for the Democratic nomination for the United States Senate in 1934. In 1952, he became a Republican and was soon appointed chair of the Inter-Governmental Relations Commission by President Eisenhower. Later, he crisscrossed the country giving speeches on behalf of conservative causes and became a founding member of the John Birch Society and a director of the national committee of America First. His political commentary, the Manion Forum, celebrated its one thousandth consecutive weekly broadcast. In its heyday, it was carried by two hundred radio stations and televised.

When we drove out to "Manion Canyon" on Laurel Road, it was just as the Professor had described it—a wooded estate on farmland with a large white house surrounded by guest lodges. Gina (*pronounced* JIN-uh) Manion welcomed us and served drinks, then we waited in the kitchen for Dean Manion to appear. After several minutes, he arrived acting every inch the dean—charming, self-assured, and in charge. While Gina prepared his drink, he told a story about the body-builder priest Bernard Lange. As a prefect in Walsh Hall, Lange once found some students gambling, he said, so Lange picked up the money and tore the deck of cards in half, a trick Manion had never seen repeated. The dean finished the story with a hearty laugh worthy of his golden voice.

Sitting down to his drink, he was all business, announcing he needed to "clear the air" after all the ridiculous stories being spread about Washington Hall. Our interview had to be conducted properly, he emphasized. That meant modeling it after the one he did for the Eisenhower Oral History Project, in which he had talked about his term as commission chairman very informally, and corrections and additions followed. For our purposes this evening, he insisted on starting with deep background, which would not be tape recorded.

He began by telling how he came to Notre Dame in the first place. Because he had a Catholic degree, he reasoned he should apply to Catholic schools. He had not even sent a formal application, just a letter of inquiry, when President Cavanaugh wrote back—here the dean bellowed—"Dear Mr. Manion, welcome to Notre Dame!" The letter closed with the words, "expecting to see you in the fall." To Manion's dismay, there were no specifics—no salary mentioned, no contract—but he decided it would be a good job nonetheless. When he arrived on campus, he was met, ironically, by Mr. John Cavanaugh, the future priest and Notre Dame president (the second so named). Cavanaugh was secretary to Father Burns, who had succeeded old Father Cavanaugh as president in the weeks since he and Manion exchanged letters.

At this juncture, we adjourned to the dining room, and I was allowed to start taping. The room was pitch black except for the low-hanging Tiffany-style lamp over the table. In the shadows I could make out dozens of photographs, mainly of horses.

Then our host began his story. To discredit the hearsay of competing versions of events, he first laid out the geography and identified the witnesses by name. In the fall of 1919, he said, several people, mainly adjunct faculty, lived on the third floor of Washington Hall, in the north wing behind the theatre stage. Their rooms looked out on the band room to the east. Dean Manion was teaching American history and politics and studying for his law degree at the time. Living in the building with him were: Jose Corona, scion of a wealthy family who was stranded at Notre Dame by the Mexican Revolution and teaching Spanish; Dan Carr, a chemistry graduate student; Jimmy Bell, an instructor of the "Minimums"; John Buckley, a law student and part-time instructor like Manion; Jimmy Hayes, an executive secretary working for a campus dean; Johnny Mangan, a laundry employee and not yet the university's chauffeur; Brother Maurilius, who sold lemonade and cake at the Huddle around the corner and lived on the floor below Manion and the others; Joe Casasanta, the assistant director of the band, who would later compose the alma mater and football songs "Hike, Notre Dame," "On Down the Line," and "When the Irish Backs Go Marching By."

This motley collection of residents became a family of sorts. They took their meals at the faculty table in the middle of the student cafeteria next door in the Main Building. From five to six o'clock every evening, they made themselves scarce while the band was rehearsing, then they returned to their rooms and settled down to work. Manion and Buckley were the night owls of the group.

As the dean was speaking, he sketched a map of the room assignments on a legal pad and asked the Professor questions to confirm or supply details, and he deferred to him on these points. This is how we learned, for example, that it was penmanship that Bell taught the Minims. Thus far, Mrs. Manion's role was confined to reminding her husband of any missing details.

One night, in November or December, the dean continued, he was alone in his room reviewing his lectures for the following day. It must have been about midnight. Out of the blue, he heard a horn—a clear, piercing single note emanating from the band room and reverberating throughout the building. It was a perfect B-flat on a coronet, as later testing would confirm. He wondered who on earth could be horsing around in the band room at that late hour. Flinging open his door to investigate, he heard nothing, saw nothing, and retreated to his room convinced he was imagining things.

The next night the horn blew again. This time, Buckley heard it. He and Manion suspected Casasanta, the resident musician,

was behind it, but though Casasanta heard it, he denied responsibility. Over the course of the next several evenings, Hayes and
Bell heard the horn, too. For a time, Corona and Carr scoffed at
their stories, until one night they heard not only the horn but
what sounded like wings fluttering under their beds.

After their initial alarm, the residents became accustomed
to the midnight horn and began treating it like a squeaky door.
They never saw anything sinister or out of place and didn't feel
physically threatened, so they decided they would just have to
live with it. Then, just when they put it out of mind, they began
to hear footsteps and slamming doors. After the horn blew one
night, they heard the front door banging, followed immediately
by the sound of someone downstairs walking, then running up
flights of stairs and turning on the top landing of their floor. Now
at last, they thought, they would discover who was behind the
mysterious sounds. But when they threw open their doors, all
they saw was Johnny Mangan in his night shirt, armed with a
club, in pursuit of the same ghost.

Worried they'd be ridiculed for believing in ghosts, Manion
and company kept the secret to themselves. For several weeks
their story was limited to the table talk of the faculty mess and
the nuns working with Mangan in the laundry. It only became
a campus-wide sensation as a result of a talk Father Crumley
gave at the Knights of Columbus in the basement of Walsh Hall.
That night there were 150 students in attendance, and Crumley's subject was the ghosts of Ireland. When Crumley reassured
his audience it needn't be scared of these supernatural events
because they took place in faraway Ireland, Buckley shot up from
his seat. Such things were not restricted to Ireland, he declared:
Notre Dame had a ghost!

The next day, Washington Hall was mobbed. Students and
townspeople alike wanted to see the ghost. Two iron beds were

set up in the band room so they could keep vigil. Several students even slept on the floor, breaking their ten o'clock curfew to do it. Many of those spending the night heard nothing and declared the whole thing a hoax, but others were converted. The horn blew for John Cavanaugh and his friend, Dan Young, two of the only witnesses of these events still alive today. They both came running to Manion's room terrified, banging on his door to wake him up. Another convert was Father Burns's secretary, Harry Stevenson. One day Stevenson was visiting Casasanta and making fun of his ghost stories. A few moments after he stepped out to use the bathroom, Manion and Casasanta heard the bugle followed by a shriek. Running to investigate, they found Stevenson stretched out on the lavatory floor in hysterics, covering his ears. After they calmed him down, he went to President Burns to vouch for their story.

The last holdout was Brother Maurilius. Early to bed and early to rise, he was the only resident never to hear the horn. He thought the other residents were fools who were drinking too much coffee. To defend their reputations, they took matters into their own hands, and this was the only bit of trickery in the entire saga, Manion swore. Maurilius had to be awakened in order to hear the horn, so one night as the old Brother was snoring, Buckley, who lived directly above him, dropped dumbbells from his top bunk and Casasanta blew a horn. Maurilius awoke with a fright, jumped out of bed, and raced down the hall with his nightgown pulled up over his knees, frantically screaming for Corona and Casasanta. He refused to go back to bed and instead went to the chapel to pray.

The next day Manion was heading to class, when he bumped into Brother Maurilius recounting his trauma to Father Charles O'Donnell (like Cavanaugh, another future Notre Dame president). Manion got a knowing wink from the priest, but

O'Donnell in his capacity as CSC provincial was obliged to hear Maurilius out. Maurilius wasn't interested in O'Donnell's offer to inspect the building—he wanted an exorcism! Manion heard that someone later performed a ritual of some sort with a hyssop and some holy water, though he never witnessed it personally. In any event, that was the last of the ghost. After a six-month run, the horn never sounded again.

Here the story ends, but after we broke for dinner, then finished eating, I began my cross-examination, presenting Dean Manion with a competing version of events. I reminded him that Charles Davis claimed in the *South Bend Tribune* that he was the ghost, and he had tricked everybody by threading a tube through the wall and into a trumpet mouthpiece in the instrument cupboard. Manion rejected this story out of hand. Davis didn't even live in Washington Hall the year in question, he said. Maybe not, I replied, but was there still a way to harmonize the two versions of events? Perhaps Davis simply wanted to play a trick on his friends, Jim Clancy and Jody Shanahan, so he blew the horn for them, believing the only horn ever to sound was his, not the one you reported. But the dean didn't budge: his little family was there all the time, and it would have detected an outsider's interference. Besides, he said, Davis couldn't have piped anything through the walls, because the first thing Father O'Donnell did was to have janitors check the building, and they ruled out a common-sense explanation like the wind blowing through the eaves. Manion expressed surprise Davis would have the audacity to fabricate such a tale.

The thorniest issue of the entire episode had to do with chronology, it seemed to me. Davis claimed the ghost appeared in 1920-21, a year later than Manion's rendering would have it. Published accounts in the *Dome* and *Scholastic* appeared to corroborate Davis's dates, but the Professor backed up the dean's recollection that Manion moved into Sorin in 1920, the year *after* the strange goings-on in Washington Hall. The Professor had been in Chicago in 1919-20 and so he missed the whole controversy and never heard anything about it once he returned to campus. If this chronology was accurate and the ghost was heard in 1919-20, Davis could have been describing a hoax perpetrated a year *after* Manion had left (in 1920-21, in other words). If Manion's dating was off by a year and he was actually living in Washington Hall in 1920-21, then either he was taken in by Davis's prank or he was in a good position to disprove it, as he now insisted on doing.

Whichever dates were correct, the dean made short work of rival accounts. He reiterated that no one ever *saw* anything—a galloping horse, a ghost, a bird—they just *heard* the horn. Everybody wanted to think it had to be a bird call or a squeaky door or scampering rats, but there was no getting around the unmistakable sound of a single, pure note on a horn.

The Professor was getting bored with this second round of details, so he drifted off to the kitchen to visit Gina. Bits of their conversation filtered through the Dutch doors, and my ears pricked up when I heard her say, "You must write your memoirs, Paul." That was a topic more interesting to me than any ghost story. I strained to hear more but could only make out the Professor complaining he couldn't type and Gina saying he should use a tape recorder the way she does with her projects.

After nearly three and a half hours at the Manions, the Professor put on his overcoat to leave, but the dean got his second wind and began describing his experience as the administrator of Colonel Hoynes's estate. Then for my benefit he delivered a discourse on states' rights and the taxing powers of the federal government. Finally, he explained how the Washington bureaucracy had stymied the work of the commission he chaired.

Back in the car, as we drove back along dark country roads, the Professor commented, "I think your question about whether Pat ever had nightmares about the ghost surprised him."

The next day, when I deposited the tapes in the archives, Father Blantz teased me about the drinking that could be heard on them. It is true that the clattering ice cubes rendered some passages unintelligible, but I was still able to summarize the transcript for the dean. He sent a telegram urging me to publish my "digest" as soon as possible, and I did so in the *Observer*.

Although the Professor had listened politely to his friend's story, he remained a skeptic.

"I thought you believed Pat Manion about the ghost of Washington Hall," I said.

"I believed him, but I never had any part in it. It was a purely fictional thing to my way of thinking always. I always thought it was ridiculous and I could never abide Manion and those boys who lived there were so sincere about it. I spoofed it all the time. You see, most of that happened the year I was trying to be a banker in Chicago. I was out of the picture."

$\left[20\right]$

Between the Library and Me

AN OLD FACULTY FRIEND, Lee Flatley, phoned the Professor with disturbing news: Father O'Neil had cancer. How did Flatley know? It was general knowledge, he said.

The Professor was infuriated. He'd been kept in the dark and now regretted not pressing for more information sooner. Yet he couldn't quite believe Flatley's news or at least didn't want to broadcast it. A faculty widow phoned for an update on O'Neil, and the Professor said, "I don't think it's cancer, but it's something, something in his back. He did fine through the operation but was very angry to be kept in the hospital four extra days due to the snowstorm in Boston."

The next afternoon, Tom and I stopped by for a chat, just as we had done countless times before. After ten minutes, in a manner that was also routine, we announced we were off to dinner. But this time the Professor snapped at us. "You don't even come to visit anymore," he said. "You're treating me like I'm a pit stop. You bring in all these people, disturb me, then leave. At night, I'm all alone here and you're all off at that damned library."

We were dumbfounded. *Where was all this coming from? Since when were there schedules to follow? Since when were our visits timed?* I tried making excuses but really didn't know what to say.

At quarter to midnight, I returned from the library, somehow forgetting that afternoon's scolding. He was still in high

151

dudgeon, though he didn't reprimand me, at least not right away. I was alone this time and he was already in his pajamas. He sat on the edge of the bed with his wooden slippers. "This has not been my day," he muttered. "I don't know if I can go on. I think my feet are getting worse. I can't even move them. Look." He tried wiggling his toes. "And my fingers: they don't work either." He flexed them for me, then said softly, with determination, "I'm going to have them try an operation on one of my hands. If they can improve one hand, then I'll have them do the other."

"It looks like you took a shower tonight," I said.

"Yes, and I'm exhausted. These clogs are so heavy. Say, I heard a boy telling me about some light slippers he thought I'd like. I forget what they're called." I described flip-flops to him. He frowned.

As I was speaking, Big Boy and Bill knocked at the door, and the Professor returned to that afternoon's theme. "I can't stand all this late night traffic," he said. Just as he began describing my hurried dinnertime visit, Tom walked in the door. Now outnumbered four to one, the Professor changed topics. "Tomorrow I'm having a little party at six o'clock until about nine for a very good friend of mine, Mr. Stritch, and a woman he knows. She has wanted to see my room for two years, and I've put her off until now. Now out, all of you, out!" Propped up in bed among his pillows, he raised his right hand and like a bishop made the sign of the cross in benediction. We said goodbye and collected our coats from the vestibule. "And don't come back at such late hours!" he cried out after us.

A few days later he told me he'd been missing a lot of sleep lately and feeling dejected, but he thought he'd finally figured out his problem. After thinking long and hard about it, he concluded the real source of his troubles was—me! My friends and I were keeping him up too late, he said. We were the ones responsible for his sleepless nights and sour moods. That's why we would have to change our ways and observe the visiting hours he was instituting forthwith. From now on, we would be permitted to visit him between ten and eleven at night. "Now decide between the library and me," he said.

The Professor or the library? Wasn't that always the choice—between studying like a hermit and living a full life? In our ambition to do well in school, we had to decide how much we could afford to socialize. The Professor was always teasing us for studying so much. "Why don't you get away from the books and relax?" he'd say. "In my day, we watched movies for free over in Washington Hall." He didn't understand we only made it into Notre Dame because we stayed focused on our studies, and we did actually have a social life most weekend evenings and did attend all the football and basketball games. I will admit I was writing papers, doing readings, and studying for tests between 7:00 and 11:30 p.m., Sunday through Thursday, most weekend afternoons, and on and off weekdays between classes. But now the Professor was asking me to sacrifice ninety minutes of prime study time (10:00-11:30) that couldn't be made up later because the library was closed and the dorm was too noisy.

Mulling over the implications of his ultimatum one day, I received a rare summons from him. He phoned to ask that I drop by before my one o'clock class, offering no explanation why and insisting I come alone. Entering his room, I could tell at once he was upset. "I have a secret that you mustn't share with anyone," he said. "It's not to leave these walls." He paused. "Father Gerber's secretary, Bert, said that Gerber had gone out to Boston to see Father Dan and consult with his doctors." For all the cloak and dagger, this news seemed anticlimactic to me, but to the Professor it represented an ominous turning point, and he needed to get it off his chest. That was all he had to say. I could go to class now.

Late that afternoon I came back to see how he was doing. Two prank fire alarms had sounded the night before, and as usual he'd slept through the bell, which tinkled softly like an old-fashioned telephone. I promised if there had been an actual fire, we'd have come down to save him. On cue, he picked up a newspaper describing a recent fire at Syracuse University. "I'm sure Mr. Byrne will fill us in on it. He'll probably send me some clippings with pictures. You know, I haven't seen PRB since the trip I took to see Stretch O'Connor the last time before he died." Then he added, "I hope you've told no one about Father O'Neil."

"No one," I said.

"I called Dan's secretary and she had talked to him during her vacation in Florida. Dan said he'd return April 20th or even a bit earlier, which was much later than he told me. I told her about Little Gerber's trip out to Boston, which came as a surprise to her, and she took it as bad news. Father Dan had hoped to be here to preside over the annual festival for the international students, but he'll have to miss that now. Someone who is high up in the hierarchy and paying the bills must have sent Gerber to Boston to bring Father Dan back to campus. This is a bad sign. In all my years here, I never knew of a priest being hospitalized away from campus for as long as he has been."

Over the next several days, there was a constant drip of dire prognosis. "I talked with some people, including Mr. Manion," said the Professor, "and now it looks like cancer. Father O'Neil's going to be taking radiation treatments which they tell me are very severe and painful. I just don't want to be around if he dies." Then Father Gerber returned from Boston with more news. "Father O'Neil is worse than we thought," the Professor said. "He's been taking radiation treatments several times a week and doesn't really care what happens. He wants to come back once more to say goodbye—figuratively, I mean—to those foreign students of his that he'll never see again because of graduation. He'd be able to come back here just for a short visit, then have to return to Boston for more treatments." Another bulletin followed: Father O'Neil had undergone a second operation for a tumor.

By this time, the Professor was resigned to the inevitable: "Well, I think we've seen the end of poor Father O'Neil," he told me. "And that will be hard on me. Dan and I have done a lot of things together."

We dropped the subject of Father O'Neil for the time being, and he reverted to another familiar topic: "You're visiting me at quarter to midnight," he complained, "and yesterday you didn't come at all!" His parting words to me were: "I want to see you tomorrow. You are guilty of a sin, the sin of neglect."

The next evening I did not neglect him, nor the next, nor the next, and I was careful to observe his curfew. He had my attention now, but I did not know how long I could bend to this whim of his, and I hoped I could settle back into my routine without disrupting his, even though the chances of compromise on either side seemed remote. What I didn't fully appreciate at the time was that visiting hours and Father O'Neil were interlocking issues. He lost sleep over Father O'Neil and my late visits. Without sleep, he lacked the emotional reserves to handle either of these sources of anxiety.

One day the *South Bend Tribune* provided a welcome change of subject. It was speculating about possible candidates for provost, months after Father Burtchaell's surprise resignation last August. Of the three mentioned, only one was a priest, Father David Burrell, one of "the three Bs."

"They'll never give it to a layman," said the Professor. "Burrell will get it."

"Isn't the board of trustees filled with lay people?" I asked. "What if they want a lay provost?"

"Fortunately, the board only gives the appearance of having the authority, but Reverend President Hesburgh does as he pleases. He has the real power and runs the school. I think it was a mistake when they sold out to that lay board of trustees in the first place, because now we are simply no longer Catholic. We are a good school, but no longer Catholic. We're just like all the rest now."

"Do you think you'll be coming back next year?" I asked, returning to a topic he raised almost weekly ever since I'd known him.

He hesitated. "I would like to, but some people don't want me to stay. I am no longer productive, you see. I thought that after George Shuster died, they might give me a job, but they didn't."

"I can't imagine anyone would want to see you leave."

"I know two who do."

"Who?"

"I won't *tell* you. Coming back, you see, involves so much difficulty. I have to arrange for my car to be brought back to South Bend from Blairsville, though I have several friends who will do it at a moment's notice. I fly them out and they drive me back. But 'getting ready to get ready to go' takes a week. It takes a lot out of me.

"Sometimes I think I made a mistake in not leaving at vacation time. I don't want to be left all alone in this big hall all summer. I'm afraid I would die here. That's the way it happens—don't laugh. The average age for men is only three score and ten, and besides that, my heredity is bad. Don't look to your parents for heredity. Look to your grandparents. Grandfather Fenlon was killed at an early age in a horrible train accident, but two other grandparents died at seventy-four and seventy-five. So, you see, I'm living on borrowed time."

As our visit wound up, he said, "Well, I'll see you tomorrow, unless God takes me as an angel in the night."

"And you would look down upon the barbarians of Sorin Hall?"

"No. I will fly up to reclaim my third-floor tower room!"

He could be forgiven for thinking death was stalking him. A few days later another friend was picked off. "It's been a hard, tiring day," he told me. "A dear old friend of mine, Art Haley, died today. He was about my age. He was eighty. I remember him from the first class I taught here. He came in right after World War I, with his pants and hat. He had to work to go to school. He told me he had a younger brother who was smarter than he, so the brother went through Notre Dame first. He was in one of Father Zip Zip Zip's business programs. They got you through in just two years and turned out some fine accountants. It was located in the Main Building, where today the cashier's office is.

"But 'J. Arthur Haley,' as he became known, started out as a student manager under Rockne. He graduated in the 1920s. Then he was made business manager in the Athletic Department. He loved it there, but J. Hugh O'Donnell put him in charge of public relations, a department O'Donnell had just invented. He didn't like it as well as the Athletic Department, especially with all its fringe benefits, but he stayed there to manage it.

"Art was a quiet, sweet, kind man. His friendships helped bring in a great deal of money for the university. He headed all of the fund drives, and even got Morris to donate the money for the Inn. He was famous for being the technical adviser on the film *Knute Rockne, All-American*."

Two days later came the funeral.

"Did they play the alma mater?" I asked.

"Yes, the Glee Club sang 'Notre Dame, Our Mother,' though

I don't like it, because it brings back memories of many boys whose funerals I've attended. The song is very emotional for me, though I've requested it for my own funeral. And I want a closed casket, too, so people aren't making remarks like, 'My, he looks so natural.'"

On my next visit, I came to see if he was coming to the *King Lear* film in the Engineering Auditorium. He was standing by his dresser and said, "I'm surprised you're not here ogling these photographs of my home in Blairsville."

"Remember? I saw them last month and I thought you didn't want to hear my repeated oohing and ahhing over them."

"When we had houseguests and our four bedrooms overflowed, I used to go up and live in the tower. The basement was finished, so we have it and the first and second floors as living space now. I was born in the same room in the back of the house that I slept in this past summer, not my usual room. I want to die in that first-floor room where I was born."

"You don't want to do *that*!"

"Why, I think everyone should get to choose where they want to die." He rustled through the drawers, then turned to me. "Now, if I should die, and you know, I am eighty-one years old, here is where I keep my credit cards and papers, and you know the eyeglass case where I keep my watches and ring."

He decided against the film because it required a long walk in the rain. "Well, go off to your movie now and I'll see you tomorrow. Remember, I told you I want to get up to the third floor again this year, before you all leave for spring vacation. There are some things I want to see, and I have some questions to ask *you*!"

Questions for me? That would be turning the tables. But two days later when he visited, he had no questions or anything he wanted to see. Instead, we engaged in our usual banter. "I was over in the alumni office yesterday," he said, "and a man with a set of false teeth like George Washington's asked me if I was going to be here for the reunion of the class of '28. 'It's their fiftieth, you know, and you were there last year for the '27.' 'Yes,' I said, 'I think so. I really don't know.' So he said, 'We're having a big round frontispiece of you in the program.' 'Well,' I said, 'In that case, I'm not going to be here.' So he turned around and said he'd write to the secretary not to put the frontispiece in."

"Why don't you like all this fame?"

"I don't like it at all."

"Do you just not like your picture?"

"No. I never take a good picture; these glasses are so thick you can't see my eyes."

He spied my copy of Dick Sullivan's memoir about Notre Dame, picked it up, and began reading aloud. I told him many people on campus thought he should be writing his own memoir.

"Well, just tell them not to hold their breath."

"Why?"

"Because I don't intend to do it."

"Well, wouldn't it be good if I wrote it up?"

"Yes, you can write it up, but you wouldn't sell ten copies. It would be a waste of your time."

"Oh, but I'm sure we'd sell more. Remember the professor you've met, Dennis Moran?"

"Oh, yes, yes."

"He's the one so interested in you. He knows I am a Sorin Hall addict, with all of my stories about you, and he was the first one to say that most of the histories written about the school really don't tell the stories of the people, besides a few like Rockne and Hesburgh and Sorin, or explain why Notre Dame was different from other places."

"They've always concentrated on, and made the money from, the publicity from, a certain group of people," the Professor said. "But I think Moose Krause has been here long enough that he's almost a legend."

"Well, *you* are a legend."

"Yes, whether I like it or not."

"Because right now, the historical thing about you is that you are the last—"

"Yes!"

"—of the whole group."

"Well, if you can outlive everybody then you become some-body. Now, come on, Philip, you have your work to do, and I'm getting out of here."

Coming down the stairs, we stopped for groups of students racing up the steps, before passing "our naked chapel" and returning to the familiar surroundings of 141. "You know Samuel Johnson there?" I asked, pointing to his Toby Jug on the mantle. "You have a lot in common with him because for twenty years Boswell followed him around writing down all that he said. So you can have compassion for him."

The Professor laughed. "See you later."

"See you later. Bye."

$\left[21\right]$

Who Is Charlie Phillips? (1924-33)

THE NAME CHARLIE PHILLIPS came up often in conversations, so at one point I finally had to ask just who he was.

"My dear friend Charlie Phillips came here as what you would call today a lecturer-in-residence. He had a name on the West Coast, because he edited the *San Francisco Monitor*. He was known for that and for *High in her Tower*, a little volume of verse that was partly inspired by the view from his own room in Sorin, with the woman character looking down from a tower. He also wrote a novel, *The Doctor's Wooing*, but it failed miserably. We always thought this was a bad title, but we never told Charlie because we didn't want to hurt his feelings.

"Charlie liked Sorin, but at first he didn't like it. Originally he was assigned to a student room, 333, then one day I walked out to the porch and saw Father Charles O'Donnell, who asked how Charlie was doing. I said, 'He's not very happy here. He's got a student room and still has many more of his books on the way.' O'Donnell said, 'Oh, my, we'll have to fix that.' So shortly afterwards in that first year he moved to 201 and got the adjoining little room in 203. The next year, somehow he got 341, and he was the first one that got a telephone in this hall.

"Until the 1920s, we had to use the pay phone in this building. I never had a private phone until then and it's the same phone number I have today. I never thought of asking—no one

161

around here ever thought of asking—if we could have a phone. Charlie was the first man who had the guts to ask. He was aghast when he came in to find there wasn't a phone outlet for him. He had been a journalist and he was writing a series of articles for the *South Bend News-Times*, earning a little extra money, so he needed a telephone like all journalists do, all newspaper men. So he said, 'I'm going to see Father O'Donnell about it.' And we said, 'Well, Father O'Donnell brought you here, so go see him.' Surprisingly, we were granted permission, though we had to pay for the installation. And that was when Charlie said, 'I'm going to put the extension down in your room.'

"So a wire was strung along the transoms of half a dozen rooms between my tower in 355 and Charlie's in 341. Any boy who ever thought of it could have just reached up there and snapped the cord, but never did. Charlie was deaf, very deaf, and couldn't hear the bell about half the time. Then some engineer had the smart idea of putting in an electric light that blinked when the bell would ring. And Charlie would look up from his writing or his work, and the light would be blinking and he'd answer the phone. Sometimes I had to answer the phone for him or run down to his room and point at the blinking light.

"It was a good system, but the phone was such a novelty that students were constantly asking to use it. This got to be so inconvenient that I finally had to put an end to it. I remember once a boy named Bob made a call from my room to a girl and she fainted! I don't know what he said to her, but I gave him hell for it and told him not to use my phone to call her again. The girl in the phone booth was Mary, and she and Bob got together and got married. Bob became a judge and later she suffered a terrible thing; she was burned in her nightgown. But she was a pretty girl!

"One of Charlie's ears was deaf from improper care when he had scarlet fever as a child. And then years later, when he was traveling—he was employed through the Knights of Columbus as a journalist reporting on World War I from Poland—he was in a very bad train wreck, and the good ear was smashed. His head was squeezed, he said, and he became totally deaf in that ear. We always had a hard time getting him to hear us. In class, he knew they were talking but not about what. I know some students took advantage of him, because I know boys who bragged about it. But his voice was normal, and unlike most deaf people he didn't raise his voice and scream.

"Yo Yeager was a senior on the third floor and he used to yell down the hall, 'Fenlon, I need some soap. I need some shaving soap.' He always forgot to buy it, and I always gave it to him, and he never paid me back. At his end of the hall, it would have been easier to ask Charlie, but Charlie couldn't hear a thing.

"He wore a bow tie a lot and a Norfolk jacket. I remember how he would retire to his room early on Tuesday nights rather than go into town with us. 'I have my Dante class tomorrow,' he would say. 'I must prepare for my Daaa-nn-tay' is the funny way he would say it. But the big surprise came one day in a little gathering he had with three friends, including me. One of us made a reference to 'we four bachelors,' and Charlie said, 'I'm not a bachelor.' This was a shock to the rest of us. Later the subject was raised again, and Charlie said, 'All I'll say is that she's at St. Catherine's in Washington.'" Here the Professor pointed to his temple and spun his finger, indicating a mental institution.

"I remember that Dick Sullivan married a girl in the log chapel in 1932. Father Carrico married them. The only reception so to speak that they had was a little thing afterwards in Charlie Phillips's room. Charlie, the couple, the bridesmaid, and I were the only ones in the room. Charlie fixed some coffee and rolls for us that morning. He had a little hot plate, just as I did, though he wasn't very handy in the kitchen. He had what they call a samovar that he picked up from God knows where. It was a gun-metal color, like an urn. He hadn't used it much, but it had a top on it, and on this special occasion he thought he'd try it out. He boiled the water in it, then proudly poured it, and *plop, plop, plop*—three rusty old nails fell out of the bottom of the thing!

"The only book Charlie wrote entirely from his 341 room, and he killed himself doing it, because he never saw it in book form, was that damned biography of Paderewski, the famous Polish pianist. The cane I have now he used when he was in Poland doing research for the book. He told us he climbed the mountains of Poland with that cane, and we always used to ask, 'How many mountains did you climb, Charlie?' I doubt he put himself through any great exertion.

"The book on Paderewski didn't really sell well; it was only his death that boosted sales. Charlie was busy trying to get the page proofs of the thing done so that he could go home for Christmas. He was a man who worked at a nervous pitch and energy all the time, and he was utterly exhausted, though otherwise in perfect health. A few days before the Christmas of '33, after classes that afternoon, we were both leaving for the holidays, and we said our parting words at the top of the third-floor stairs. He asked, 'Is there anything you want me to bring back?' 'No, just bring back yourself,' I said, and he replied, 'That may be difficult enough to do.'

"I wasn't really looking forward to going home because my mother had only just recently died. I took the four-something or other out of Plymouth to Blairsville. I was home only a few days when someone told me they read in the *Chicago Tribune* about Charlie's death. I was asked if I knew and I said, 'No, I'm completely shocked.' I immediately took the train back to the place where I knew Charlie wanted to be buried, his birthplace, New Richmond, Wisconsin.

"After Charlie left South Bend, he'd spent a night in Chicago. Nobody knows where he went though. Wherever it was, presumably it was there that he contracted the fatal disease. After staying in Chicago, Charlie went to visit his sister Eva in Minneapolis. He was dining there on the first day of his arrival when he suddenly got up from the table and bolted to the bathroom. He stayed there several minutes, so Eva called through the door to see if he was alright. Of course, it was difficult to make herself heard because Charlie was deaf. Finally, they got him to lie down in the bedroom and within minutes he was unconscious. He was rushed by ambulance to the hospital and died the next morning. The coroner's verdict: meningitis.

"Father Cavanaugh was very distressed and hurt by Charlie Phillips's death. He was supposed to meet me and a few others for the burial. But he took ill and because he could not attend, Patsy Carroll was sent as his representative, and it was he who delivered the eulogy over the body. Charlie had few enemies, but if he had known Patsy was there, he would have gotten out of his grave. Of all the CSCs, he disliked this one the most.

"Charlie's brother Frank and sister Eva came here in 1934 to find a will. The two of them spent hours going through *all* of Charlie's books but could never find it. They went into a tizzy and fought greedily over all of Charlie's things; it was terrible. Eva took most of his rare book collection, which had valuable first editions inscribed by their authors. She also took other personal items except for the fireplace. She offered that to me, but she took the artificial fire with her.

"She was usurious—all she did was ask Charlie for checks. She thought he was wealthy, but he worked constantly writing newspaper columns, magazine articles, little poems—some for only fifteen dollars—just so he could send money to her. Charlie was vexed when he finally visited her apartment. There was a maid in a uniform waiting on her as if she were a wealthy woman, while her poor brother was literally working himself to death for her. As a widow she came back to Notre Dame a second time years later looking for work. She saw President J. Hugh O'Donnell, who was quite fond of Charlie, and he got her a job in Chicago as a sorority mother.

"I had a letter recently from a distant relative of Charlie's, a Mrs. Heiting, who wanted to visit me to talk about him. Apparently, she had passed through South Bend last year and seen the *South Bend Tribune* story about me. So I dined with Mr. and Mrs. Heiting at the University Club, and she surprised me by saying Eva was adopted and many of Charlie's brothers died mysteriously at an early age. We couldn't understand why Charlie had such a devotion to someone of such extreme selfishness. Anyway, I told stories about our beer party with G. K. Chesterton, and she took copious notes, so I was most impressed by her, but her husband couldn't care less. They came back to my room after dinner, and I showed them Charlie's cane and the poetry book inscribed to me. I wanted to show them pictures of Charlie, but all I found was *this*."

He handed me a Christmas card, which I opened and found blank. "Now open it all the way up," he said. Inside was a handwritten poem in ornate black script, "Jerusalem Beasties, by Charles Phillips."

"I have no idea how I came by this. I had never heard of this poem and couldn't find it when I made a quick check of his other volumes of verse." He speculated this was an unpublished poem, and then he pulled out a copy of Phillips's book, *Back Home*, to show me Charlie's inscription to Eva dated November 26, 1911.

On the flyleaf of another book there was another dedication—"To my dear friend Paul Fenlon, for having been born.

Charles Phillips 31 July 1925." "I remember watching him write the inscription on my birthday," the Professor said, "and I've always laughed at it. He had such nice, bold handwriting. He wrote all his works by hand, then dictated them to his secretary, a marvelous baby-faced boy now living in Chicago. I've kept all my correspondence with Charlie, but the bulk of it is in my attic at home."

"The campus histories don't have much to say about people like Phillips, do they?" I asked.

"Yes, they only talk about the bricks. You know, after Charlie died, many of the students wanted to leave his room just the way it was, perhaps turning it into a library, a quiet room. He had so many visitors and friends among the students who used to visit that room constantly. Of course, his sudden death over the Christmas holidays only enhanced their emotional attachment to the room. They wanted it preserved just as they had remembered it, but then of course Eva came along and took all of the books and the fireplace came to me. The room lost all its charm. The next year, just as I predicted, some ordinary person just moved in. But it's hard to blame later generations for not remembering his room, because they would not know who had once lived in that room. They would say, 'Who is Charlie Phillips?'"

[22]

Alone

IN THE WEEK leading up to spring break of my sophomore year, I noticed the Professor was out of sorts, and he confessed as much. He wasn't just fatigued or worried about Father Dan, as he had been the past four months. No, now he had a new physical complaint every day, it seemed. He was waking up with unusual chest pains, he told me, and his left arm sometimes went numb. His memory was fine, but the literary allusions, wordplay, and ironic remarks that were staples of our conversation were now lost on him. He'd give a bewildered stare and ask, "What?" as if he was hard of hearing or I had said something untoward, though when I explained the joke, he'd comprehend it right away, brighten, and laugh.

These days he was also prone to falling asleep. The two of us would be reading in silence except for the occasional sound of a page being turned or his rocker moving back and forth. Then the room would become very still and I'd hear his book slip in his lap. Whenever I observed this out of the corner of my eye, I recalled his repeated warnings he could drop dead at any moment. But then he'd wake up and go back to his book, not bothering to check if I had noticed.

This was all distressing to me, especially the numbness, which he said might be the early sign of a stroke, but I didn't know what to do. He and I were both worriers, I told myself, so perhaps this was just another thing we were fretting over needlessly. Wouldn't

169

one of his adult friends—someone like Mr. Stritch—take action if that was necessary? On the one hand, I knew he was under the regular care of a physician and still had the mental acuity to self-report any serious medical symptoms. On the other hand, I knew I had more daily contact with him than almost anyone else, and if there was a turn for the worse, I would likely be the first to recognize it and have to report it up the chain of command. Part of me didn't want to acknowledge his mortality or believe that this might be the beginning of the end or that when the end did come it might look exactly like this.

On at least four occasions this week, the Professor asked me to stay in Sorin over break. I had a bad cold, he said, and besides, he could use the company. How very odd, I thought, suddenly to need my attendance, imagining I would give up a sunny week on the beach and time with my family. When it became clear I had no intention of changing plans, the Professor made a fuss over my departure. I knew it would be hectic as we got closer to Friday afternoon, with break starting then, so Thursday I began to say goodbye early, in a roundabout way. He saw my drift and would have none of it, interrupting me, "Are you going to see Dr. Fitzsimons tomorrow?" a reference to my class with historian Matthew Fitzsimons.

"Yes."

"Now you're leaving tomorrow right after your class or right after Andy's class? Then you have time to see me before you leave." That, he made clear, was the end of that. The next day we said our goodbyes, and he added, "Now send my regards to the family, and your grandmother especially."

A week later, sporting a tan, I found the Professor's inner door open. He was standing in profile at his dresser, not four feet in front of me, yet he was unaware of my presence. I knocked. He turned in my direction. The noonday sunshine reflected off his lenses. He smiled, exhaled as if he had been holding his breath for my return, and made for me, leaving the dresser drawer open. I said "hi," and he gave me a little hug. "Glad to see you," we said in unison.

"How are you doing?" I asked.

"I've been depressed in a way. It was awfully lonesome here." He summed up his week: he had a visit with Professor Fitzsimons and tea with Sister Jean Lenz; he couldn't watch the Notre Dame-Duke basketball game with the Boehms due to the ice storm Holy Saturday; he spent Easter with the Manions; he did a spring cleaning that turned up two applications for admission, dated 1905 and 1907, in a pile intended for the archives.

The Professor knew I was late for lunch and class, so he let me go on the condition I return in the evening, which I did. My knock caught him lifting a shot of Scotch to his lips. He was in his retirement chair and greeted me with a smile, but within minutes he was wheezing and out of breath. He said he'd been doing a lot of running around and was getting ready to go out with Myron Busby.

"You're trying to do too much," I said.

"You're right, Phil. Say, do I look pale to you?"

"No. Why do you ask?"

"I don't know what's the matter with me. Lately, I have been very fidgety. I feel like something is going to happen to me very soon. I've had these pains in my chest. I really don't want to go out tonight, but I must. Myron has been very good to me, and I should go."

Huffing and puffing, he complained how hot the room was, and I pulled his turtleneck over his head, replacing it with a lighter one. I told him it was foolish to go out, but he insisted. In a pitiful, weak voice, he said he wanted to see me later tonight.

Presently, Busby arrived with his little blond son. He rushed in seeming not to notice the Professor's distress, introduced himself, grabbed the Professor's medicine from the green pill box on the dresser, and left. This all happened so quickly I was caught flat-footed, standing alone in 141 with nothing to do but lock up.

Later that night, my phone rang. The Professor knew I was bone-tired from my travels but wanted to know when I was coming to see him. I trudged down the stairs. He'd calmed down by now, describing a pleasant evening with the Busbys. As we sat there, he read the paper, offering occasional comments, until at last, on this, our third visit of the day, recognizing we were both exhausted, he let me go. On my way out, a couple steps beyond the threshold, he usually called something out to me, but this was the first time he did this just to extend the evening to keep him company. "Hey, Phil," he asked. "Do you know what today is?" He proceeded to tell me what happened on this date in history, drawing me back into his room for ten more minutes.

The next day, to my surprise, all was sunshine, the result of a good report from his doctor. "'Have you had any colds this winter?' the doctor asked me. I answered 'no,' then Dr. Egan asked whether I would mind taking a new shot they have for pneumonia. I said, 'Of course I don't mind. You're the doctor. I'll do whatever you say.'" Well, I thought, *the chest pains and numbness couldn't have been so serious if you left with just a shot and a pat on the back.*

Though the medical crisis might have passed, the Professor was soon in the doldrums again. For the first time since I had known him, he was bored. Father Dan wasn't back from Boston yet. Mr. Stritch was out of town. Doris was in Rome. "I don't feel as if I have enough to keep me busy," he said.

And then one evening, the Professor went missing. On a hunch, I checked the public restroom, where I found him struggling to get from the shower to the chair stationed inches away. I offered him an arm and he sat for ten minutes to regain his strength for the walk back to 141. "The shower is too much for me, Phil," he said. "I can't undergo many more of these."

"Why don't you have them put a shower in your bathroom so it would be easier on you?"

"They said it couldn't be fixed. Besides, you know, I'm only living in Sorin by the grace of God. They're going to kick me out soon anyway, so I don't want to press my luck." To hear him tell it, he could find himself at any moment sitting on the sidewalk, his possessions piled around him. Try as I might, I couldn't get him to put this silly idea out of his head.

Back in his room, I was astonished by what I saw. There on the bed was a stuffed animal, a St. Bernard complete with brandy keg. I tried not to crack up laughing. *Where did this come from? Has this been in your dresser all this time? Is it a gift? Something new you brought back from Blairsville?* As sorry as I felt for him, I couldn't believe he needed this nursery comfort to make it through the night. "Do you sleep with this?" I blurted out.

"Yes," he said, indignant the question had to be asked. He was so tired or so consoled by the dog that he let me leave without protest.

Another day, he said to me, "I think my walking is getting worse. I'm deteriorating. Look at how often I am tired or get winded, how much energy is required just to take a shower. I once planned on staying at Sorin indefinitely, but now I think this may be my last year. I may just return in the fall to see my friends again then leave for good in December."

I didn't want to hear this, but I still had a few weeks before the end of the semester to persuade him otherwise. He dropped the subject for now, though it was always threatening to come to the surface. As this visit ended, he was fishing through his medicine cabinet, when he pulled out what looked like a test tube with a metal cap. "Do you know what this was used for?" he asked, as if this were a quiz.

"I have no idea."

"This was used during Prohibition," he said, enunciating this last word for effect. "We got these from the boys over in the lab. We used to fill them up with liquor and"—demonstrating—"hide them in our coats." I asked whether he could spare one of these for me as a souvenir.

"I don't know," he said. "It brings back so many fond memories. I'll have to think about it."

Three days later, when he handed it to me, I had a bit of news for him. I had gotten wind of a plan by some student politicians to create another student lounge by removing a wall between room 119 and Colonel Hoynes's old quarters in 123. I had already told the powers that be this was a bad idea. If they wanted to knock down walls, why not do that in the south wing, which was originally one large room housing the law classroom, before it was hived off into bedrooms in 1917? No thought was being given to the historical importance or tradition of these rooms. There were also plans afoot to renovate the basement this summer. If the administration was looking for more social space, why not restore part of the basement to its original use by reconstructing the Sorin subway?

"They just don't have any respect for the history of these rooms," I said.

"No, they don't," he said. "I suspect they are already plotting for my room after I leave."

"I hate to say it, but you're right to be suspicious. A week ago, I overheard someone say he was 'waiting for Fenlon to kick off so I can make a TV lounge out of his old room.'"

"I'm not surprised."

"Maybe one day your room could be turned into a museum. That's what you already call it—the museum." The Professor did not scoff at the idea, but pointed out the impracticality of it, just as converting 341 into a memorial to Charlie Phillips never worked out.

$\left[\,23\,\right]$

The Thirties (1931-38)

THE 1930S WERE FILLED with memories of unforgettable characters like Charlie Phillips and Pop Farley, but the Professor wasn't finished with them yet:

"In 1931 or '32, I was on summer vacation in Wisconsin and I received a phone call from Red Brennan wanting me to change a grade for a boy he had on the basketball team. And when I got back to Notre Dame, Daddy Carrico, the department chairman, asked me, 'Professor Paul,'—he was the only one I allowed to call me 'Professor Paul'—'is it true that last week you were called about changing a boy's grade?' And I said, 'Yes, it was, Father.' And he said, 'Did you do it, Paul?' 'I certainly did not, Father.' 'Good. Otherwise, we might have been losing your services at the university.' I didn't change the grade because, first of all, of course, it was not ethical. Besides, I didn't like the boy.

"Daddy Carrico was very well-known. They tell the story of a letter being addressed to 'Father Carrico of Notre Dame,' and Carrico got it. That's right, not even 'Indiana.' He showed me the letter himself. When we were supposed to switch to daylight savings time, and Notre Dame refused to go along because the priests would be getting up at four in the morning, Father Carrico was the one who declared, 'Notre Dame will always stay on God's time!'

"Red Brennan was rector here, but did a bad job because he didn't want to take responsibility for this hall. He was the most educated man of the entire CSC order, and they tried to promote him, but he wouldn't allow it. He was lost because he hit the bottle.

"Father Brennan played baseball professionally and was a hero-worshipper of athletes and very popular with many of them. He said Mass so quickly we thought he was wearing his track shorts under his cassock. He was also a great bridge player. We used to play in my tower room and when he saw he wasn't going to win, he just threw down his cards and quit.

"I remember some of my best friends in the class of '31 used to spend time in my tower room when I would go across to sleep in my bedroom. They would stay in the tower working on their papers. Now that was Phil Angsten, Bob Baer, and that outfit, and they were '31. And I think the class of '35 did it, because Hank Wurzer, Johnny Neeson, Sam Murtha, and those boys used to come to my room to study, and they were on the third floor.

"When all the lights went off at ten o'clock, there was only one light in each alley of the corridor. And the boys would try to bring their chairs out and sit in front of their doors to study, but if there was a priest walking around, prefecting as they did in those days, they didn't stay there very long.

"At about this time, right after the outbreak of the Depression, very surprisingly, the faculty received a small pay hike. It wasn't much, but we weren't getting much pay anyway. The poet-president, Father O'Donnell"—who wrote the lyrics to the alma mater—"was trying to pep up the university, get better professors. I suppose some of the faculty would have left if there had been a large pay cut, but most of us wouldn't. Jobs were hard to get, remember, and we were loyal to the school. At the faculty retirees dinner, Father Joyce said this school wouldn't be where it is today without the sacrifices made at times by its faculty. You see, back then we didn't think about such things.

We didn't complain or cause trouble like some of these current faculty members. Besides, I've never had to worry about money. My entire life I've had money.

"Before the Depression, I was paid a hundred dollars a month, including room, board, and laundry. O'Donnell's pay increase was more than fifteen dollars a month, but a little later we had to pay for our own meals. Charlie O'Donnell was fair and I always respected him.

"There used to be a newspaper stand at the South Dining Hall, and O'Donnell once banned *Time* magazine because it described him as 'smallish, precise, and bespectacled.' Anyway, because of his arrogant manner, there was a considerable faction against O'Donnell. His probable successor was his number two man, Vice President Michael Mulcaire, who came from Ireland. And so they were called 'the poet and the peasant,' and it stuck. One day Mulcaire appeared drunk in public. After that, the anti-O'Donnell group sent Mulcaire off to Oregon, then appointed Cardinal O'Hara as his successor. Charlie O'Donnell was determined to live out his term of office despite his terminal illness and the faction against him. He died the night of commencement, June 4, 1934, and Acting President O'Hara signed all of the diplomas that year.

"Father Con Hagerty was on the golf course in a foursome right behind Mulcaire and his group. And the peasant was in the middle of a sand trap swinging away, swearing 'goddamn s. o. b.!' Father Con did not allow swearing and so he stepped up to Mulcaire and asked, 'Father, where did you learn those words?' And he replied, 'Why, in the novitiate, Father!'

"It was very well-known that when Con was a prefect in Walsh Hall the boys out in the corridor would yell 'goddamn sonofabitch!' and then run back into their rooms. And Hagerty would be out of his room in an instant to punish them. He would send them down to the rector right away, and if they were prep students, they had to leave school permanently. Thank goodness the college boys did not have to leave.

"Con Hagerty used to visit the Manions often. He would call the house ahead of time so Mrs. Manion could call off her awful dogs out there at the Manion Canyon. Then up over the hill Con would appear, and he'd call out, 'Do you have any buttermilk to offer a poor, tired priest?' And Gina would answer, 'No, but I have something a little stronger.' And so he would come in. Hagerty was a great friend of the Manions. Pat financed his last books because he couldn't get them published himself.

"Sometime before 1934, when Charlie O'Donnell was president, the great *J. Hugh* O'Donnell was prefect of discipline. Later J. Hugh became president of this university, of course. But there is a story I like to tell about him. In those days, the prefect walked the streets of South Bend to keep boys out of the taverns. One day Hugh accosted a student outside a tavern and chased him all over town. Now O'Donnell was a large man, on the football team as a student here, but by the time he became prefect he was out of shape. At last he cornered the poor boy in an alleyway. 'Buddy, I am a trained athlete and you cannot escape me!' So typical of J. Hugh, so pompous.

"The boy today is a prominent lawyer, so I can't tell you his name, but he was suspended for two weeks, as I recall, which was rare but customary in such cases. During that time the student could attend no classes and was not allowed to make up the work, though some professors cheated on that. He lived one block down the street from my aunt in Woodstock, Illinois, and his father ordered him to spend the two weeks in a Chicago hotel. He couldn't go back to that little town, because they would say, 'Why aren't you at school during Lent?' or something like that.

"We had other prefects of discipline who were famous, too.

Father Mizer once had a boy arrested for drinking off campus. The next day, outside of the old post office across from the Knights of Columbus, the boy got out a horse whip and attacked Mizer. The boys who gathered around the fight quickly broke it up and the boy was arrested again. It was quite a famous incident. This was sometime in the 1930s."

***

"They had a write-up of my old friend, Haig," the Professor said.
"Who?"
"Al Haig."
"The general, Alexander Haig?"
"Yes, Al Haig."
"Nixon's chief of staff?"
"Yes, I told you, *Al Haig.* I knew him via the Neesons. Johnny Neeson, Sr., class of 1903, lived in 333 Sorin, and his son, Johnny, Jr., class of '35, lived in the same room. Johnny, Sr. graduated as an engineer and a year later went to Philadelphia, where he worked in the office of the city engineer under Republicans and Democrats alike until his death. He was the only man to know every pipe and passage under the city. He was a member of Notre Dame's first board of trustees. His wife's sister was Alex Haig's mother. So Junior, who died two years ago, was Al's first cousin. When young Haig's father died, Senior was named guardian, so they were always together. Once I went with Junior to visit their place on the shore, in Atlantic City. You know, every summer half of western Pennsylvania is in the Atlantic Ocean at once. There I remember playing with Al Haig when he was about ten years old.

"He was a fat little fun-loving boy. If you'd asked me, I wouldn't have said he seemed particularly intelligent. He was just ten, as I said. Later, Alex applied to West Point and failed, but he was persuaded to go to Notre Dame. Even though his mother was a Catholic, Alex absolutely hated Notre Dame. He lived on the first floor of Lyons in the center of the building. I rarely saw him. He only came to me when he needed money, and I would contact his guardian, Johnny, Sr., who would send the money. At the end of freshman year, he applied to West Point again and this time Senior's influence got him in. Alex was very ungrateful to Notre Dame, hated it. I don't think Haig would even remember me, but when Senior died, he split his money mainly among the three Haig children. Junior was not pleased.

"But I met many people through my good friends the Neesons, including that man, 'He-e-e-e-re's Johnny!'—Ed McMahon from the Johnny Carson show. Neeson's wife and other prominent women from Philadelphia hold the biggest card party in the world to raise several thousand dollars for charity. And one year, for some reason, they got McMahon to be there, and he came out to the Neesons' beach house. They had a reception line for him and we'd each come up and be introduced. So I met this Ed for the first and only time, just shook hands with him; that's all.

***

"At Notre Dame the faculty had to use the summers to do our studying, because there wasn't any other time to do it. There were no such things as sabbaticals then. You had none of these faculty taking off as they do now. So I shopped around and went to Harvard in the summer of 1936. I sat in on [George Lyman] Kittredge's Shakespeare class there. He was a little, white-haired porcelain chap, who looked as though he might break in two at any time. I spent two summers at Harvard and two at my beloved Bread Loaf in Vermont. Robert Frost lived just six miles away from Bread Loaf and he gave poetry readings for us, which everybody enjoyed very much, but he drank too much.

"In the summer of 1938, I went on my famous European trip. I only made it to Europe once, I regret to say. At that time I was one of the first to own an electric razor, and before getting on the plane I had to explain to the officials that it was not a hand grenade, though it looked like one.

"My traveling companion was Tom Madden, a professor here. He and I stopped by the Holy Cross House in Rome, and that's where I first met Ted Hesburgh. He was a seminarian studying there. I didn't notice anything very much about him then, but I really got to know him later, when he was the chaplain of Vetville after the war.

"In Munich they took our passports, and poor Tom was so worried that he never slept a night in Germany. He paced all night smoking cigarettes. We were in Vienna exactly one year before World War II started. A guard with a gun stood at our hotel. We all made faces at him, but he wouldn't break. I also remember we were on a boat in the Rhine and there was a statue of Hitler. Everyone came up to it and clicked their heels and saluted it like *this*. I was laughing and joking about it, but Tom told me to be quiet or we could be arrested. It was a dangerous time for Americans to be traveling in Europe.

"Tom Madden and PRB and one or two others were allowed to teach for a few years after turning sixty-five, because the retirement benefits were so poor. But poor Tom didn't get a chance to enjoy his retirement. A few years after his teaching, he died, and his mother outlived him, if you can believe that. There was only a sixteen- to eighteen-year age difference between them. Now Delia was born in Ireland and came here at an early age, which meant leaving her family. And once she left Ireland, she never kept in touch with them, so when Madden and I made our trip, Delia asked us to visit her family. We stayed in Ireland for four days to visit with them. Now here's the only story, and I thought it was funny as hell. I talked with one of the sisters and she, of course, had horrible teeth, all dirty, some missing. And she only had one question, which she kept repeating, 'Does Delia have her own teeth? Does Delia have her own teeth?' That's all she wanted to know, after all those years.

"But Tom was sort of a mama's boy, you know. His mother lived with the rule that he could not drink any liquor, and for many years Tom wouldn't. Finally, we convinced him to drink some sort of wine, a mild port, I think. But even then, he only drank it in our presence on the condition that we never tell his mother. And here he was, a grown man!"

$[24]$

The Party

MY FRIENDS and I had planned a party, and we didn't expect the Professor to accept our invitation. But he must have wanted a distraction from his medical complaints and low spirits, so he agreed to attend. At 10:15, Tom and I came down to escort him to our room. The Professor had already reached his two-Scotch maximum with Mr. Stritch, but I suggested, for old times' sake, that he fill up one of his Prohibition-era tubes. Instead, he filled a half-pint flask with Scotch and water.

He grabbed his cane with one hand and the banister railing with the other. We started up the stairs, with me at his side and Tom following behind. On the second-floor landing, we encountered three freshmen on his Most Wanted List for their crimes against the peace and quiet of the hall. They were taken aback to see him on their turf, but they smirked as we passed by. The Professor ignored them, focusing instead on his own labored footwork.

On the third floor, we were three abreast, with the Professor between us. As we made the final turn, we could see the party was in full swing. At the end of the corridor, last room on the left, was our 301 turret room, and dead ahead was a large window leading out to the fire escape. People were milling about, eating and drinking; some sat on a couch we put under the window; some danced in the darkened tower room; others were shouting over one another to be heard. The disco-style strobe light in 301 flashed into the hallway as the floor trembled to the beat of the music.

"Oh, my," said the Professor, taking in the scene. He smiled as we made our way down the hall. The noise didn't bother him as much as I thought it would, but as he got closer to the action he repeated, "Oh, my." Then he turned to me. "Better hide this." I covered the flask in the palm of my hand.

Once the partygoers caught sight of us, they quieted down. Guests who had never seen the Professor before, seemed wonderstruck. A few giggled nervously. Someone rushed to turn the music down, and we got the Professor settled on the couch. He looked up at us, beaming at everyone standing there as they were introduced. Then the music was turned back up and we poured him his Scotch. He wanted nothing to do with the punch specially concocted for the occasion.

He chatted amiably with the students he had just met. "Louise, I'm glad you're at St. Mary's," he told one girl. "My sisters were there, you know." Big Boy's maiden aunt was sitting next to him. (Big Boy's friends would substitute her name in the Latin chant *Agnus Dei*, so at Glee Club rehearsals it was not the Lamb of God but *Agnes Dailey* who took away the sins of the world.) A stout woman in her sixties, Agnes sank so deep into the lumpy sofa that the lightweight Professor was pulled down against her. The two began an animated conversation.

At that point a student named Nick wandered down from his room uninvited. Under normal circumstances he wouldn't have much to do with the Professor, but this night he had one beer too many. He was so amused by the sight of the Professor next to Agnes, who was still dolled up from her bridge party, that he grabbed a camera to take their picture. "Use the yawn technique," he instructed, motioning for her to put her arm around the Professor while pretending to yawn, a method for making the first 'move' on a date. Luckily, Agnes either didn't understand or didn't hear him, and we hustled Nick away before the Professor got wind of this gentle mischief.

After twenty minutes, the Professor was ready to leave. As we reversed course, we passed the rectress of Walsh Hall on her way to the party.

"Hi, Paul."

"Well, hello, Sister Kathleen."

Turning the corner past 315, we saw the door to 341 open at the far end of the hallway, so we went down to see Father Green.

The Professor had not been in that room for many years. He marveled at it, pointing to the spot on the east wall where Charlie Phillips's fireplace used to sit. We turned off the lights to look out the window at the dome lit up, just as the Professor sometimes did in his room.

"Do you have any idea who our new rector might be next year?" he asked. Father Green didn't know. "This is six years in a row that we've had a new rector," the Professor went on. "Why don't you do something about it? I'd much rather have you downstairs again."

"Why, that's the nicest compliment I've had all day. Thank you, Paul."

"We need continuity. Why don't you stay?"

Father Green just laughed, adding, "I hope it only takes one person to take you downstairs tonight, not five, as in Chesterton's case."

"Yes, you know Chesterton visited Charlie Phillips in this very room. I think he was up here from ... oh, let's see, his lecture got out at ... I'd say from quarter past nine until half past two. And in all that time he never had to go to the little boys' room."

"A great man!"

"Chesterton himself said it was all in the plumbing."

I took the Professor downstairs. "You can just return my flask to me quietly tomorrow," he whispered. After a few more steps on solid ground, he said, "Now you go back to your party. Thanks, Phil." And with that he disappeared into the vestibule.

This wasn't such a bad time for the Professor, I thought, these waning days of my sophomore year. His attendance at our party was proof of that. For all his physical ailments and emotional strains— which were real and not to be discounted—the Professor still had his independence, saw his friends regularly, kept to his routine, and remained mobile thanks to his cane and his driving privileges. As a conversationalist, he had stamina, too, never flagging under my close questioning. He was like a spigot left running: the stories poured out of him one after another, seemingly without end.

We were now both very comfortable with story hour. On one occasion, I recall him leaning back, smiling, and saying, "I remember that Rockne said—" and I interrupted, taking the words out of his mouth—"any man who takes four years Latin and four years Greek—we don't have to worry about him." He was delighted I could parrot this line about F. X. Disney's academic eligibility.

But as much as I tried convincing myself otherwise, the Professor's physical condition was worse than I thought. One day he went to the doctor complaining of indigestion, shortness of breath, and leg pain, and returned with a prescription for his nerves. This new medication, I learned for the first time, was on top of the two sleeping pills and tranquilizers he was already taking. I would never have guessed he needed so much medication just to fall asleep. I had assumed those bottles I always saw him fumbling with in the medicine cabinet were for the garden-variety infirmities of old age, not psychological problems. Or then again, maybe anxiety and insomnia *were* the common infirmities of old age.

What, I wondered, did a prescription for "nerves" mean exactly? It sounded like something out of the nineteenth century: a Victorian malady, a gentleman's complaint, an affliction of the nerves requiring the rest cure. But I had to remind myself that the Professor *was* a relic of the last century. Like those well-to-do Victorian forebears, was he having trouble adjusting to the travails of modern life? I tried to lighten his mood with a jesting remark, but the Professor said his medicines were no laughing matter. When it was time to leave, he said, "Yes, I'll see you tomorrow—if I'm still alive."

It was a close-run thing. The next day he passed out at church and was rushed to the hospital. I was in the thick of final exams and hadn't had the chance to see him that day. By the time Father Green heard the news, it was late at night and he didn't want to wake me up, but he found Big Boy, who told me about it the next morning. By then, Myron Busby had already dropped off the Professor's belongings at the hospital. Father Green told me the Professor ought to stay away from Sorin at least until after graduation, when the hall would be quiet again.

Late in the morning, Big Boy and I drove out to St. Joseph's Hospital. As we pulled up, my first thought was: *This is where they took Gipp, and this is where he died.*

The Professor was in the Constant Care ward, room 371. "Big Boy? And Phil? Is that you?" He grabbed our hands and held tight. He was mumbling as he seized the oxygen mask, mistaking it for his eyeglasses. He hit his forehead with it, then his nose, then his cheek. His first coherent words were: "Don't tell Father Dan about me. He mustn't know I'm here. It wouldn't be good for him." *Here you are, you may be fighting for your life,* I thought, *and your first thought is for Father O'Neil. How these friends keep their illnesses secret from each other!*

He was in such a pathetic condition, so feeble, so helpless, I felt sick to my stomach. His right hand had an IV, and his bare chest had several monitors. Wires and tubes were helter-skelter. Above his head was a screen with his heartbeat and other numbers flashing in orange. His rosary was wrapped around the bedpost, just within reach. He was grateful to be in the new wing of the hospital, he muttered, and glad he had what amounted to a private room since the other bed was unoccupied.

Then a young nurse entered the room, asking, "What do you want now, big guy?" After some effort, we understood he wanted his glasses, and once we put those on he looked much better. She brought his lunch. He complained he was used to eating two hours later than this, but we helped cut up his turkey and open the ice cream for him. He was a slow and sloppy eater. The nurse made the mistake of saying, "Is that okay now?"

"Please don't say that word," he replied sharply.

"Do you want me to say 'alright?'"

"Yes, thank you, that would be nice." We tried apologizing for him: "He's an English professor and you're lucky he doesn't have his red pen with him."

We unloaded a sack of things from Sorin, including the *Chicago Tribune* and a new book on the history of St. Mary's College. Then I pulled out my Prohibition-era tube filled with Scotch. Before I could say a word, he burst into laughter; his old laugh was back—something the sedatives couldn't suppress.

As he ate, he told us what had happened. "I had not been feeling well at all yesterday morning. At Mass, I was going to communion, when I felt like I was going to fall down. My knees were weak. The left side of my face was all tingly and my left leg ached. Those are the first signs of a stroke, you know. So I just sat down there in Putty Crowley's pew and said, 'I'm sick, Putty.' And she said, 'I thought you looked sick, Paul.' And we got that man who's suing the university—"

"Danehy?" I asked, referring to Professor James Danehy, whose lawsuit was challenging the compulsory retirement policy.

"—Danehy, that's right. And he drove us to St. Joe's here. Oh, and last night we had that awful thunder and lightning. The room just shook. Then this morning I called the Dunns to tell them what happened to me. And they thought I thought I was coming out to visit them *today*. They asked as a joke whether I was insane or had had a stroke. I told them I would be out of here in a day or two and I hoped I could still make the trip we had planned together. Then Doris phoned to say *she* was very sick in bed with a cold. Then Stritch called, saying this was 'the goddamned worst time' for me to get sick: 'I have never been so busy. Why, this is the busiest week of my entire life!' He had that wedding Saturday.

"Poor Tom was so upset. My bad timing reminds me of my friend, PRB. When the new library was set to open, he was responsible of course for the big move from the old one. It was almost inevitable that PRB would not make it to the library's grand opening. And it was one week before the dedication that he was walking around one of the lakes and he fell and broke his leg. So on the day of the dedication, I remember visiting him in the hospital. Looking back on it, he said he could not have timed his accident more perfectly, because he was spared so much work. The only part of the move that really worried him was his beloved Dante Collection, which Father Zahm had put together. And without Byrne there to super-vise, they put all of those priceless old books in general circulation for the students! Yes, I know: eventually they retrieved all of the volumes and today they're together again."

As he was speaking, I noticed his storytelling had the effect of reviving him. I recognized that volunteering stories was a re-flex reaction he had whenever I was in his company and a way of anticipating my questions. Here it also might have been giving him a sense of control over alien surroundings, restoring a sense of normalcy. Whatever the case, whether it was the stories or simply the medicine wearing off, he was slowly returning to his old self.

As the Professor was discussing the Dante Collection, he had been playing absentmindedly with the wires fastened to his chest. By now they were hopelessly tangled with his scapular, a black-and-white miniature of the Blessed Virgin that hung by a green string around his neck. He was amused by what he had done, until a red light began to blink and a buzzer went off. A different nurse, seven or eight months pregnant, came in to investigate. She was not pleased. As she was checking the dials and picking through the wires, the Professor introduced us. "Phil here is from St. Petersburg and Big Boy is from Montana. Take your choice." She looked down at her tummy, smiled for the first time and said, "Oh, I think I've already made my choice."

Once she left, we shared some gossip: the new rector next year was going to be a thirty-seven-year-old seminarian. "Why, that would make him the first layman in the history of Sorin Hall," he said. "So there *will* be some changes in Sorin next year."

While he spoke, I watched the flashing orange digits above his head. I didn't understand what they meant, but they didn't seem affected by anything he was saying or doing. They were in the seventy to ninety range, but once jumped to 135 and later dipped to sixty-five when he started to doze off. He was drifting in and out of sleep, sometimes clawing for his rosary. *Was all of this normal?* I wondered. *Why can't he stay awake? Is he going to die here and now?* In a lucid interval he managed to balance his oxygen mask and glasses on the end of his nose, and he listed the things he wanted Myron Busby to bring him later in the day. He shook our hands again and said, "I'll see you again, if I'm still alive." Everyone laughed, but I didn't find it very funny.

The next day I returned for a visit and Tim came with me. The door to room 371 was open and we could see both beds all made up and empty. My heart sank. *Don't tell me that ...* but the pregnant nurse spotted us, smiled, and said the Professor had been transferred to a private room in the older part of the hospital.

We arrived at room 663, just as Paul Boehm was leaving. The Professor was much improved but complained no one would say what was the matter with him. He was angry with a nurse for returning late with a blanket, and he rang a bell non-stop for at least thirty seconds to get her attention again. He said he had phoned Tom and Betty Casey that morning, and Father Joyce had visited earlier. Tim and I stayed for half an hour, then Father Gerber dropped by and we left.

When at last the Professor received his diagnosis, it made perfect sense: "They say that I am in the hospital for 'anxiety neurosis' or in layman's terms 'a fidgety attack,'" he said. Looking the term up, I found it described his symptoms to a T: insomnia, irritability, indigestion, excessive worrying. He hadn't always suffered from these ailments, so far as I could tell, but they had come to a head in recent months, with the Caseys' financial problems, Sorin Hall almost uninhabitable, and Father Dan apparently dying of cancer. My own late night visits must have played a role as well, I felt with a tinge of guilt.

I had never thought of him as being nervous or high-strung, yet he did have those bite marks on his watch, come to think of it, and he did once say of my friends, "When you bring in that big crowd, it makes me nervous. I like it more often when you come in alone. I'm not nervous with you." Regardless of how far back this problem went, at least we had a better idea of what we were up against now.

The following day, his fourth in the hospital, the Professor didn't seem quite as sharp, but otherwise there was nothing to report.

On day five, a great storm cloud gathered in the western sky, but the rain stopped by the time Big Boy and I arrived. Finals were over, so I was coming to say goodbye before leaving for the summer. Today I learned the Professor had an enlarged heart. Every day, it seemed, another secret from his medical file was revealed. He was still experiencing shortness of breath brought on by the heart condition, but his doctor had good news for him: he could go home tomorrow, meaning he might be able to go to Illinois to see the Dunns after all.

"Have you had any visitors today?" I asked.

"Oh, yes, several." The most noteworthy was the beloved campus chaplain and writer, Father Robert Griffin, a shy, mountain of a man wearing his flat cap and checked jacket.

"Did he bring Darby O'Gill?"

"No, he didn't bring his dog."

"Was he wearing the 'Snoopy' vestments from his Urchin mass?"

"No. I was so afraid when he tried to sit down on that little chair you're on that he'd break it and fall flat on the floor."

The Professor showed us two bouquets of bright yellow flowers that he planned to donate to the hospital chapel. One came from his friends the Corbetts; the other was signed "Notre Dame English Department."

"Well, Professor, I have to go," I said at last. He hated this phrase and teased me about it, but I really did have to get packed to drive back to Florida. As we shook hands, tears welled up in his eyes, magnified by his lenses. "Well," he said, "have a safe trip home, and maybe we'll be together in the fall again. Goodbye. Thanks again, Phil, thanks for *everything*."

Whatever our parting words might have lacked in drama, the weather made up for in special effects. Bright sunshine finally broke through the clouds to light up the room. Everything was dazzling white—sheets, walls, gown—much as I imagined the Transfiguration. The Professor thought I had already left the room, but at the doorway I turned around for one last look, fixing this scene in my memory. He was propped up in bed staring straight ahead, alone, lost in thought.

Would I ever see him again? He appeared to be on the mend, but he was still so frail and old. Was his doctor leveling with him— was the Professor leveling with me? Would he make good on his vow "this is my last year"? If he survived this health scare, would I see him next in Sorin or in Blairsville?

[25]

Mourning

IT WAS AN ANXIOUS few weeks before I learned the Professor was out of the hospital. "Almost everything I've heard so far points to good news," Dennis Moran wrote me. "I saw him in the University Club last week and he *looked* well." It was another three weeks before I received firsthand evidence of his recovery. "Dear Philip, Just this far + typewriter gave out," the Professor wrote in a note responding to my get-well cards. "I've read Ms. Once," he continued, referring to an updated version of my hall history—"much has to be scratched out."

And then, because his script looked like Morse code, I had to read the next line several times. I couldn't make the entire sentence out, but I *thought* it began, "Since Father Dan's death on 9 June...." I read and re-read these words. If that's what he was saying, the Professor must be devastated, I thought. It pained me to think how he must be suffering. How would he be able to live without Father Dan? This latest emotional upset would put him over the edge, wouldn't it? And poor Father O'Neil—what a good soul he was, just fifty-eight years old. I didn't know him well, but he was the Professor's dearest friend and now he was gone.

The note went on as if lightning had not struck: "I'll try to have typewriter fixed. Always my best to you—See you Aug. I hope!! Paul." So he's well enough to contemplate returning to Notre Dame: that's good, I thought. And those exclamation

195

points tell me he isn't completely disheartened. I took the Blairs-ville postmark as a favorable sign, too; it meant he was well enough to travel.

Three weeks later, the Professor wrote again, further easing my mind. There was a comforting familiarity about his corre-spondence—the jumpy typewriter line disappearing off the end of the page, the return address missing his street name and num-ber, the stamp affixed sideways. Strangely, his letter had nothing about Father O'Neil. After answering some of my factual ques-tions about campus history, he asked who the new rector of Sorin would be. He was starved for information about Notre Dame. All that Stritch had said on the phone was that summer school enrollments were disappointing.

The Professor told me he "had enough of hometown by now" and was making arrangements to return to campus. "I'm depend-ing on you and your little crowd to help me," he said. His cousin accompanied him to Pittsburgh to get a new prescription for his glasses: "I can't see out of these old ones very well … and when I can't read or write I'm in trouble." In closing, he said, "If I'm all right hope to be back by time classes resume. Bestus always, Prof. Paul."

Back at Sorin for the fall semester, I came down the stairs one morning to find the vestibule door ajar. Elma was out in the hall-way with her supply cart. No, she said, she hadn't remembered opening the door. We looked and found the inner door open as well. I knocked. "Edward, is that you?" the Professor called out, thinking it was the janitor. He greeted me nonchalantly in his pajamas, explaining he had arrived late last night with the Bus-bys. Elma came in to make sure he was all settled and then left. We laughed. She'd made up his bed using the wrong sequence of blankets and sheets. Mind you, there was a strict sequence to be followed.

"How is your health?" I asked.

"I don't think I've recovered yet from Dan's death," he said. "I hadn't seen him in six months and I didn't want to see him when they brought him back. I missed the funeral, too. Dan was flown back in an ambulance airplane on Thursday. I had never heard of an ambulance plane, but Hesburgh sent one out to get Father Dan. They put him in the hall that's for the priests. He was suffering greatly, they say, but he said he just had to get back to campus. That's what he wanted to do. And the next afternoon he died. It was a shock to Betty his sister because Dan had been expected to live longer. But it wasn't violent, apparently. Dan died quietly. Now that was on June 9th and the funeral was on the Monday. Some young fellow who had never met Dan gave the eulogy, which they said was very good.

"And another poor friend of mine died, F. X. Disney, class of '23, a wonderful friend of mine. I don't know if Chet knows yet; I'll have to call him. Oh, and Margaret died—Mrs. Dick Sullivan—the day after Dan. I went to the 'wake,' though I hate calling it that.

"For a week this summer I had to live in the Morris Inn, but I went back home a few days later. I returned here earlier than usual—last night—because of that little grandnephew of mine. He nearly drove me crazy. He was playing with my St. Christopher medal and ripped it from the rearview mirror. I almost killed him. I must have my medal to drive.

"A family I know is driving my car back. I flew. I had an hour layover in Cleveland and all of a sudden I heard, 'My God! It's Paul Fenlon!'" The Professor pinched his nostrils to get the imitation right. "He was from New York, and we had a delightful time."

Out in the corridor, we found the new rector talking to a student. Once David Porterfield's eyes met the Professor's, he excused himself from the student and stepped our way. I introduced them.

"Professor, I'm very glad to meet you, sir," he said. "We're happy you're back with us for another year."

"Well, I'm glad to meet you, Father."

"Oh, I'm not a priest, not a deacon, not anything—but I *am* a CSC."

"I see. Now I'll have to speak with you later. I've got to get dressed now."

The conversation ended there, but it would be many days before the Professor could accept the change of rector—or the death of his friend.

"We have a new rector, a new horse," he announced the next day, as if I needed reminding.

"Are you going to ride him?"

"I don't know, but I think I will break him in."

Later, he said, "They didn't play fair with us. They had to know Father Dan was coming back to Notre Dame, because arrangements had to be made. They knew Dan was dying and he knew he was dying, but they didn't tell us. Dan was determined to die at Notre Dame, you know. He came in at seven o'clock Thursday and at four the next afternoon I got the call saying he had died. Tom Casey was here but had to be back by Monday, the day of the funeral, to keep his job in Pennsylvania. Several priests convinced me to go with him rather than stay here for the funeral."

As he was talking, the bells of Sacred Heart began to ring. The Professor's eyes lit up. "We have a pope!" he cried. "We have a pope!"

"Maybe it's just a wedding."

"No, it's those bells! We have a pope!" The Professor bolted from his seat and almost knocked me over getting to the television.

He watched with a boyish grin as I tried the channels. Sure enough, a late report broke news of a surprise choice of Paul VI's successor.

Later in the evening, the Professor went to Corby Hall hoping to pick up more details. "A man came running and yelling down the stairs like a madman. 'Who is he? Who is he?' I told him, 'John Paul—Luciani.' 'Never heard of him. Never heard of him.' He had been taking a nap, as the CSCs do."

Meanwhile, the process of settling in continued, as the Professor began a new term in Sorin. Already he was making a favorable impression on the new freshmen, who dreamed up a fantasy about his secret life: "We call him 'Spike,'" one of them told me. "He climbs into that beat-up brown car and drives to a garage in South Bend. Then he gets on his Harley-Davidson 1200 and takes off."

Every time the Professor returns to South Bend, he spends his first few evenings going out to dinner with friends. Last night it was the Manions; tonight it would be me; tomorrow it would be Mr. Stritch. He was in no hurry, however, to dine with the rector. "I am free after Sunday, but I don't want to get too chummy with him. The last Father that was really my chum was Father Burke."

He decided the two of us would eat at Eddie's. "I like it because it's been going for decades, an unpretentious place where trains run by as if they're going through the front door. When I phoned Eddie, Jr. to make reservations, he was surprised to hear from me but promised us a good meal. As a young faculty member, I was allowed to go to Eddie's because it was on the east side of town. During Prohibition, we were forbidden to go to the west side, where Alby's was, but we went there anyway."

"Here, you have a wrinkle on your coat," I said.

"Leave it. Tonight I want to stay a little sleazy." He told me *sleazy* was a favorite word of his.

When we pulled up to the nondescript building, I expected

to enter a dark, windowless room with suspicious characters loitering at the bar. What I found instead was an ordinary greasy spoon—Formica table tops, tile floors, napkin dispensers with salt and pepper shakers and steak sauce. The Professor was hoping to be seated on the "sleazy" side of the restaurant, but the proprietor, greeting us warmly, put us on the more respectable side next to a large window.

The Professor asked about classes I was taking, what was new with me and my friends. I told him I was still living in Don Miller's tower room but had added another roommate to form a triple, which meant two of us had a bunk bed in the room across the hall, 302, and the other had the turret. He reminded me 302 was once his room, joking, "You have violated my sanctum sanctorum." Then I asked about his plans for this year.

"Well, I would like to get back to Father Blantz's oral history project to finish those interviews with him."

"How far along are you?"

"Just as far as the Burns administration." We nursed our drinks a little while longer, then he said, "Last night I was at the Manions. The table talk was so political! It was like being at the Kennedys.

"Say, Phil, is the corner of my lip drooping?" He pointed to the left side of his face. "That would be the preliminary sign of a stroke, of course. That's something I can't take too lightly. Last spring when I was in the hospital, Dr. Egan made a point of saying he *hoped* to see me in September. My voice has changed, too, I think. There's something the matter with my vocal cords. My voice seems to be coming out far in front of my face."

The Professor told me he knew Father O'Neil was "up there" in heaven. "I never saw a man in my life who loved life as much as Dan did. He always had such long-range plans. I don't think he ever thought he'd die. He thought he was indestructible, and so it

seemed he was. He used to meet some of the most well-to-do people, marrying them and so forth. He married a man who opened a
clothing business in Fort Lauderdale. Dan told another friend to go
there and say he was a Notre Dame grad to get a 20% discount. So
the man went and looked at some trunks and they cost forty-eight
dollars. He phoned to tell Dan he lived in high society!"

"How do *you* know so much about clothes?"

"I know the fashions because I read about them. Leisure suits
are out—*bang!* Ties are thinner. Button-down shirts are in."

After dinner, at Sorin, we spotted a friend of Father O'Neil
talking to the rector. The Professor rushed up to ask—almost ac-
cuse—him, "You were with Dan in the last days before he died?"

"Yes, I saw him the day before he died," the priest said.

"Last night I was a little upset with Gina Manion because I
hadn't been told the truth about Dan. I'd been told 'he's improving' and 'he's getting along,' when he actually wasn't."

The priest was flustered to be put on the spot and tried defending those reports, though not very convincingly, I thought:
"He really became much worse only after the plane ride to South
Bend. There were two storms during the flight. They gave him
medicine for it, but the medicine killed him."

The Professor pressed for more information but realized he
was getting nowhere and gave up. He turned to the rector and
said, "I have been here since 1917. We have had numerous rectors in the last few years. Are you going to stay?"

Mr. Porterfield laughed. "Oh, yes, quite a while—for the
duration."

"What is 'the duration?'"

"Seven years."

"Good!" Then the Professor added, "I'm afraid this is my last
year here."

"No, sir, I think you'll be here for a long time," he replied.

Back in his room, the Professor found a note from the rector informing him Brother Boniface had died. So another name
was added to the Professor's litany of the dead, and I began to
wonder whether he was entering a perpetual state of mourning.
"You see, now I've suffered two big deaths," he said. "I had to get
over Kerndt dying and now Dan; it's hard." *Kerndt Healy died
eighteen years ago, Professor!* "T. Bowyer, F. X., George … they
aren't quite the same as these two. You don't realize the hole it
leaves inside me." He paused for a moment. "But the only time
I get lonely is when I'm inside Sorin Hall all by myself with the
building completely vacant."

[26]

The Infirmary

THE NEXT DAY, this mood had lifted and the Professor was more cheerful than he'd been in months. What could have wrought such a change? He anticipated my question, smiling before he could get the words out: "Well, now I know that Dan is dead," he said. "I visited the cemetery today. He's buried right next to the oldest member of the community, Con Hagerty. I've been dreading that visit, but I finally got it over with."

He spoke as if this was a longstanding ritual of his. Whatever its origins, its immediate impact was marvelous to behold. Suddenly, what his talking, letter-writing, and prayers these past three months had not accomplished, ten minutes at the cemetery had. The graveside visit was an act of self-preservation, it seemed to me. He had to know if he didn't regain his emotional balance, he wouldn't survive. His stay in the hospital last spring taught us that.

The Professor's buoyant outlook had another source as well. He showed me last June's 1928 reunion booklet with its dedication to "Our beloved Professor Paul Fenlon" and its pictures of him. He had once wanted to quash this tribute, but now he looked on it with immense pride.

Since coming back at the start of my junior year, the Professor had been making a successful transition to Sorin. You could even say he was returning to normal. He'd reestablished ties with friends, resumed old routines, dealt with a wounding grief, and made peace with his celebrity status. He'd even begun adjusting to a new rector, finally consenting to dine with Mr. Porterfield. To hear his noncommittal report ("We were feeling each other out"), it couldn't have gone so badly. But then, not two weeks after being on campus, disaster struck.

I was returning home from the library, when I noticed the Professor's lights were off. I assumed he was just out for the evening, but under my door I found a slip of note paper. Penciled in beautiful longhand, it said:

Phil,

Prof. Fenlon had a bad fall this evening. He's in St. Joe Hospital for the night, but I hope it's only a bad bruise. I left his car keys on his desk. I will call him in the morning. Will you pls call me 232-1865.

Prof. Stritch

The next morning I drove to the hospital. The Professor extended a limp hand for me to shake. He was drowsy and muddled, just like his last hospital stay. He would be here a few days until the bruise could heal, he told me. "I fell off some steps in Mr. Stritch's backyard. We debated for two hours whether to go to the hospital. Finally, we called an ambulance and it came without all its lights going. Pretty soon there was a crowd. A woman from the neighborhood came running up to him, saying, 'Oh, Mr. Stritch, I was so afraid it was you being taken away, but it's only Professor Fenlon!' I had never been in one of those stretchers before. It was so strange; everyone was looking down at me when they strapped me in. That's the first time I was ever in an ambulance."

The next day, I returned to find the Professor on the verge of tears. Once I calmed him down, he told me he had just learned he did not have a bruise—he had a cracked pelvis. No surgery was required, but he would have to stay in the hospital two to three weeks. "Being here these past few days has confused me. I woke up once thinking I was at the Inn. You know, I stayed there a few days this summer. Then the oddest thing was one morning it was so quiet here I thought I was back home. I thought little Danny had gone off to school and I was alone with Betty. And I started calling out for Betty. 'Betty, Betty,... Betty!' Soon a nurse came rushing in. I'm sure she thought I had gone mad. I felt so foolish."

I visited the Professor every other day for the next three weeks. Big Boy, Tim, and Bill were also regular visitors. On one occasion, the Professor introduced Big Boy and me to someone as "two former students of mine." Misidentifying me in this way was not that unusual. I remember one time he said to me, "Thank you. Thank you, my son," then, trying to correct himself, "my grandson," before giving up.

On another visit, Big Boy reported hearing something like a gunshot on his way to the hospital. "Did they know the car you were in belonged to me?" the Professor asked, instantly suspecting his student enemies. Gunfire in that neighborhood wasn't out of the question, we told him, but we couldn't believe there was a student sniper tracking his car through the streets of South Bend. The Professor also panicked when the rosary Mr. Stritch lent him went missing. It was his uncle Cardinal Stritch's private rosary, in mint condition, and it didn't reappear for several hours.

When the Professor was finally able to move to a private room, he was much more comfortable. "There were so many people visiting in the other room," he said, "and, besides, as you know, I have never liked the idea of having a roommate."

Finally, the Professor was discharged and transported by ambulance to the Student Health Center behind the Main Building. The first thing he did was shower thanks on those who made the move possible. "Ted was not in when I phoned him, but I talked with Miss Hosinski to express my gratitude. This is such a lovely room. I was just beyond words when I saw it. Phil Faccenda was not in either, but he said I was a fixture here and could stay as long as I thought I could. Ted told them to ditch that silly rule about students and religious only, not allowing lay-men into the infirmary. I had all sorts of people shooting for me: Phil Faccenda, Mrs. Manion, Tom Stritch. Mr. Stritch of course went right to the top, to Ted."

For the next two weeks my journal was blank. I was so de-pressed by these hospitalizations that I didn't write anything down. I know the Professor must have had a reaction to the election of Karol Wojtyła as pope, but I didn't record it.

We were on a crisis footing, just trying to survive, not given to long or interesting conversations. I was engaged in mundane tasks like handing him things he couldn't reach, getting instruc-tions from staff, and picking up items from Sorin. The Professor was trying to adapt to the Health Center routines—meal times, nurse visits, physical therapy sessions, visiting hours. Only after he had his rosaries, prayer books, and photographs with him did he begin to relax.

There was a rule prohibiting alcohol in the building, but one day the Professor asked me to join him for a Scotch. Later, he organized a clandestine cocktail party for Big Boy, Tom, and me, and prevailed upon the nun in charge of the no-alcohol policy to join us. At this gathering, he announced he had arrived at a decision: "They can't put me here permanently or over in Brownson Hall or over in Moreau. I will either live in Sorin or I will live back home in Blairsville. Those are the only two places I will live."

That was in the future; for now he had to make the best of his temporary lodging on the second floor of the Center. There our visits began to take on the character of former times. He told me, " 'Cricket,' my favorite little nurse here, said *her* favorite person here was Father Lange! 'Oh, Father Lange was the sweetest man!' 'Oh, no,' I said. Of course, Phil, you have to remember he could charm people; he could be quite popular with some of the boys. Yes, Lange was a real charmer. He lived several years right here in the student infirmary or 'Student Health Center'—they won't let you call it by its real name anymore. He died just a few doors down the hall here."

Then one day the latest issue of the alumni magazine arrived. The Professor sat looking through it and I leaned over his shoulder following along. We took turns making comments as he turned the pages, until he stopped at an article by Chet Grant about the football star Red Salmon, and I moved to the other side of the room to sit. A long silence followed. The Professor bowed his head, squeezed his eyes shut, clasped his hands together, as if in prayer, then pressed his right index finger against the photo of Salmon, blotting out his face. He opened his mouth, hesitated, then declared: "I remember this photograph." Another dramatic pause, then: "I had been teaching just a few weeks here, when I was told to go down and see the rector. It was Father Lavin who gave me the phone. And it was our family doctor on the line."

His voice cracked. "It was...." He lowered his head and began to cry, struggling for words.

"Your father?"

"Yes, my father... and it was only a few weeks after I had gotten settled!" He broke down again, angrier than I had ever seen him. "Just *two or three* weeks! ... So he told me, 'Go ahead. Go get your sister. I'll make your train reservations.' So I went over to St. Mary's and Sarah said, 'What's the matter?' And I told her. She was surprised, too. She didn't even know of father's condition. I didn't either, to tell the truth. But we both went back home for the funeral. And that's why I missed Salmon. You see, after graduating in '05, what Chet says here is true: Red Salmon only came back here to visit once. I never remembered his homecoming, but it must have been while I was away for father's funeral. Years later, I was going through an old trunk in the attic with my sister. We came upon a photo of his homecoming—the very same one as in this magazine—and I just ripped it up." Here he made a tearing motion with his hands and lost his composure again. "I didn't know anything about it."

As he spoke, I felt mounting embarrassment and even fear. I had never been in the presence of a grown-up who was so distraught, and I didn't know what to do or how to understand someone weeping over an event almost sixty years distant. Granted, his medication, drink, and stress must have been contributing factors, but it was clear his father's death was a devastating blow to him.

Was it something more as well? Was it even more important to his psychological makeup than his homeschooled years? I believed here I had a key to the mysteries of the man if only I could unlock them. Were these tears of self-pity? Had the Professor actually been lonely all these years, somehow blaming his solitary existence on his father's abandonment? Was his fixed way of life, his intense loyalty, his independence, his talent for friendship—everything that made him who he was, in other words—somehow tied to the death of the man who once tried to thwart his vocation at Notre Dame? These questions came in the days ahead. At the time I was struck dumb by what I had just witnessed.

After a few minutes, the Professor regained control of his emotions, raised his guard, and changed the subject. Walking back to Sorin, I was convinced I had experienced something too profound to understand—then or perhaps ever. That photograph had exposed a deep psychic wound, but what did it mean?

$\left[27\right]$

God, Country, Notre Dame (1940-52)

THE PROFESSOR was always telling me to keep my presidents straight: there were two president O'Donnells and two president Cavanaughs. The second O'Donnell (J. Hugh) led the school from 1940 to 1946, including World War II, and he was succeeded by the second Cavanaugh (John J.). The Professor fondly recalled both men as well as the bachelor dons whose tenures overlapped with their terms of office. But for him the decade began with *Knute Rockne, All-American* (1940) and its "win one for the Gipper" scene starring Pat O'Brien and Ronald Reagan. The movie was filmed on campus, and the Professor was there.

"I remember looking out from my room at the mob in front of Corby Hall when they were shooting the picture of Rockne. They were using reflecting foil like the sun to light the shots on cloudy days. I played one of the extras. My friend Art Haley ran the public relations department and he got to choose the extras. He chose all of Rockne's coaches, including Chet Grant, some professors, and some students. We were each paid five dollars.

"The funeral scene took quite a while, at least a couple hours. Whenever they were ready, *poof*—these big, very bright lights went on. I remember they must have moved that casket up and down the aisle a dozen times, and the poor widow had to walk each time. The actor who played Charlie O'Donnell wasn't Catholic, so he refused to genuflect at the end of that

209

long procession. He wouldn't make the sign of the cross either, so I think they put in a double for him during those scenes. I sat next to Mrs. Layden. We sat there and listened almost word for word to Charlie O'Donnell's eulogy.

"When the filming was over, they held a banquet. I remember that Mrs. Rockne went up to the head table with that vulgarian, Mrs. Feeney, the fire chief's wife, who told a vulgar story. She was a very big woman, and she wore a fire helmet and that badge. I never saw Elmer Layden laugh so hard in my life as he did at that woman's story. She was vulgar, but I had to admit she could tell an awfully good story.

***

"Mr. T. Bowyer Campbell taught history here and awoke at five o'clock for tea every morning. Then once a week four of us would meet for afternoon tea in the fourth-floor tower of Morrissey Hall. In the group we had Paul Byrne, Tom Madden, Campbell, and me. On Monday he used to have tea for the professors and Tuesday through Friday for the boys. For that reason, he was sometimes referred to as 'Tea Boiler' Campbell.

"He owned three or four canes and wore a stiff straw hat, which looked very vaudevillian to me—very tart. In his wrinkled, worn coats, T. Bowyer always smelled of garlic. He moved off campus into a white brick house on the first street past Angela, and I only went there once to eat. He came out of the kitchen from cooking, and his famous thick tweed jacket reeked of garlic.

"He was frugal, thrifty, and even stingy. That's why he was an RA when he lived in Morrissey—to save money. I remember he was outraged when the cost of stamps changed from two cents to three cents. When I used to visit him, I only drank V-8 juice. Finally, he said, 'Come now, Fenlon, you must learn to drink tea; juice is too expensive.'

"He was really more of an Englishman than an American. He was an Anglican chaplain, but then converted, and his Episcopalian friends deserted him. In Rome he met Charlie O'Donnell, who brought him to Notre Dame. When his female relations came to visit him here, they expected to see Indians behind every tree. They were appalled that he lived in this Indiana wilderness. One of them wrote him, 'You settled in that far-distant country. How terrible!' But he used to say, 'I've come to the end of the world, but at least I'm in the right pew.'

"I'll never forget what he said about burying people in France. They bury them on top of each other over there. There isn't that much land, you know. T. Bowyer's brother married a famous French actress, and T. Bowyer resented him because he never had to do a stitch of work in his life and refused to convert from High Church Episcopalianism. The brother finally died, and when T. Bowyer received the news, he just flipped the telegram in the trash can and said, 'Oh, let them bury him on top of somebody.'

***

"During World War II the Navy wanted to buy the school for $17 million. They told us the school could be moved somewhere else, but our president, J. Hugh O'Donnell, and the Congregation of the Holy Cross refused to sell; they said, 'This is the only place Notre Dame can ever be.'

"It was O'Donnell who coined the phrase, 'God, Country, and Notre Dame,' which is carved over the side entrance to Sacred Heart. But poor Hugh! He was so earnest. 'For God, Country, and Notre Dame,' he always used to say. And the Burke brothers would just roar with laughter. Pepper O'Donnell took himself so seriously.

"He was like King Farley: he was not a learned man, but he had a good heart. I remember the absurd way in which he earned his PhD by collecting the names of all the priests in the United

States. He simply inquired at all the dioceses and made a list of names. It was ridiculous. He was only an athlete, of course, a famous athlete. He used to be mocked by the Four Horsemen in the litany that Jim Crowley wrote: *Who dropped the ball last game? J.! Hugh! O'Donnell! Who gave the game away? J! Hugh! O'Donnell!*

"But you know they tell the story about him, that he wasn't out of office very long before he was ill and went up to Mayo's. And they opened him up, and he was full of cancer. And he came back and the provincial was told about him. Gene Burke is the one who told me the story. O'Donnell was in the infirmary at the time and still in bed. Several priests were there, too, when he was told by whoever the provincial was that his days were numbered. After the provincial left the room, Hugh O'Donnell turned around and said, 'Gentlemen, let us go down to the chapel and make an act of thanksgiving'—which was one of the best things he did in his entire life. And he didn't put on a show or anything. 'Gentlemen, let us go down to make an act of thanksgiving and accept what I have been told.' And he didn't live many months afterwards, you know. And he really died a fairly young priest.

"The Navy didn't buy us but they did take us over for their training. One day I answered a knock at the door to find a couple of young naval officers all decked out with scrambled eggs on their uniforms. They were inspecting Sorin to see whether it could be turned into another of their residence halls. But they complained we didn't have enough 'heads.' I had no idea what they were talking about. They told me 'heads' were toilets. The Navy couldn't understand why we only had one head on each floor. So Sorin was taken out of consideration. You don't know how relieved I was.

"I always remember the loneliest day I ever spent, which was at Sorin on Christmas Eve the first year the Navy took us over.

The Navy made us have classes right up to Christmas Day, so on the 24th I finished teaching my afternoon classes and then went up to my tower room. Sorin Hall was a horribly lonely place for me that night.

"It was during the war that I visited Florida for the only time in my life. Gas was being rationed on one side of the state but not the other. I don't remember which side was which, but we ended up traveling mainly on the rationed side. We were near Miami when I received word that one of my sisters was very ill. I immediately boarded a train north and was surprised to find it had seats instead of sleeping compartments. I had always traveled on Pullman cars because we always had free passes, since my father worked for the Penn Central. I used to think all trains were made up exclusively of Pullmans. I was spoiled.

"My friend Tom Stritch quickly went into World War II, after graduating from here in 1934 and taking a job here teaching English. He slept in my turret room, as many of the boys during the war years would do on weekend visits. They slept on the same couch that is now in my vestibule. Stritch commanded a ship in the war and after about three years returned to the United States to head the military program at Lawrence College in Appleton, Wisconsin. Then he came back to Notre Dame.

"At one time, you know, I didn't particularly care for Stritch. I thought he was a rather cocky s. o. b. During my eleven years as assistant dean of the College of Arts and Letters, I used to help schedule courses for the next semester, and Stritch requested late morning or early afternoon classes. So I assigned him something like Journalism I at ten o'clock and Journalism II at three o'clock. When he saw where I had put him, he said, 'Why, I can't teach at these hours!' And I said, 'There are simply no vacancies.' Of course, later I told him the truth and he likes telling the story on himself.

"But then one year the chairman of the journalism department was found dead in his bed, so Stritch was made chairman. Now as chairman, you see, he could then change his course times to whenever he wanted. I asked the dean of Arts and Letters what could be done to stop him. And he said, 'What can I do? What can I do, Paul? What *can* I do?' When Stritch told me he was coming back to head the journalism school here, I said, 'Tom, you don't know anything about journalism,' and he said, 'Oh, I know, but you don't have to know anything about something to run it. Besides, we're restructuring the department.' And he did.

"His uncle was the famous Samuel Cardinal Stritch of Chicago. I knew him. He was a short man like his nephew. At the beginning of Lent when he went to Florida for the winter, we would use his house in Chicago on the weekends sometimes.

"Once I accompanied Tom to Arkansas where he was visiting some of his kinfolk. Traveling with Mr. Stritch, I learned that all women in the South are addressed as 'Miss.' Tom was always mentioning 'Miss Ellen, Miss Ellen' until finally I asked him, 'Who is Miss Ellen?' He told me it was his mother.

"Stritch was a bachelor professor-in-residence until he got kicked off campus with most of the others. When those professors were told to get a place in town, Pop Steiner said, 'Let Withey and Ryan and O'Malley and Fenlon stay.' It is through Pop Steiner's generosity that I am still here.

"In the last few years of his life, Jim Withey didn't teach, but by sheer kindness they let him live on in Walsh Hall. Stritch was made in the mold of Withey, another bachelor who taught English, the most peculiar man you'd ever seen. In his last years, he combed this straggly, kinky white hair straight back. Father O'Neil was rector of Walsh, and his suite was on the left and Withey's on the right. The only time that I ever visited him in his room, his bathtub was filled with neatly folded towels and washcloths. I asked, 'Do you ever use the tub?' He answered, 'Oh, no.' He suffered from TB, and we all went to visit him one time at a sanitarium in Michigan. Finally, they took him to St. Joseph's Hospital, where he later died."

Rev. John J. Cavanaugh, CSC was president of Notre Dame from 1946 to 1952. He was not to be confused with Rev. John W. Cavanaugh, CSC, who was president from 1905 to 1919, the Professor told me: "You know, that's what Cavvy I said when Cavvy II became more prominent: 'They're going to say he was my son.'

"The second President Cavanaugh used to live on the third floor of Sorin as a student; he was just a few years behind me. He came through like the rest of us. He was even engaged to be married but broke it off, so she became a nun and he later became a priest. Along with two others living on the third floor, Harry Barnhardt and Frankie somebody, Cavanaugh founded the Student Activities Council (SAC), a group of students working to organize better events on campus. We thought it was kind of silly, so we called it the Silly Ass Club (SAC) behind their backs. I don't know if he knew we called it that or even if he knows to this day. Father Cavanaugh's great innovation, of course, was creating all of those vice presidents in the administration. Father Eugene Burke said we had more vice presidents than the Ford Motor Company.

"I knew a priest who lived near me on the third floor here. He was in President Cavanaugh's administration, before they made Father Hesburgh a vice president. Now a friend of mine had fallen in love with a very beautiful girl, a non-Catholic, who was already married to a man in a mental institution. My friend went ahead and married the girl in Chicago and I was best man. Then they went on their honeymoon and I took the South Shore back to South Bend. Anyway, he had a terribly guilty conscience and talked to this priest, who told him not to worry about it. They've been happily married ever since, and he comes up for his fiftieth reunion this year, God willing. I've been best man for seven marriages and godfather to eleven children.

"Father Cavanaugh baptized all six of Pat Manion's children. He didn't know how to drive a car; that was the strange thing about it. There was a terrible snowstorm the day Manion's last child was baptized, and I drove Father Cavanaugh there. When I made the turn up the hill, my little Ford hesitated and putt-putted. Cavanaugh said, 'Give it the gun, Paul! Give it the gun!' I was annoyed to no end when I'd come to the same turn and Father O'Neil would say, 'Give it the gun, Paul! Give it the gun!'

"Father Cavanaugh would have preferred to have done away with football altogether. He thought it interfered with studies too much. J. Hugh O'Donnell supported football just as adamantly as Cavanaugh opposed it. Though he was no longer president, he used to play football and still had a great deal of influence. Finally, Father Hesburgh offered a kind of compromise, saying we could have both athletics and studies, and so this is what we have today.

"Now it wasn't beneath Frank Leahy or one of his assistant coaches to approach a professor about seeing to it that some boy got through a certain class. And some of the professors would do it. I remember myself being approached about changing the grade of a boy. Leahy's men found out very quickly I wasn't going to play their games, so most often they just ignored old Fenlon and I flunked some of his players. But Rockne never tried any of Leahy's tricks. Rockne didn't interfere with the boys' studies. He just left the boys alone and if they got sent out of here because they didn't study, why that was fine. Today, you know, they have special tutors for the athletes and everything. It's preposterous.

"In Father Cavanaugh's reform administration, Hesburgh

rose to the rank of vice president. It was somewhat of a surprise to everyone that so young a priest should ascend to the presidency in 1952, but it was just accepted. The last time I was in President Hesburgh's office was when I was assistant dean, when we used to meet up there occasionally." A short profile of Hesburgh had just appeared in *Time* magazine ("Prince of Priests, Without a Nickel"). "I'd say it's about 40 percent accurate. That part about him sleeping on a steel cot in Corby is utter nonsense. There are no such cots anywhere on campus, with the possible exception of Badin Hall."

[28]

More Like a Friend

THIS DAY the Professor felt well enough to leave the infirmary and go off campus for dinner. First he had me drive back to Sorin to pick up a few things, then he took Tom and me on a tour of St. Mary's. On our way to the Inn, we passed T. Bowyer Campbell's old Napoleon Street home with its twin chimneys. At the intersection of Notre Dame Avenue, he pointed out Maurice Francis Egan's "Lilacs" to us.

As his convalescence was coming to an end, the Professor began taking short walks outside. He ventured to the Main Building to cash some checks, telling me, "I want to get it in cash before I die." He was thinking of poor Colonel Hoynes, who died with thousands of dollars in checks lying on his bed.

At last, after six weeks in the infirmary, the Professor moved back to Sorin. He was overjoyed to be 'home,' though he remained less mobile, less sure of himself than before his fall. In some ways, his regimen changed little. To be sure, he didn't have the staff to assist—or bother—him, but he and I were still focused on building up his strength and avoiding another accident. Nothing else mattered.

Social niceties fell by the wayside. One day I found him eating lunch out of a pie tin at his desk. "Why, if my mother could see me now!" he said. "I just shudder to think of it."

"Why?"

"Well, this is not eating at all; it's terribly uncivilized."

"Like eating at McDonald's?"

"I've never been to a McDonald's, of course, and I never intend to go into one. But, yes, they look just dreadful; they're undignified; it's not eating."

"Did I tell you? Mr. Byrne is gone. I got word that he can't even walk, so they've put him in a nursing home. Poor PRB. I don't think he'll ever be able to write to me again. Now I'm the last of our little group. There was T. Bowyer Campbell, Tom Madden, PRB—"

"—and PIF—"

"But they didn't call me 'PIF.' I issued a decree forbidding it. I curse the day I told you my middle name."

A new edition of Chet Grant's book, *Before Rockne at Notre Dame*, had just been published with an Introduction by Dan Devine. The Professor and I went to the autograph party held in the Sports and Games department of the library. By the time we arrived the crowd had thinned out. After purchasing our copies, we walked over to the authors, who were standing together signing books. I was fascinated to see Devine close up. Eleven months ago he had won a national championship, but this year the football team had three losses. Many fans blamed him for not winning a second straight championship, and some alumni believed his lack of charisma was sufficient cause to fire him, regardless of his win-loss record.

The Professor handed his book to Chet, who wrote in the flyleaf, "To: Paul Fenlon, gallant survivor of the old days and the old ways." Next, it was my turn. "To: Phil Hicks, an old young man I prize as a newfound friend. – Chet Grant." Then he added "witness" under his own signature, so that all Devine had to do was sign his name, which he did. After shaking hands with the coach and thanking him, we left for Sorin. I have to say, I was more impressed with this function than the Professor was. For him, it was just a chance to see Chet and test his range this far away from Sorin Hall.

Back at Sorin, I was cooking up a rather different event for him. As the semester came to a conclusion, I wanted to do another interview. In the University Archives I had discovered directories listing the name and room of every Sorinite dating to the 1920s. I didn't know when or if I'd get another chance to ask him about this material, but I correctly judged he still might submit to close questioning despite his precarious health.

Unlike the last time I tried to do this, the Professor was now positively tranquil as I threw scores of names at him in what must have seemed like a game of 'stump the professor.' For almost every name, he had at least a line or two for me—"he was well-liked by the students," or "his classes were chock-full," or "he's failed terribly; he looks like a walking ghost of his former self today," or "he is very, very ill—a stroke—dying in St. Joe Hospital, but a nice man, a nice fellow."

The Professor remembered the center and captain of the Four Horsemen team, Adam Walsh, who was living in Sorin and carrying on a romance during the summer school with a girl he ended up marrying. I was surprised how many professors and priests once resided in Sorin. One of them, he told me, had been forced to leave Canada and live at Notre Dame due to a new CSC rule that applied to American-born priests. For good measure, he named three or four other priests affected by the same rule, even though they had nothing to do with Sorin Hall. In offering these details, was he just showing off? Whatever the case, it was a bravura performance, even by his standards.

J. Arthur Reyniers, who later developed the germ-free lab on campus, was listed as a second-year pre-med student in Sorin, but the Professor didn't know him. Did I have the right

"Wenninger" living in Sorin? The only Wenninger the Professor knew was Francis, the dean of the College of Science, "a tough German who would laugh at almost anything." Haggar Hall was once named Wenninger-Kirsch Hall after him and another biologist-priest, Alexander Kirsch. "It was awful to take away the names. I remember the day we dedicated it and they were so proud of the fact they had a building. Now they've taken the names out of the bricks, just like they did the Hoynes College of Law when they made it the Crowley Hall of Music."

The Professor did not recall Moose Krause living here but did remember some of the football stars of the '40s. Creighton Miller was listed in 41, and later in 102, 301, and 47. "Could have been. He was around here, I know that." Johnny Lujack, the Heisman Trophy winner, was listed in 117 in the fall of 1946. "He and Creighton Miller were very much in this hall, but as to what room they were in, I don't know."

Only at the forty-five-minute mark of the interview did the Professor show any sign of impatience, but I pushed on to the next name. Father Bill Toohey, at present the director of Campus Ministry and a charismatic campus preacher, was listed as Sorin's chaplain in 1961-62. "Well, if he were, I wouldn't know about it. He came back from the war. He was a chaplain in the Marines, you know."

Thinking back on all the Professor's stories, I noticed most dated to the mid-1930s or earlier and seemed to dry up afterwards. What about the 1940s, '50s, and '60s? The campus had to be just as interesting in those years as before. "Most of your memories cease at about the time of Charlie Phillips's death, don't they?" I asked. "Doesn't that seem like a long time ago?"

"Well, yes, it seems like Charlie lived a long time ago. I remember those early, memorable years more than the past few decades, which just flew for me." Granted, he didn't take much interest in athletes, but he didn't even notice the stars of Ara Parseghian's teams living in the same building with him—Reggie Barnett, Tom Clements, Dave Casper, Jim Lynch—though he told me I had overlooked someone: "What about my friend George Kunz? He lived in Captain's Corner."

"Did you know him well?" I asked in reference to the All-American tackle and co-captain.

"No, I remember him, that's all. I just remember seeing him on the porch, back and forth."

"Did he ever come in this room to talk to you?"

"No, no, never to my knowledge. I think it was George Shuster who one time said about him that he was one of the few athletes who was a thoroughly good boy."

While the Professor was speaking, he paged through a pictorial history of the campus. "Okay, that's all I've got," I said. "Do you have any other statements?"

He did not answer, still engrossed in the pictures. "You see the funny stiff collars we had to wear in those days?" he said, before snapping to. "Well, that's quite a long interview!"

"Well, thank you."

"Now I need to wind my watch. You and Big Boy stepped out of here last night and neither one of you wound my watch, but I wound it a little bit and I think it's kept going." He handed me the watch. It was quarter to five; the bells outside had just gone silent.

This hour provided me with lots of trivia but no great revelations. As a matter of fact, I now began to wonder whether there were any revelations left to be revealed. Were we reaching the limits of his memory? He wasn't repeating himself, but when I reminded him of an old story or personality, I couldn't squeeze any more out of him. And so I stopped trying. It would be unkind to tax him any further, I decided, especially since he was still recuperating. Now I could be more like a friend to him and less like a reporter. He would have to volunteer stories from now on, because I wouldn't be demanding them anymore.

Our friendship had been forged in storytelling. Our common interest in campus history was what brought us together. So what was going to happen, I wondered, now that those stories occupied so little of our time? Already I sensed a shift in the balance of power taking place. When the Professor was healthy, he had been the generous one sharing his stories and submitting to my queries. I was indebted to him, and he set the rules. But now he depended on me to get through the day, all at a time when he was less able to repay me in stories. I was in charge, and he didn't enforce 'visiting hours' anymore.

It was terrible, wasn't it, to think of friendship in these terms, tracking who owed what to whom? I never made such a strict accounting, thank goodness, but in the back of my mind I thought, *I owe him so much for indulging my interest in Sorin Hall, so now it's my turn to help him, even if this caretaker role is new to me and real work sometimes. His friends are dying off quicker than he can replace them. He needs a friend and I am here for him.*

Then again, maybe the Professor was going to get healthy and we would return to a more equal plane. He was still full of surprises. The day after the interview, he accepted an invitation to a student Christmas party upstairs. Cracked pelvis or not, he was determined to climb to the third floor, and he enjoyed himself for nearly an hour there, nursing his Scotch, though refusing the eggnog.

The day before he flew back to Pennsylvania for the holidays, Big Boy, Tom, and I were helping him pack, when a student knocked at the door. Could the Professor stop by Dave Porterfield's room? The Professor looked at me. "I'm suspicious," he said. "This message seems ominous."

Volunteering to check it out, I knocked on the rector's door. When it opened, I saw forty or fifty students crammed inside. They pulled me in, and I found a space behind the door. A minute or two passed, then the Professor arrived. At once, a graduate student stepped forward, raising his voice: "Professor, on behalf of the residents of Sorin Hall, I would like to present this to you. Merry Christmas, sir." He handed the Professor an official Notre Dame plaid sport coat. The Professor was effusive in his thanks. "Won't you try it on?" the emcee asked. Three students helped him with the coat, then everyone broke into applause.

"I hope I sound better to you than I sound to myself," he said, "because I've just gone deaf." There were some snickers at this remark, some of them not very friendly, but whether his ears were ringing from the ovation or not, the Professor, in some unaccountable way, started to make a speech. "We have a good group of boys at Sorin this year," he began, his voice breaking and tears welling up. "They have been unusually good to me and I'm very thankful to them." Then he turned to the latest campus controversy: a proposed lottery to determine who would remain on campus during the ongoing housing shortage. The Professor offered a point-by-point critique of the proposal, just what the room wanted to hear.

As he spoke, I thought, *This is a side of you I've never seen before.* Even with his hoarse voice, he sounded like a seasoned public speaker, but then I had to remind myself that of course he knew how to do this—he spent forty years in front of a classroom. Even so, he was extraordinarily skillful in gaining the sympathy of the audience. This was a window into what it must have been like to have him as a professor, I thought, maybe the only one I will ever have.

Why give this speech at all, especially with everything else on your mind? Why not just say, "Thank you very much. Merry Christmas," then walk out the door in your sport coat? No, something else was going on here, it seemed to me. Didn't this performance harken back to his heyday as a bachelor don, when he was devoted to the interests of his students? Lately, some of them had proven disloyal, but he was still on their side; he was still their friend; he still wanted to be popular with them.

"Now you boys must have your parents write to Father Hesburgh about this lottery thing," he continued. "You've got to stick up for yourselves. It's a horrible thing—that lottery—and it must be stopped." More applause followed and then, without another word, he shuffled out of the room. As he did so, I saw someone rest his cheek on a friend's shoulder and say, "Aw, didn't that make you feel all warm inside?"

Just as I suspected, the rector had press-ganged these students to the event. As they were filing out, I recognized two of them as the vandals who had kicked out the panels of half a dozen doors in the basement last night. I remember the rector sorting through the splinters now heaped on the courtyard dumpster.

[29]

It's Alright, Paul

AT THE END OF FEBRUARY, the Professor had not yet returned from the holidays, and he phoned me late at night, after the long-distance rates went down. He wanted to take advantage of the weather in Pittsburgh to fly back to Indiana next Saturday, he told me. I warned him that this was the night of the hall's semi-formal dance, and it could be a madhouse. This didn't deter him, but his voice cracked nervously, and he admitted as the date of his departure neared he was worrying as usual about "getting ready to get ready to go." He told me Dale Harkcom had died. "I attended all four years of high school with Dale. He was the only friend I had in Blairsville that I could really drop in on. He died a week ago yesterday, but he wasn't a Catholic, of course. Sprawled out on the floor of the kitchen: that's the way they found him. I had been with him just the night before." As the Professor was hanging up, he added, "Mr. Byrne is not doing well at all."

The theme of the dance was "Sorin—A Tropical Paradise." The decorations committee outdid itself, stringing artificial palm fronds from the ceiling and christening the women's restroom "The Ladies Lagoon." My roommates and I kept a lookout from our perch on the fire escape, and at quarter to nine Paul Boehm's big luxury car rolled up behind Sorin. Through the car's rear window, we could see the top of the Professor's head in the back seat. The Boehms bustled about, taking care of the luggage.

227

Then, with a little help, the Professor emerged from the car and headed up the back steps.

Tom and I waited for him to get settled, then went downstairs, passing the Boehms on their way out. The Professor was in the vestibule, fiddling with his luggage on the couch but unaware of our presence. "Hello, Professor!" I said. He turned, stretched out his arms and cried out, "Oh, Phil, *hello!*" He was thinner and his hair shorter than in December. There was Scotch on his breath, which meant they'd stopped for dinner on the way from the airport. "Good to see you," I said. Then he saw Tom with me. He embraced him as well. "Tom, hello!" He told us he wanted to get to sleep right away. "We'll talk later, but you go pick up your dates now."

The next day, the Professor attended the 4:15 Sunday Mass in Sorin Chapel. To his profound embarrassment, the visiting priest asked the assembly to "pray for Professor *Fen-uh-lawn*'s return to the hall," and everyone responded, "Lord, hear our prayer," even though he sat there in plain sight.

I was helping him unpack and noticed again the snapshots of his home in Blairsville. He said, "In the bed back home as a child I slept with my head at the north end of the bed, and I did it the same way last summer. You know, there's an old thing that says that's supposed to bring you good luck. But in my old room, where you are living, 302, I slept south, just as I do in this room. And you must sleep the same way, don't you? In that room it's about the only way, since you can just reach up from there to turn the switch off and on."

"So you slept south in Sorin many of these years and despite that you survived."

"Yes, I did. It's just a superstition, and you know I'm very superstitious. Why, just recently I sat down to a table and then found out I was the thirteenth one there."

"So what did you do?"

"Why, I got up and left, of course."

Now that he was settling back in, the Professor was visiting friends again. The Manions were up first: "Pat has a big engagement in Washington, D.C. this weekend with that Mrs. Schlafly, or whoever she is, who is fighting against that women's lib thing."

"The Equal Rights Amendment?"

"Yes! She asked Pat to speak at this banquet."

"Is he against the ERA?"

"Oh, my yes; he's agin it."

"Is he well enough to go?"

"Yes, he is. You really don't have to be that healthy to give one of those speeches. Remember, Pat's whole life is that sort of thing. He is an orator, with a style people don't use anymore, in the manner, I always thought, of William Jennings Bryan. Manion uses all these gestures, you know, and has a bombastic way about his words. I saw Bryan during one of his campaign trips. He ran for the presidency three times, you know. Pat heard him, too."

Spring break and Easter came and went, and the spring semester wound to an uneventful conclusion.

I finished my exams and packed for the trip home. The night before my departure, the Professor returned from dinner with Mr. Stritch. "Be sure to stop by before you leave tomorrow morning," he said, before adding something I had never heard him say: "But remember: I *never* say, 'goodbye.' I only say, 'so long.' I *never* say, 'goodbye.'"

The next day, sure enough, after giving me a hug, he said, "so long." Yet this rule about not saying goodbye sounded crazy to me, since I couldn't believe he didn't use the term all the time. Then again, that would be just like him, wouldn't it—never letting go of his friends, never conceding a permanent break from them? In this case, was he simply refusing to admit we might never see each other again?

As it happened, he sent four letters to Florida in quick succession, each stuffed with clippings. Many were updates on campus events. Helen Hayes was awarded the Laetare Medal. Father Blantz won the Sheedy Excellence in Teaching Award. Students protesting recent tenure decisions demanded an overhaul of the tenure process. There were lighthearted pieces in the mailbag, too—some cartoons, a column on losing socks and another with the headline "Professor takes aim at bastardizing of English" (*bastardizing* double-underlined in red).

The Professor complimented me on the photos I had taken of him ("great") and wanted reprints. He asked me to read an article about Harvard's new core curriculum ("very good!"). He also told me, "I've buried two old friends: Tom Dunn of Morris, Lee Flatley former prof. here 1929-37. Been very upset by it." He reminded me he was marking the one-year anniversary of Father Dan's death.

After writing this flurry of letters from Notre Dame, the Professor drove back to Pennsylvania "with Busby at wheel." Then I heard nothing more from him for weeks. Beginning to worry, I sent a letter to his Walnut Street address in mid-August and waited for a reply.

In the meantime, I moved into 15 Sorin, a triple in the basement, also known as 'Captain's Corner.' By a defunct tradition, captains of the football team once lived here. The first piece of mail I received at my new address was from Tom Casey. "Uncle Paul asked me to drop you a line," it began. "Uncle Paul is now under doctor's care here in Blairsville. He is doing fairly well but his age is taking its toll. He gets around well but isn't too strong. He plans to get back to Notre Dame but the date depends on the doctor's recommendation. We're hopeful that he can make it back. Uncle Paul asks that you go to the Post Office and get all his 2nd and 3rd class mail. They can continue to forward his 1st class mail to Penna. Also, I am enclosing clipping concerning the death of Mr. Manion ['Clarence Manion, 83, national political figure, dies']. Uncle Paul felt that you would be interested. Perhaps you could call him some evening. It would cheer him up. Have a good year at ND. Uncle Paul talks of you in glowing terms so thank you for your kindness to him."

I phoned Blairsville later that day. Naturally, I wanted to talk about how and when he would return to Sorin, but all he wanted to talk about were his dead friends: "Now I am so glad that you and Pat got together to do that story about the ghost of Washington Hall. Pat got to see that story out in print before he died and I know that made him happy. They found him on the floor, next to his desk, you know. He died of a stroke. I talked with Gina on the phone and she told me I must not come out to the funeral. It would upset me too much.

"I had a fall, and there are other things I have to say that I cannot talk about over the phone just now. I am having a lot of trouble with stairs. Tom and I just got back from a little walk and it went pretty well. I still have a walker, you know." *No, not a walker!* I thought. *I don't want to see you like a crippled old man.*

"I am going to my doctor tomorrow and I'm hoping he will have some good news to cheer me up. I want to come back sometime in October, I think. As a transition to Sorin, I can stay at the infirmary. I will have to write Sister Marion to see if she can make room for me over there."

And so it came to pass. Five weeks later, the Professor returned. After spending the night in the infirmary, the first thing he wanted to do was visit Sorin.

A month earlier, the rector had approached me about making repairs to the Professor's room. The university had been trying for years to fix the crumbling ceiling, but the timing was never right until now. The only problem was how to do it without disturbing all the Professor's keepsakes. Our solution was to photograph

everything first, map out the position of the furniture, and remove the mementos and smaller pieces of furniture. Next, the
workmen put the larger pieces in the center of the room, draped
a tarp over them, plastered several sections of wall and ceiling,
applied a fresh coat of paint, and installed new carpeting. When
they finished, we replaced the Professor's possessions, checking
against the photos and drawings. We took equal care not to tell
him what we had done. We wanted it to be a surprise.

At the appointed hour, we made our way to Sorin, a little
group that included his niece Betty and Mr. Stritch. When we
entered 141, the Professor expressed satisfaction about returning
to his old room, but noticed nothing out of the ordinary. He chit-
chatted with us, oblivious to his surroundings, until we couldn't
stand it any longer. "So, Professor, do you notice anything different about your room?" I asked.

"About my room? No. Why should I?"

"Look up at the ceiling there," I said. His eyes widened, he
grinned, and his face lit up. "Why—how did you do this?" he
asked. As we explained, he stood there smiling, shaking his head.
Then he sat down on the bed and looked up at us, scanning our
faces. "How much better I would feel, if I could have just *one*
night's rest on this bed," he said, vowing to return to his room as
often as possible.

In the weeks that followed, setbacks delayed his return. He
had a fall while walking alone outside Corby Hall one day. On
an earlier occasion, I had seen him walking by himself and I ran
over to chastise him for doing something so stupid. I couldn't
understand why the staff would let him out on his own. Or had
he escaped? Within days of the first fall he fell again, this time in
his own room, but in neither case was he hurt.

One night, after regaining some confidence in his mobility, he
took Big Boy and me to dinner downtown. There he unburdened

himself. "When you get to be my age and you have no independence—they took my car away from me, you know, and they won't
let me walk anywhere outside alone, because of those two falls—
then it is just not worth it," he said. "So I think I will sign off."

"Sign off?"

"Yes, I said 'sign off.' I didn't say, 'I don't have anything to
live for' or 'I don't want to live,' but this is just not the way to do
it. Besides, I'm afraid I don't have a place at the infirmary. It is
true that Father Hesburgh sent me a second letter this summer
offering the infirmary to me again. I think he sent it because he
was coming back from California on a plane with Pat and Gina,
and I think they asked him to repeat his offer. But this letter
has the stipulation that the infirmary is free for me to use while
recovering *to go back to Sorin*."

Of course, returning to Sorin was the Professor's goal all
along, and sprucing up his room provided an extra incentive
to schedule some sleepovers in 141. "At Sorin," he said, "I had
many more visitors than I do here, because it was so easy for any
of the boys to stop in at night. Remember the way you used to
come in and we would have such nice chats, Phil? It's good for
me to be around all the life, the running and yelling of the boys."
That's changing your tune, I thought. *Now you're nostalgic for the
rascals who almost drove you out of the building?*

"I have always mixed better with the younger crowd than
with my own. Back in my day, when everyone would light up
their cigarettes, I would say 'no,' because of the coward that I
am, and they would say, 'Well, pack your trunk and go!' I was
a sissy about smoking, in a sense, and everyone smoked on all
occasions." *So this is another piece of the puzzle falling into place,*
I thought. *Snubbed by your peers, you spent more time socializing
with young people. So in a way, your aversion to smoke nurtured your
extraordinary rapport with students and might even help explain why*

you get along so well with another young person—me. "My father used to smoke cigars, and long after he was dead my mother would say how she would love to smell that cigar smoke again, but I wasn't willing to take up the things."

The Professor's desire to get back to Sorin was all well and good, but he realized he would have no nurses there and no supervision. Who would help with the pills he had to take at breakfast, lunch, and dinner? Where would he get his food? How would he get around campus, to say nothing of South Bend? At this point, he couldn't even walk without assistance, "especially on windy days," he said, smiling. Taking these variables into account, the Professor said, "I should never have come back. I should have stayed in Blairsville."

I tried to talk him out of it. Surely, I said, the best course of action is to live on campus, where you have friends at least. Besides, the infirmary is the only place that can take proper care of you now. You need to hang on, take advantage of Father Hesburgh's offer while it lasts, and hope you get well enough to return to Sorin.

But he insisted, "This has to be my last year. Maybe I'll be back next spring, but I don't know. People want me to stay through Christmas here on campus, then go home. Gina and Doris have both of course invited me over for Christmas, but I always remember the loneliest day I ever spent, which was on Christmas Eve at Sorin and I don't ever want to spend a night like that again here in the infirmary."

For the rest of the semester, long after we pushed back our chairs and left the restaurant, the debate continued. He argued with me and my friends; he argued with his own friends; he argued with himself. In each instance, he returned to the same issues: the ups and downs of his health, the practical considerations of where best to live, the fears and memories stirred by his recent difficulties, the need to read the minds of the powers that be. During one of these discussions, he divulged what he hadn't wanted to repeat on the phone two months earlier: "Over the summer I suffered what was called a 'cerebral thrombosis' or a 'mini-stroke,' as my doctor calls it. One morning at the breakfast table I tried to pick something up and I just couldn't. That side of my body did not work. So they called an ambulance for me and I rode to the hospital. And the problem is, once you've had one, you can have others, too, Dr. Egan said. I remember my poor mother, who had six or seven strokes. That went on for about five years, before she died very quietly in 1933."

He told me this one Friday afternoon of a football weekend. The weather wasn't half bad, so the Professor decided he wanted to get out and enjoy the festive atmosphere. We walked from the infirmary to Sorin and back. On our shortcut through the Main Building, several people greeted him, everyone over the age of forty in fact, and many by name. As we got closer to Sorin, we came upon a stream of people leaving Sacred Heart Church from a wedding. Then I heard a car creeping up from behind, turned around, and saw the crowd parting for a silver sports car. I raised my voice above the chatter, "Professor, it's Father Hesburgh coming up alongside us."

"What?" he asked. Before I could answer, Hesburgh shouted, "Hello, Paul!" The Professor lurched backwards, I caught him, then he leaned forward towards the rolled-down window. "It's good to see you up and walking around campus, Paul," the president said.

"Oh, Father, I tried to get a hold of you and I'm so thankful, I'm so—" The words tumbled out like a well-rehearsed speech, but Hesburgh interrupted, "It's alright, Paul." As introductions were being made, the driver of the car stretched out his hand to shake: "I'm Tim O'Meara," he said. Then they pulled away, stopping momentarily for the bride, who bent into the car for a kiss from Father Hesburgh.

As soon as the Professor regained his composure, he asked, "Who was that man with the peculiar accent?"

"That was our provost, the South African mathematician."

"Oh, so *that* was our provost!"

Later in the day, once he had more time to reflect, he was very pleased. "How lucky I am to have run into Hesburgh like that. 'Good to see you walking around campus like this,' he said. So he knows I'm trying to get well."

A few days later, there were other positive developments to report. "Today has been a good day for me," the Professor announced. "I visited that nice eye doctor, Dr. Hall. He adjusted my new glasses somehow so that I can finally see out of them. He did all of this probing of my face and said my nerves were recovering from my illness. He said this thrombosis throws your whole system off balance and it takes a while for your sight and balance to recover. But he said I might be much better in a month and back to normal, 'good,' in three or four months. So it was good encouragement, which I needed."

Who knew? Maybe the Professor's condition was reversible and he could return to Sorin after all. This was the hope at least, yet in the weeks that followed he remained hostage to the infirmary. No decisions were made about where and how he would live, except that he would fly back to Pennsylvania for Christmas. So on a Sunday in mid-December, the Professor headed back to Blairsville, never having spent a night in Sorin Hall.

[30]

A Spring Day

AFTER THE HOLIDAYS, I didn't hear anything from or about the Professor until February, when he phoned me from Pennsylvania late at night. His voice was strong, and this was usually a good barometer of his health, yet he complained he walked slower than ever now and was getting almost no exercise because it was too cold to go outside. He blamed the cold for his loss of dexterity, too: "I think I'd be in my room all day trying to get dressed, if it weren't for Betty. She's been wonderful to me." After chatting about several things, he came to his point: "Phil, I don't think I will come back."

My heart raced. *So this is how it all ends? Betty will return to collect your belongings and you will be gone forever? I may get out to Blairsville to visit you, but you will just wither away there?* "It would be too much work," he continued. "And my family here is all agin it."

Until this moment, I hadn't realized the Professor was waging a battle against the Caseys, not just his declining health. With my ear pressed against the receiver, I tried to be patient, not to interrupt, but I was determined not to resign myself to this outcome. Something inside me revolted against the idea. Call it selfishness or blind impulse, but I was adamant that he stay in Sorin. It wasn't my decision to make, of course, but I felt there was something fundamentally unjust about his living anywhere but

Sorin. He had to stay in Sorin at all costs, because he wouldn't survive long anywhere else.

In the tug of war between Blairsville and Notre Dame, more was at stake than whether he would be returning for the spring semester. We were also fighting over where he would die. He'd been thinking about this question for some time now. His literary sense told him that lives, like stories, ought to end where they begin, and he'd made a case for dying and being buried in Blairsville. But my historical sense told me someone who lived three-quarters of his life at Notre Dame ought to find his resting place there as well. I knew he hadn't ruled out this second possibility completely, because he once said, "I don't know whether I want to be in the CSC burial grounds or not."

As these thoughts crowded in on me, the Professor seemed to draw back from a final decision, indicating he still had an open mind: "Anyway, before I do anything I will have to get the doctor's approval, and I will be seeing him tomorrow. I've gotten calls from Gina, and of course she wants me to live in that converted sanitarium near her place, Healthwin. And Boehm and Stritch want me in an old men's home. But if I go back to Notre Dame, it will be to Sorin Hall, not that infirmary way out there.

"My doctors say I must eat regularly, at the same times every day when I take my medicine. Dr. Egan looked into Meals on Wheels, but they don't deliver on weekends and I need to eat on weekends! Our rector Dave is supposed to be working on my future eating arrangements, but he has done nothing yet as far as I know. But Father Hesburgh was supposed to have told him, 'do whatever you can to make Paul happy.' Maybe Mr. Stritch can work something out with Corby Hall's kitchen so that food can be brought over to me. Of course, they insist on not letting me drive my own car, but if the weather warmed up I might be able to walk to my meals at the cafeteria."

Blairsville also had drawbacks, he acknowledged: "Life here at home really isn't that good. I have so little to do that I spend much more time in front of the television; I've finally given in and broken my vow not to watch TV. With this cold weather I've been cooped up here. I haven't been to church in four weeks! And there is that little monster, that nephew of mine. He's so spoiled! I swear, he destroys in seconds what I have preserved for years. But I better keep my mouth shut.

"At least here I can get up and go to bed when I want, 9:30 in the morning and 11:30 at night, but there are so few people around. I think I'm depressed. And my memory has been impaired; I've lost something. They tell me about things that have happened recently and I don't remember a thing about them. Different events that I do remember I can't put in the right order."

"You're having trouble because of your isolation," I said. "You can't make those connections to people that you are so famous for—when people married, where their hometowns are, when they were born or died."

"Yes, I love people and I've made many great friends."

As we went back and forth, he seemed resigned to defeat or didn't understand the magnitude of the decision he faced. I had to get through to him that this was his life we were talking about.

I didn't think I was making any headway; he was being stubborn and so was I. But then—whether his mind had never really been made up or he was just warming to the idea of returning to Notre Dame—he made a complete about-face.

"What I'd like to do," he said, "is come back during your vacation this Easter, then stay through for your commencement. I'd like to see some people and spend time visiting with them. Then we will all go out together. That will be it for me—for good; I won't return. I am really so anxious to get back."

Relieved as I was to hear this, I'd only won a battle, not the war. I didn't like the idea of giving up on Notre Dame, but I was glad he would be there for my last five weeks on campus—time enough perhaps to convince him to stay on. With this immediate crisis averted, one question remained: could he preserve his resolve and stay healthy enough for his promised return?

Two months later, praise the Lord, we were still on schedule. A brief note heralded his arrival: "Phil, The Professor arrives Wednesday April 9 at 5:37. I aim to meet him. Can you come, too? After we land him we'll all go to the U Club and dine (on me). The 'companion' is due to turn up next morning; let us hope the Professor won't garrote him on the first day. T. J. Stritch." I laughed aloud at the image of those arthritic hands expending their last ounce of strength strangling an orderly for disrupting his routine.

Over the past two years, as the Professor's physical condition worsened and old friends had come to his aid, I saw more and more of Mr. Stritch. He was a short, pear-shaped man who walked with a waddle and had a lovely rumbling voice, a refined southern accent that almost sounded British. He spoke in arresting phrases punctuated with "damn" and "hell," reminding me of a professional actor or radio personality. He'd make an ideal emcee, I once told the Professor, only to be informed this was exactly the role he played on campus and off.

Mr. Stritch and I waited an hour for the plane before it touched down in the drizzle. Once the rest of the passengers were off, out came the Professor, pushed across the tarmac in a wheelchair with his cane on his lap. He was alert and in good spirits, yet we noticed he was disoriented in terms of time sequences and names. Physically, he seemed about the same, which is to say he still had difficulty getting around.

We went straight to the Club for dinner, then to Sorin. We

met his new helper right away but didn't know what to call him. Was he a companion? An orderly? A valet? A nurse? Ron was in his mid-twenties and worked as a hairdresser on campus. He was hired to help from seven to eleven in the morning and seven to eleven in the evening, and he seemed conscientious enough.

We left the two of them to get acquainted, at Mr. Stritch's suggestion. In private, Mr. Stritch expressed doubts about the new arrangement. "I don't believe it will work," he said, "but we must give it time." He told me the Professor's return owed everything to Father Hesburgh, who had issued the orders: "Do everything you can to make Paul happy. After all, he's been a one-man alumni association for over sixty years. Have all the bills sent directly to me." But according to Mr. Stritch, the university was dragging its heels. Paul Boehm was the one who had to hire Ron, and Mr. Stritch had to bring lunch from the Pay Caf every day and ask Ron to deliver dinners from Corby Hall.

I was glad to have Ron providing a safety net for me, since I didn't want to be at the Professor's beck and call when I was busy with other things. But I timed my visits with the Professor not to overlap with Ron's hours, figuring it would be awkward having him in the room with us. In those first conversations together, the Professor rehearsed what he had said on the phone two months before, saying he'd met with strong opposition from home about returning to South Bend but had decided the effort was worth it. "I came back primarily on account of you and your little clique," he said. "I think I'll graduate with you. As long as I'm here, I expect to get in a good deal of visiting with each of you, some quiet time alone."

It was gratifying to think our friendship weighed so heavily in his calculations. Was his immense collection of friends so depleted by death and illness that my "little clique" remained one of the few attractions left at Notre Dame? Whatever the case, he was orchestrating a dramatic departure for himself. If he was going to leave the university, he seemed determined to take us with him or at least leave in our company. For a man who had spent over seventy years living according to the rhythms of the academic calendar, it was appropriate that he should choose graduation to make his final farewell.

During his absence, one of his friends had deteriorated badly, and the Professor was angry Mr. Stritch had kept the news from him. Paul Boehm, who would normally have had airport duty the night before, was going blind. When Boehm finally visited the Professor again, he was led around the room by his wife, unable to see a foot in front of himself.

Although it was heartbreaking to see Boehm in this state, the Professor's return to Sorin was otherwise well-timed. The president of the hall, Bart, my suitemate from freshman year, had been looking for an excuse to have a social event. When I mentioned this was the seventy-fifth anniversary of the porch, it became our theme. I enlisted the help of several Sorinites to organize the "birthday" party. They set up a makeshift sound system and hung red, white, and blue bunting from the porch roof and in a corkscrew around the columns.

It was a cold, wet day, but we had a turnout of about sixty dressed in the school uniform of jeans and sweatshirts. I hosted the event from the porch, while the crowd huddled near the barbeque grills waiting to eat. The traditional story of the porch, I said, was that Colonel Hoynes was going out for a night on the town when students on the third floor doused him with water. To prevent this prank from being repeated, the porch was constructed. Many people, including the Professor, had cast doubt on this legend, I told the audience, but material in the archives suggested it was probably true. After my talk, some students sang a vintage song about the drenching episode, and one dressed up in a Civil War uniform and stood at attention while two others dumped water on him from a third-story window. The weather kept Mr. Stritch and the Professor away from the show, but the Professor peeked out of his window to watch.

As the weather improved that spring, the Professor made a habit of pacing on the porch for fresh air and exercise. "This porch has quite a history, as you well know," he reminded me. Shortly after the anniversary celebration, he and I spent a particularly memorable afternoon there. It was a crisp, sunny day such as northern Indiana experiences perhaps a half dozen times a year, a day of utter relaxation before final exams. Students were out in the front yard under the towering White Elms. Several were sunning themselves; a few were tossing Frisbees, running and shouting like children let out of school; others were on the steps talking. Bundled up in two sweaters, the Professor sat with me on a bench. He was remarkably happy and relaxed as he received visitors. The rector stopped by for several minutes. Later, the assistant rector, a man destined for high administrative office, Father Edward "Monk" Malloy, paid a call. As a wedding let out of Sacred Heart, several passersby also stopped to say hello. One fellow came up and said, "The last time I saw you, you were sitting on the same spot, forty years ago!"

Holding court on the porch while the boys frolicked on the lawn: was life on the Fenlon tennis courts ever so carefree as this? For a few hours, he forgot his infirmities, the difficulties of the last several months, his uncertain future. This is how I liked to remember him: the center of attention, telling stories and enjoying conversation, deferred to, at ease. They were moments to savor and extend. I clung to them, not sure how many more would be granted him.

$\left[31\right]$

O'Malley's Shadow (1952-74)

FROM 1952 ONWARD, we enter the Hesburgh years at Notre Dame, and by this time Frank O'Malley is a star in the English Department. The Professor is competing with this younger colleague for popularity with the students now, though he recalls other remarkable people in the modern period as well:

"I was a very good friend of John Towner Frederick. It was he who gave me this old desk chair of mine. He was the nicest man you'd ever want to meet, but at the same time the most homely looking—but you quickly forgot that. He wasn't 110 pounds dripping wet. He taught English at Northwestern, lived in Chicago, and took the South Shore railroad to Notre Dame two days a week to teach classes, during which time he lived over the arch at Lyons Hall.

"He was very religious, but not Catholic, of course. His first wife was an Amazon type of woman, very manly. She smoked incessantly and one day was crossing the street for cigarettes and was hit by a cab. She had no ID at all, so they took her to the Cook County Hospital, where they'd take anybody, and later she died. JT was home that night, very concerned she had not returned. He questioned anybody he could find and finally at the drugstore the druggist said the woman injured in the accident might be his wife. He discovered it was so, once he traced her to the Cook County Hospital.

"Leo R. Ward, Dick Sullivan, and I went up to Michigan for her funeral. It was right on that awful Lake Superior. This must have been 1970 or so. They had just made the changes at Vatican II. I remember that after the Our Father, I said, 'Amen,' but I was interrupted by 'For thine is the kingdom, the power ...' since I was so used to saying the prayer the other way. They never let me forget it. Later, Frederick married his brother-in-law's widow, who I believe is still living.

"The fiction that he wrote focused on the home state he loved so much—Iowa. He was a great teacher of American fiction, a scholar who believed in regionalism and started a magazine called *The Midland*. His protégé was Ruth Suckow, who shared the same regionalist qualities. His favorite author was William Dean Howells, and he considered *The Rise of Silas Lapham* by Howells the first American novel."

The Professor pulled three of Frederick's books from their shelf. As we paged through them, several reviews, letters, and clippings fell out, and one caught my attention, a slip of paper folded in three with a yellowed piece of tape running its length, addressed to the Professor. We opened it up and read: "Paul—Please check with Jim (the colored man) or Frank (Hawaiian student) working in the hall—to move you downstairs tomorrow, Tuesday. If you set the time + supervise it may help, but don't move anything yourself. Father McD C.S.C." The Professor explained this note had been taped to his door, room 355, by the rector, Thomas McDonagh, with instructions for the big move down to his present quarters in 141.

"In the summer of '62 I was living in Howard Hall, in a one-story affair in the northwest corner of the building. The next time you go by Howard, you go look at it. There I had those awful gallbladder pains at night, just as my mother and sisters suffered from them, but today the only foods that really bother me are chocolate, bacon, and corn on the cob.

"After my gallbladder operation, my doctor asked me how often I went up the stairs in Sorin. I said, 'I don't know.' He told me I must have a first-floor room, so I told Father McDonagh, 'I guess I'll have to find another room in another hall.' But Father McDonagh said he'd get me a room on the first floor. There were two boys in 141 he didn't especially care for, and he made a deal with them. In a trade for their one room, he gave them my two old rooms, 355 and 356. So one day, these two and a couple of their friends carried all my stuff down those stairs. That fireplace was a real problem.

"Later, I was forced out of this room, you know. For two summers—six weeks each—I had to live in Fisher Hall, because the nuns had moved into Sorin at that time. I wanted to stay here and I explained that down here I had my own bathroom and my own short exit out of the building, so I wouldn't see them and they wouldn't see me. But they didn't buy that, so I had to leave. The Sisters were so delightful, but they took over this hall and threw me out.

"Father McDonagh was one of the gentlest men I ever knew—the last rector of Sorin Hall who deserved the title. He was a companion of Father Hesburgh, and they spent four years in Europe together. McDonagh was one of their bright men. He had his degree from Rome, then they released him. I think he taught here three or four years, let's say, and then he went to Wisconsin and got his PhD in economics. He came back here to become chairman of the department and then they made him rector.

"McDonagh wasn't tough; he was a gentleman; he was agreeable. The boys respected him and they wouldn't play any smart tricks on McDonagh. Well, after they took him out of teaching, he was religious superior over here like Little Gerber is today. And he was an excellent superior, so they had it all settled: when they held their Provincial Council in Portland, Oregon about ten years ago now, McDonagh was slated to be provincial. And just like Bishop Heston, McDonagh, not simultaneously, but a couple of years apart, had to change planes in Denver. Heston was one of our CSCs who became a bishop over there in Rome— he was so valuable during the Vatican II thing, you know. This seems strange, but it's a fact: McDonagh had a heart attack in Denver because of the altitude and Heston had a heart attack, too. The only difference between Heston and McDonagh was that Heston died within several weeks.

"Heston's sister was a nurse and she flew out immediately. His brother is still living. I just talked to him not long ago. He and George were very close. But Father McDonagh was spared, and they couldn't possibly think of making him provincial after his heart attack. He's Hesburgh's age exactly.

"You know, Hesburgh said to me the night I got my little parchment from him, when I was out of here fifty years, which was what? Sixty-nine, wasn't it? I graduated in '19. When you're out fifty years and still living, they call your name and you go up and they give you a little piece of parchment, which tells you you did this and that. So when he gave it to me, he said, 'I don't know what I can say about a person who was here two years before I was born.' He laughed and so did I."

The Professor had a couple more memories of the very recent past to share. One involved a famous incident when Sister Jean Lenz confronted a hundred naked students invading Farley Hall at the height of the 'streaking' craze. "Yes, I had never known what streaking was, but a few years ago I happened to be out of my vestibule in the hallway, when six boys ran by without any clothes on. They were wearing sneakers; that was it. Their bare bottoms were showing and everything. Chip, my dear friend, asked me later if I had seen those boys and I told him I had. I asked what they could be doing and Chip said, 'streaking.' Then he said the boys were on their way to a girls' hall. When I heard that, I nearly died!"

Another vivid memory from this period involved the end of the Frank O'Malley era: "I saw they were going to close the cafeteria all day Easter, and so I had to go to the Morris Inn. It was one of the very few times I decided to have my breakfast before going to church. I was eating at the Inn when the waitress said, 'Mr. Fenlon, do you know Mr. O'Malley?' 'No,' I said. 'We do not have much in common.' 'He was in for breakfast earlier and did not seem very well at all.' And so I supposed she had smelled more than the usual couple of snorts on him.

"Then that afternoon I had heard that two boys picked him up outside of Lyons Hall. He had collapsed there and we thought he'd die right away, but he fooled us. He was told, 'Stay off the hard stuff, or you will die.' And he did for a little while. He decided to shape up, but then he started drinking again. And O'Malley held on for about six weeks until he finally died in May, either from cancer or booze. He drank himself to death. They had him lying in state in O'Shaughnessy Hall, then buried in the community cemetery near the big monuments in front.

"O'Malley bragged he had six martinis before dinner. He could have lived if he had just taken better care of himself. The seniors elected Senator Everett Dirksen class fellow one year, and we all met him at a dinner at the University Club. He and O'Malley had a drinking contest and O'Malley lost. Dirksen would fill up a water glass with some strong liquor and then drink it like water.

"Frank O'Malley was in this hall only very briefly during the war years, when he was forced to move out of Lyons because the Navy invaded us and the 'ninety-day wonder boys' were living in

Lyons, Howard, and Morrissey. He lived where the old law school used to be located, on the south end of our first floor. You take a right and go down that corridor, then count one, two, three doors down on the left. It's the room with double windows, a horrible room that looked out to Walsh Hall. O'Malley was most unhappy at Sorin. As I recall, he had to use the common can here, but over at Lyons, of course, he used to have his own bathroom.

"Joe Ryan lived in Lyons Hall over the main entrance on the second floor. He had to listen to the boys every night coming in. The loose door was noisy; it would *bang, bang, bang* all night long. And above him was Frank O'Malley dropping his books on the floor, *bang, bang, bang*. Poor Joe got it from above and below.

"Frank O'Malley did his MA work on Willa Cather, but like me he didn't go on for a PhD. He was greatly devoted to her, just as I was; she was my favorite author. I met her once, just by chance, when she was teaching at Bread Loaf. She was a largish, very mannish woman who never married. And she died in her chair in her apartment in New York, writing, from a heavy stroke. She taught and published first in the Pittsburgh public schools, but I'm afraid that her readership has declined. She's too tame for the present-day crowd—too much of a lady. This generation doesn't understand her subjects.

"Ed O'Connor was Frank O'Malley's student, a well-known graduate of ours, and he wrote *The Last Hurrah*. I didn't teach him, but I remember many years ago eating in the Pay Caf when he returned to Notre Dame. He was in his thirties or forties at the time. Every morning he'd eat and wait for Frank O'Malley to come in. He'd consult about his novel and go over the draft with Frank. Of course, O'Malley never got out of bed before noon. O'Connor died not long ago in Chicago. He lived in an apartment with little shops downstairs and walked down one day and just dropped dead.

"Many people here were caught up in a kind of O'Malley cult, but I think he's overrated. In fact, I don't agree with him on many things. I never was in the O'Malley crowd, never, never. I escaped all that, the mystical, mythological student following that O'Malley had. You know, his strange assignments made him into a hero of the freshmen. He always mumbled; nobody could understand him. Nobody knew him because he wanted nobody to know him. But I remember him as a student of mine—he had awful, wispy hair, like straw."

With these dismissive comments, the Professor's long series of reminiscences—stretching from childhood to retirement and highlighting my visits with him—came to an end. Fittingly, they concluded with the death of Frank O'Malley in 1974, for in most minds the names Fenlon and O'Malley were automatically linked as the old bachelor dons in English. Yet I had been slow to appreciate just how important O'Malley was to the Professor's world and at the same time how different he was from him. Only at the end of my four years was I in a position to step back for a moment to compare the two and see more clearly just who the Professor was—and was not.

Despite the Professor's denial to the waitress that Easter Sunday, he and O'Malley actually had a good bit in common, and not just a devotion to Willa Cather. They were both popular classroom performers known for their taste, exacting standards, and memory for names and hometowns. They both shared a strong Catholic faith and a long tenure in the English Department. Both counted Mr. Stritch as a friend.

However, the Professor was thirteen years older than O'Malley, and in many ways they did present a stark contrast. In one-on-one encounters outside the classroom, the Professor was at his most gregarious, while O'Malley was prone to awkward silences and blushing. The Professor had his two-Scotch rule and never lit up; O'Malley drank to excess and chain-smoked. The Professor taught courses like Short Story and Victorian Novel 'straight up'; O'Malley mixed theology and philosophy into his Modern Catholic Writers and his Philosophy of Literature. The Professor had an open-door policy in Sorin; O'Malley was a recluse in Lyons. The Professor said he was a legend whether he liked it or not; O'Malley said, "I'm not a legend; I'm a myth."

From everything I could gather, Frank O'Malley was a guru. Students approached him like an oracle and memorized whatever he said. They were told to "redeem the time." By contrast, the Professor sneered at mantras like this one. He was no guru. His followers were friends, not disciples. He wasn't an intellectual like O'Malley either. True, he was an intelligent, educated man, a remarkable teacher with a flair for the dramatic, but he was much more interested in people than ideas. After all, many of his stories were just high-level gossip, as he freely admitted: "I love gossip, you know. That's the way you get to know people, by the gossip, the ins and outs, especially the outs. All these little stories I pick up have been passed on by word of mouth and they are interesting to many people."

He loved people and entertained friends with his tittle-tattle, and yet in the end he preferred to live by himself. His solitary existence might have bred eccentricity—that occupational hazard of academic life—but he was actually rather conventional, especially in comparison with peers like O'Malley. Even his student tormentors never made fun of him for being strange. They mocked him precisely because of his propriety, his enforcement of the rules. That's one reason why O'Malley grated on him: "He never wore a hat no matter how cold it was and he never sat down when he visited my room." In the Professor's book, this was bad manners, pure and simple, and he criticized other faculty members on similar grounds, even friends: Fitzsimons for refusing to wear a hat or coat in the dead of winter ("he was imitating Chesterton, or at least we always thought so") and Ed Fischer for taking his daily constitutional at 5:30 in the morning ("he's an oddball to my way of thinking").

As for me, I had a high tolerance for social misdemeanors like these and valued idiosyncrasy. I was already something of a Fitzsimons groupie, scribbling down his God-like utterances, savoring his ceremonial bows and the spectacles dangling from the corner of his mouth. Fitzsimons was less eccentric than O'Malley, but I thought to myself that if I had arrived at Notre Dame a decade earlier, I might well have succumbed to his charms as well. In the event, I came to befriend a very different type of bachelor don, one I now understood to be living in the shadow of Frank O'Malley. It was O'Malley who received write-ups in *Time* and *Newsweek*, not the Professor. He was the one people were still talking about six years after his death and who always seemed to get better press than his old teacher.

By most accounts, O'Malley was a great man, but I would like to think that in his own way so too was the Professor. I sought him out for time travel, not wisdom, and yet by the example of his life he imparted deeper truths just as surely as if he spoke from behind O'Malley's desk. Wasn't he teaching the importance of faith, perseverance, and loyalty—the value of friendship, tradition, and storytelling? I hung on every word of his stories just as closely as O'Malley's students transcribed his lectures. If my own experience was any indication, perhaps, after all, student devotion to the Professor, then and now, *had* risen to the status of a cult, though a different kind from O'Malley's. Only one question remained: was I to be its last high priest?

[32]

Waning Days

NOT LONG AFTER that lovely day on the porch with the Professor, I was paging through a bulletin of faculty news, when I came across a proposal to improve pensions. "You see, of course, for many years, we didn't even have a pension," the Professor said. "That's why I think Father Hesburgh has been so good to us lately, and why he's been so good about letting me come back and taking care of it all. They feel a little guilty about neglecting the faculty for so many years. And now he's trying to make it up to us in cases such as mine."

With his tenure in Sorin Hall apparently coming to an end, the Professor was in a reflective mood, pondering the happenstance responsible for his longevity as a bachelor don. He came to see that his success was due to a combination of skill, patronage, and luck. As we have seen already, his eminence as a don led Pop Steiner to keep him on campus with three others when the rest of the dons were kicked out. Later, Father McDonagh made room for him on the first floor when he couldn't climb to the third anymore. Now Father Hesburgh was making a concerted effort to keep the Professor on board. Was it because of Hesburgh's own friendship with the Professor? His guilt over the way faculty had been treated? His concern for public relations? The simple goodness of his heart? Whatever the reasons, Father Hesburgh looks more and more like the hero of our story.

The Professor was fortunate to live at a time when universities were not overly troubled by legal liability, and top administrators could allow a frail old man to live in a dilapidated building lacking handicap accessibility. In addition, the Professor had good relationships with every one of these administrators: the executive vice president, Father Edmund Joyce, the general counsel, Phil Faccenda, and the vice president for business affairs, Father Jerry Wilson. In the end, of course, all that really mattered was Father Hesburgh's generosity, and the Professor had known him since his days in the seminary.

Another link in this chain of fortuitous circumstances, I had not realized until now, was George Shuster. After leaving the presidency of Hunter College, Shuster had come to Notre Dame to serve as Hesburgh's special assistant. "George was the one responsible for me staying on here," the Professor told me. "I retired in 1962 and was ready to go back to Pennsylvania, but George said, 'Hold it! You're going to stay here. There's work for you to do in the alumni office. Now I can't offer you much in the way of a salary, but I'll see to it that you get your quarters here for the rest of your life.' So maybe this is why I have been given my room back this year."

The Professor was now raising new possibilities. Was he only here because an informal contract stipulated it? Originally he had no real interest in staying on? He only did it as a favor to George? Otherwise, he would have returned to Blairsville without giving it a second thought? It was disheartening for me to think this might be the case.

In any event, word was spreading that the Professor was back on campus and this might be the last chance to see him. Several people took advantage of the opportunity. His dear colleague Richard Sullivan dropped by to visit. A former student phoned to check on him. Father Blantz called about interviewing him for the biography of George Shuster he was writing. Someone from the archives asked if he was ready to resume the interviews they had started.

The Professor welcomed the attention, and there was more to come. The rector, together with some students outside my immediate circle, decided to inaugurate an annual teaching award named after him. Between the Christmas sport coat, the mass petitions, the redecoration of 141, and now this, you couldn't say the rector wasn't doing what he could to make him feel special.

The awards dinner was held downtown on the top floor of the tallest building in South Bend, and we all dressed up. Sorin residents chose one honoree from each college: Arts and Letters, Science, Business, and Engineering. The winners received plaques, as did the guest of honor, who quipped that students in the audience ought to try living with him in Sorin for another sixty years. After the presentations, Father Malloy gave a talk. He said alumni returned to campus year after year not just to see the Golden Dome, Sacred Heart, or Sorin Hall, but to see the people, and they flocked to see the Professor. Father Malloy thought the Professor could show no "greater testimony of love than to live among his students" for so many years. The Professor was moved by these words, indeed by the entire occasion. He was proud of his plaque, too, and anxious to find a place for it in his room—no small achievement.

The next day, we read in the *Observer* about his big night ("Sorinites Honor Professors"), and I had a chance to walk him over to La Fortune where we sat by the fountain. He made a point of getting out for a walk every day now and he enjoyed taking in the bustle of campus in such good weather. He was tickled to see so many students wearing gym shorts, boys and girls alike: "It's just as old Bernie Lange used to say, 'They come to college and revert back to their infancy.'"

Final exams were about to begin, so I couldn't visit the Professor as often or as long as usual, but once they finished we entered into that glorious interlude between finals and commencement known as senior week, a period of late-night parties, daytime get-togethers, and off-campus trips. While my friends and I were busy squeezing one last week of fun out of our four years, the Professor began complaining he was bored and that Ron and Larry (the weekend orderly) were late. The truth was they were not even scheduled to appear. "Remember, Professor," I said. "Seven to eleven in the a.m. and seven to eleven in the p.m.: those are the hours. The rest of the time, you're on your own."

"Yes, Phil," he said, "but when there isn't much for me to do, it seems like all I am doing is waiting, waiting for people to come to move me or feed me. I can't do things on my own anymore." This wouldn't be so bad if there was just a week to kill, but the Professor had decided on a new timetable. He no longer planned to 'graduate' with us exactly, if by that he'd meant adding his car to the caravan of vehicles heading out of South Bend. No, now that he'd settled back on campus he wanted to stay longer, indefinitely in fact, as he had not yet set a departure date. This being so, he worried about boredom over the summer once "the group" was gone, with nothing to look forward to besides the interviews for the archives.

I suspected Mr. Stritch was behind the change of plan. When I ran into him on the third floor of O'Shaughnessy, he rehearsed all the reasons why the Professor ought to remain in South Bend, whatever he does, whether in Sorin Hall, a hotel, or a nursing home. He scoffed at "this nonsense about returning to the womb, to that house in Blairsville." Now it looked as if the Professor had come to his senses about where to live.

Mr. Stritch was about to go on a trip to England and Scotland, and this only heightened the Professor's fear of loneliness.

Already the Professor was looking seven months ahead to Christmas, and he was still haunted by the memory of that day in 1942, "the loneliest day of my entire life." It wasn't the first time he'd brought up the episode, but now he reminded me it was during the war and Notre Dame had classes through December 24th. Returning to his room in the afternoon, he spent the following day there without another soul in the building.

That experience obviously scarred him, but I had to wonder why it was so debilitating, so fresh, almost forty years later. Was he recalling an earlier, more foundational trauma, not a single day but months of loneliness he vowed never to revisit? In other words, was he thinking of his six-year-old self alone in bed with his leg suspended in the air, listening to the children play outside? Was he thinking of the three years that followed, when he couldn't go to school like everyone else? To ensure there would be no repetition, especially after the bad year at the bank and his father's premature death, hadn't he created so many friends he'd never be lonely again? Didn't he make his tower a shrine to them and his absent family? The Christmas of '42 was a recurring nightmare that called to mind just how fragile the life he had constructed for himself actually was. Whatever plans he made for his final years, that kind of loneliness had to be avoided no matter what, he made clear.

While he was marking the days to Christmas like a boy expecting coal in his stocking, I counted the days to graduation. With eight to go, he and Doris Shuster got into a car accident. When I heard the news, I went straight to his room and found him carrying on as if nothing had happened. He and Doris had eaten at Bishop's Cafeteria, he told me. She was driving his car home in the rain, when she ran a red light. She got a swollen lip when her head hit the steering wheel, but he suffered nothing more than a scrape on the forehead. Neither one was wearing a seatbelt.

The police investigated the crash and had them checked out at the hospital, but the Professor insisted on returning to Sorin rather than spending the night there. Speaking to me now, he became increasingly agitated as the realization set in that he could have been killed. He was more distraught in telling the story than in the immediate aftermath of the accident, when, he told me proudly, "I was calm."

The day after the accident we went for a walk. Lately, excursions like this one had been nerve-racking for both of us, because he had no faith in my ability to prevent him from falling. Whenever he lost his balance or grip on a handrail—even near his bed, where he had a soft landing—he'd cry out, "Phil, I'm scared." "I'm right here, Professor," I'd say. "I can catch you. You're so light I could even carry you back to Sorin if I had to." He'd smile, but the fear remained.

We reached the far end of Walsh Hall, before turning back. Then he started slumping to the left and dragging his foot. I quickly put my arm around him and the two of us somehow made it back to Sorin. Had he just suffered another stroke? Sitting on his bed, he put himself through the tests the neurologist had taught him. First, he asked me to grab his hand as he squeezed mine, then he began opening and closing his mouth. Next, he blinked one eye, then the other, alternating back and forth. He did very well, I thought, though I demonstrated even greater self-mastery by not bursting into laughter.

Presently, Larry arrived. He said the muscle weakness was due to a back strain from the car accident that made it difficult to stand straight. I wasn't persuaded by the diagnosis, but the Professor was, and soon he was steady on his feet again.

Just as alarming to him as this health scare was a newly arrived letter from Betty. Initially, it appeared Tom had lost his job, but when we reread the letter together we found this was not the case. "You know, if that happens, Phil," the Professor said, "then I *have* to go back to Blairsville, because they will have to depend upon my money."

While all this was going on, Ron failed to show up one day. Though it was the first time either attendant had been absent or even tardy, the Professor was shaking he was so angry with them. However, he knew how to get his revenge. He went on strike. "If Ron won't show up," he said, "then I won't take my medicine. Only Ron can give me my medicine."

"You *have* to take your medicine," I told him, arguing long and hard before he finally gave in.

"Well, if this medicine kills me, it will be your fault," he said. "They say your medicine is a very important part of your recovery. I'll take it this time, but you must check on me in the morning to see that I'm alive!" I was familiar with his histrionics and love of routine, but now he was trying my patience.

The *South Bend Tribune*'s story about the car crash, buried on page twenty-nine and mercifully brief, concludes this sequence of events. Once I learned no one had been seriously injured, I was amused by the whole incident, just as Father Blantz was. He said that Doris refused to give her age to the investigating officer, and the Professor tried to distract him from that sensitive subject by taking him to the other side of the car to point out non-existent dents and scratches. We tried to picture the two of them in their prim attire sneaking out like underage drivers for a joy ride at twenty miles per hour, chatting merrily, oblivious to their surroundings ("Doris, aren't we on the wrong side of the road?" … "Paul, what else did Gina say to you?"). Readers of the *Tribune* could be forgiven for thinking Paul and Doris had been in some kind of illicit rendezvous that was only discovered when the accident put them on the police blotter and in the papers.

But the Professor may have had the last laugh. "Of course,

Doris Shuster lied about her age in the *Tribune* for the story on our accident," he told me. "I remember I found out her age when I was in my room watching television with George. A news flash appeared that Father Philip Moore had just died, and without thinking, George said, 'Why, he was the same age as Doris.' Then he realized his mistake, covered his mouth, and told me not to breathe a word of it. But the story she is fond of telling concerns their marriage. George's parents were oldish, you know. Anyway, Doris remembers the father of the groom's first remark to George upon seeing Doris: 'Why, George, a child bride!' And she has repeated that story from that day to this. She liked to think of herself as a child bride, which, of course, she was not."

[33]

Three Watches

AMIDST THE HIGH SPIRITS of senior week and the Professor's wild ride, as graduation approached, I harbored an uneasy feeling, not just these past few days but the entire semester. Anticipating my departure from Notre Dame, I wasn't sad about leaving a place that meant so much to me. Nor was I anxious about what my future held. Rather, I knew that somehow I was going to have to say goodbye to the Professor and admit to myself that our paths were headed in opposite directions.

Unlike his future, mine was very clear, at least in the immediate term. For the next two years, I was going to be in graduate school with an eye to becoming a professional historian. I managed to get accepted to the University of Cambridge, located just a few miles from my birthplace. My goal was to be *a* professor but not *the* Professor. My model, if I had one at this time, was Fitzsimons, a scholar of British history and a family man. I wasn't crazy enough to imagine myself as a bachelor don, a role, besides, that was going extinct.

Some of the dons were easily mistaken for priests, and I wondered—but never asked—why the Professor had never become a priest. He'd already adopted a spartan bachelor existence, which looked an awful lot like taking vows of poverty and chastity. The only thing missing was a promise of obedience to a religious superior. By refusing to do that, he'd preserved his all-important independence but sacrificed the rich communal life he might have shared with the Holy Cross Fathers. As they grew old, he pointed out, the priests had a community to look after them. Given half a chance, he said, he'd love to join them in Holy Cross House. Instead, he was forced to shuttle back and forth to Pennsylvania or call in special favors from friends. Those friends helped compensate for losing this potential second family when his own family was so small—just a niece, her husband, and their son.

The Professor always made little asides about how good the priests had it, without idealizing them entirely. He clashed with several priests over the years and knew well the infighting that went on. Yet I always thought his stories about them, taken as a whole, amounted to an affectionate tribute to the order, and his respect for the institution verged on awe. A name came up once and the Professor told me, "He was unfortunate. The less said about him the better." Then he lowered his voice to a whisper, bowing his head: "He left the order." Leaving the priesthood was an almost unspeakable scandal to him, filled with shame and more terrible than divorce.

Again and again, as I thought about the Professor's unique position, I returned to the image of him fifty years ago high in his tower watching Father Eugene Burke's story hour with its hearty laughter echoing across campus on summer mornings. How well this scene symbolized the mixture of jealousy and detachment that characterized his relationship with the Holy Cross Fathers. The Professor painted an idyllic picture, yet one tinged with envy, for he looked out of his tower at a camaraderie he could not share. He was most vulnerable to loneliness at that time of year, when most of the students and some of the faculty regulars were away. He knew each of those priests, counted several among his good friends, and shared his own moments of merriment with them. Yet he wouldn't dream of coming down from the turret and walking fifty yards to join them on the Corby porch. He lived among them, to be sure, but he was not one of them. Although many priests had been on the faculty and labored side by side him doing much the same work, he would always inhabit the border-lands, not quite a priest and not quite a layman either.

I realized that once I said goodbye to this extraordinary man, I would not be seeing him for over a year. Traveling back and forth across the Atlantic was expensive, so I would be staying in England until next June. I had to ask: would the Professor still be alive then? I put my hopes in the rudimentary support system that would remain in place after I left, especially in Big Boy, who was staying on for his master's degree. The Professor was nothing if not a survivor, I reminded myself, so he might surprise us all by hanging on for many years to come. Even so, I felt like I was abandoning him, like his survival depended on me being there. *I had never signed on to be your caretaker*, I told him in my imaginary dialogue. *It's not as if you were a parent and I had a duty to nurse you to health. I have a life to live—you can understand that, can't you?*

After our friendship had thrived for three and a half years, here at last we came to the issue that divided us: soon, one way or another, we would have to go our separate ways, because I had a future and he didn't, or at least at the rate he was declining he didn't. He told everyone he was about to die, but I thought I was going to live forever. And while his whole life was Notre Dame—as his decision not to book a return flight confirmed—Notre Dame was only one part of mine, and I was ready to leave it behind. In contrast to the Professor's once boundless circle of friends, mine was narrow, perhaps too narrow, chafing under the daily routine in Sorin, so I was ready to break out and make new friends elsewhere. In this business of friend making, he remained the master and I the novice.

Our own friendship began because his watches needed winding. If I had paid more attention to them, I might have understood elements of his personality that were only now coming into focus in the dwindling days of our time together. Recall that he had two watches: the gold pocket watch from his father and the Swiss wristwatch from Father Dan. I used to ask myself why he had two watches. Now I thought I had an answer: he needed them, at least symbolically, to balance out his loyalties, his attachment to family and to friends, to Blairsville (the pocket watch) and to Notre Dame (the wristwatch). Of the two timepieces, the pocket watch was richest in meaning. So much of the young Paul was reflected in that shiny graduation gift: his family's affluence, his academic prowess, his bond with his father, his fitful anxiety traced along the gnawed markings of its cover.

He kept an obsessive eye on his watches, lest they run down. He knew he didn't have much time left, but he acted as if winding his watches gave him more time. In a sense they did. We who wound his watches provided the companionship and help with chores he needed to survive.

While he clung to those watches like life vests, he teased me about mine because it was still set on Greenwich Mean Time. This was more than tsk-tsking a schoolboy foible. Behind it I detected resentment that my attention was focused on a wider world, that my ultimate allegiance lay elsewhere. My watch reminded him that after graduation I wasn't sticking around, and it reminded me of my promise to return to England. It was set five hours ahead—already I was living in the future.

Although we were about to set off on different trajectories, I tried to help him stay true to his own course in Sorin, right up to my last hours on campus. The day before graduation, my parents and I attended a reception hosted by the university's top brass. The president, the provost, and a few vice presidents formed a receiving line. Once we ascended a stairway to the awaiting dignitaries, I made the most of my few moments with the great man to lobby for the Professor: "Thank you, Father Hesburgh, for all you've done to keep Professor Fenlon in Sorin Hall."

"Well, it's the least we could do after all he's done for us," he replied.

The day after graduation, it was time to say goodbye to the Professor. Given his declining health and my time abroad, we both knew, I think, we would likely never see each other again. Neither of us wanted to acknowledge this and so we tried to act as if this was just another semester coming to an end.

I knocked on the inner door at about nine o'clock, a time of day I rarely saw him. He was cleaning his teeth, putting back his dentures, checking his smile in the mirror. The atmosphere was tense with emotion, but he remained composed. We simply embraced, exchanged a few good wishes, and I left. My excuse for not lingering was that my brother and mother were waiting in the corridor for the eleven hundred-mile trip ahead of us. His excuse was that I'd caught him in the middle of his morning routine. But was it really that? Or had he timed our farewell this way to make parting less drawn out?

We both knew what needed to be said but couldn't quite bring ourselves to articulate it—my thanks for his friendship and the hours he'd shared with me, my prayers for his health, his gratitude for my support these past few years, and so on. But knowing what needed to be said, we knew it didn't have to be said. Besides, if we didn't admit this was *goodbye*, we could hold out hope it was *so long*.

Making my way out the vestibule, I wondered whether he'd remember our custom one last time. I counted *one, two, three. Wait*, I told myself. *Here it comes*. Then, sure enough, he called out after me, "Scratch your pen a little!" These were his last words. Scratch my pen? At first, I took this to mean *study hard at Cambridge*, but in the car, on the first leg of our journey towards Indianapolis, as the miles passed by with growing monotony, I decided he was saying *write me, keep in touch*. Much later, I found yet another meaning. Was it too far-fetched to suppose he was encouraging me to write up his stories, as we had discussed so often?

As it happened, I was to scratch my pen in each of the three ways he might have intended to be understood. Most immediately, I wrote him a letter soon after getting home and I received a quick reply. "If only you could see Sorin Hall at the moment," it began. "You would even forget you lived here and *liked it*." Right after graduation a team of workmen had invaded the building for a remodeling project that left his own room in disarray. At reunion, "I had many callers only to be ashamed of my present quarters."

The Professor's typewriter was still broken, so he was dictating his letters to an unnamed scribe. "I'm writing this to you from the Porch where I am sitting for warmth as all records of temperatures have been broken," I read in an unfamiliar hand. "You are the only one of the group I have heard from. Those last few days (of the group) have been hectic. And I hope when you are going to England in October you might stop off this way.... Give my best to all the family. Let me hear from you again and I just might reply.... Sincerely The Old Prof.," under which he put *Paul*.

We spoke on the phone a few times that summer, but his next letter said not to try reaching him in Sorin because he'd moved to the infirmary due to the extremes of temperature. "Last p.m.," he wrote, he "met Father B. in front of big church and had a chat mostly about you and your future plans," but otherwise he hadn't "seen any of our friends in the library" or "heard from any of the boys in the group.... Wish you could enjoy these somewhat dull days." The big news was St. Edward's Hall "burnt almost to the ground." It was in all the papers and even Betty saw it. "Rumors are flying about how many things have been discovered since the fire. For example, a package of old letters that had been placed in the cornerstone. You would have a heyday if you were here." Before closing, he added: "If you want to be one of the historians come and look."

Setting down the letter, I looked at my watch in frustration. Did he really think that I was going to get on a plane, return to campus, pick over the charred bricks of St. Ed's, then discuss it with him like old times? Or that I would drop by to see him on my way to England just as easily as I used to bound down the stairs to his room? The Professor didn't realize there wasn't a chance of this happening. Going back to visit him now, just two months after saying goodbye, was the furthest thing from my mind. He didn't realize how difficult it had been for me in those last moments in 141 to break away and begin mourning his death. I felt sorry he'd misread me so badly. I wasn't coming back—at least not anytime soon.

He still knew me well enough to appeal to my vanity, my self-image as the campus historian. Yet that was a role I was putting in mothballs, and I didn't have the time, interest, or money to book a flight to Indiana. He'd have to be content with being a pen pal for now. I was too busy with my summer job and preparing for my trip. He was still digging around in the past while I was fixed on the future.

[34]

This Good Man

IN CAMBRIDGE the academic year begins in early October, and on a frosty night my cab pulled up to the Porter's Lodge. The college was quiet, as I had arrived a day or two early to get settled. The porter gave me a key and we piled my things onto an ancient wooden wagon. I pulled it across Grange Road to the rambling three-story house that was to be my home for the next two years. My room was on the second floor in the back overlooking the garden, and I received a warm welcome from the nine other graduate students in residence here. It didn't take long to adjust to my new surroundings—at least I didn't have to remember to set my watch on English time.

Those first days were filled with exotic experiences: being summoned by a gong for a talk by the head of the college, a distinguished historian whom we addressed as "Master" and who asked about Father Hesburgh; feasting at the matriculation dinner in formal gowns amidst the glories of our paneled hall; making my way through stalls in the market square to another college for my first supervision; attending lectures in the architectural showpiece of the pyramidal glass History Faculty; queuing in front of a van for fish and chips wrapped in newspaper and sold by a man with a thick Italian accent.

Cambridge was living up to my high expectations, as I reported in a series of postcards and letters to friends back home.

271

I couldn't place overseas calls directly from my house, and the alternative, an international collect call, was prohibitively expensive, but my parents did make a few calls to me, which I answered on our one phone under the stairway. After a few weeks in Cambridge, I began receiving replies to my letters, but I had not heard back from the Professor yet. *Patience*, I said to myself: it takes at least five days to get there, then my letter will sit in the Sorin mail room until someone picks it up for him, then he will have to find someone to take dictation and he can't do the whole thing in one sitting, and then it will take five days for the return journey, and—

Then the phone rang. It was late one evening and I was struggling with my weekly essay, this one on eighteenth-century Russia. "Phil, it's for you!" a housemate yelled up the stairs. *How odd*, I thought. *This isn't one of our scheduled phone calls.* It was my father's voice on the line. "I have news about the Professor," he said. "The worst has happened." *I know what's coming. How can this be? Now I know why I haven't heard back.* I listened as he relayed what few details he had. He mentioned Big Boy had phoned him trying to get in touch with me, but otherwise my father and I didn't have much to say. We exchanged some words about what a fine person the Professor was and how lucky I had been to befriend him. After hanging up the phone, I returned to my room, fighting back tears. Why not admit it?—I had a good cry.

Dear Lord, I prayed, *thank you for the life of this good man. Grant him eternal rest. Bless his family and bless Notre Dame. Hail Mary, full of grace ....* These words came easily to me, but I was at a loss to explain how the phone call left me feeling. I was shocked because I hadn't even heard the Professor was ill, and part of me really didn't believe he would ever die. This was only the second time I had ever grieved like this, so it felt like my grandfather had died all over again. I had a heart-sinking sadness as if a part of me were cut away.

After picturing the poor Professor facing and then succumbing to death, I thought about Notre Dame. With the Professor gone, the school was now separated from part of its history, perhaps forever. What secrets, what stories, had gone to the grave with him, I could only imagine. Yes, he had given some interviews, and yes there were people on campus with long memories of his life and times, but in my four years, I reasoned, I must have amassed the greatest anthology of his short stories. Now I bore an even greater responsibility to preserve everything he had said to me. In doing so, I told myself, I would be honoring his memory—his memories—and he would live on. Notre Dame would be made whole again with this rupture of oral tradition mended.

Once I finished this mixture of prayer and reflection, I came back down to earth. The first thing I did was go to my trunk and pull out my journal for one last entry, two brief paragraphs recounting the phone call ten minutes earlier. I began, *Cambridge 10-11 p.m. phone call ...* and finished with the words, *the last I ever spoke with the Professor was on the phone a day or two before his 84th birthday, when he spoke of the excitement of St. Edward's Hall burning.* After closing the journal, I found some scratch paper and began jotting down ideas for an obituary I had long contemplated writing. Catherine the Great would have to wait until morning.

The week before, I later learned, the Professor had deteriorated sharply. Earlier that fall, he had suffered a series of strokes, and in September he'd been moved from Sorin to Healthwin Hospital. There the rector visited him to administer the last rites, and Doris Shuster used to give him spoonfuls of homemade jelly. On Friday afternoon, as his condition worsened, he had visits from Miss Murphy and Mrs. Stoddard, names barely recognizable to me. Mr. Stritch couldn't come because he had a role in the dedication of the Snite Museum of Art. Sister Jean Lenz visited, then immediately warned Big Boy he had better hurry, so he skipped class to get to the hospital. Over the dinner hour, the Professor's only company was Big Boy. Conscious but robbed of speech, the Professor was listening to him read poetry when he died.

I was grateful this man who so feared loneliness had a friend with him at the hour of his death. I looked upon Big Boy as a surrogate for all the friends, like myself, who wanted to be at that bedside but couldn't be.

On Sunday—the day of the phone call—there had been a wake in Sorin Chapel. Mr. Stritch spoke, and the Professor lay in state there until the funeral the next day. By all accounts, the crowded funeral in Sacred Heart was a fitting celebration of his life. "Paul would have fussed, but I am sure he was pleased," Father Blantz wrote me. Father Joyce said the Mass and delivered the eulogy, paying tribute to the Professor's "gift for friendship" and recalling his own experience taking Short Story with him. After communion, the body was incensed, a final prayer offered, and "Notre Dame, Our Mother" sung. The Professor's coffin was walked to the community cemetery, "just right, I think, in spite of his own wish to be buried next his mother," Mr. Stritch wrote me. "But think of all the alumni Hail Marys he will get here." The Caseys had nixed Blairsville to accept the honor extended by the Holy Cross Fathers.

After I finished writing my remembrance of the Professor, Dennis Moran arranged to have it published in *Scholastic*. I drew on my journal for quotations and themes, and concluded by asking whether in pursuing its high ambitions the school still had a place—I mean, besides the cemetery—for extraordinary campus figures like my deceased friend. I sent a letter of condolence to the Professor's niece, enclosing a copy of my tribute.

"Thank you so very much for remembering us—and him," she wrote back. "So many of the letters and telegrams went to the University and Father Hesburgh, naturally .... I found that your obituary seemed to penetrate to the real Professor whom you knew better than I expected." She remembered as a small child thinking of herself as some kind of heroine because she had a famous uncle. "I have missed him in so many ways this summer—and at Christmas. He was always a part of my life since my first remembrance of anyone, being my mother's older brother." She had the rector save the Professor's Charlie Phillips cane for me and offered to give me any of his letters that weren't already deposited in the University Archives. "What else would you like?" She hoped her husband and son could meet me sometime and asked that we stay in touch. "I do hope you consider writing about Uncle Paul," she said in closing. "There would be much of human interest to write about .... Bestus always, Betty Casey."

By a curious irony, the Professor had died three days after the US presidential election. In the wider world beyond Sorin Hall, two presidential elections formed the bookends of our four-year friendship. Politics wasn't a subject he seemed very interested in (another contrast with O'Malley), and I didn't know if he had a favorite in the political contest being waged as his life slipped away. Yet this election result was one of a number in recent years—those in Britain and Vatican City, in particular—that signaled a shift away from some of the permissive values celebrated during my time at Notre Dame. A sea change like that does not happen on a single day or coincide precisely with the birth of a new decade, but if the Professor had been able to appreciate these larger concerns outside his hospital room, he might have taken satisfaction in believing he had survived, albeit by just three days, some of the madness of the last decade and a half. He had withstood the last wave of barbarians: the 1960s were finally over. "At least more of the boys are getting their hair cut now," I could imagine him saying.

[35]

Getting It Over With

THE JOURNAL of my Notre Dame years was a treasure to me, and the summer between Notre Dame and Cambridge, I purchased a steamer trunk to protect it for all the journeys to come. On its maiden voyage, the trunk was flown to London, then transferred to the baggage car of the train from Liverpool Street to Cambridge. A couple years later, on Labor Day weekend in Baltimore, it rode in a station wagon up Charles Street to Johns Hopkins, where I was beginning a PhD. Two years later, it went to London for a year of dissertation research. As I unloaded it at Mecklenburgh Square, near my headquarters in the Reading Room of the British Museum, a handle broke on one overstuffed suitcase but not the trunk. After three more years in Baltimore, it accompanied me to South Bend, where I was starting a job, of all places, right across from Notre Dame at St. Mary's College. Within a short time, I was married, and my wife and I bought a house not far from campus. It was here, at last, that the trunk and journal—and I—came to rest.

I had preserved the journal intact but I hadn't done anything with it. Just as I once chose to study in the library rather than visit the Professor at a reasonable hour, so now I concentrated on my work and neglected to spend time with the journal. I told Betty Casey I didn't think I could write a book about her uncle after all. She said she understood, but whenever I saw the trunk it reminded me of my failure to follow through. My solution, ostrich-like, was simply to keep the trunk out of sight.

Not that I'd ever forgotten the Professor. Every year since he died I've commemorated the date of his death in my pocket diary, the only such date in it. For many years, I had a color photograph of him with Chet Grant on my desk; now the only daily reminder I have is the novelty item he gave me—a giant clothespin labeled *Big Deals* that was once paired with a smaller desk organizer, *Little Deals*.

In thirty years, I'd never spent more than two or three minutes looking at the journal. Then one autumn, while on sabbatical, I decided to do my share of cleaning out the basement. I wound my way through piles of toys, clothing, and furniture accumulated by our four children. I lifted two banker boxes off my steamer trunk and began sifting through a series of souvenirs dating from childhood. When I got to the journal, I smiled, but as I held it, it didn't feel like it belonged to me anymore: it belonged to Notre Dame. I needed to return it to its rightful owner. Before handing it over, however, I decided to take one last look. I sat down on one of the bottom stairs in the middle of the vast concrete room and opened it up. As I flipped through the pages, his voice came back to me:

Excuse me, boys; say, could one of you help me with my watches? They need winding and I can't do it myself. I've got terrible arthritis, you know...

Because of my leg, I never went to school until I was nine. I could never kick a football or use my leg for much in sports, but my father built the famous Fenlon tennis court for me in our backyard. People used to come from everywhere to play on that court. My mother had fits the way it used to dig up the lawn, but I know that I survived and healed so well due to her prayers...

I say a prayer every night to Father Irving that he'll let me be his altar boy in heaven...

The university chauffeur was a little Irishman named Johnny Mangan. He lived on the top floor of "Cadillac Hall." Johnny with his brogue always called the students "kids"—so improper. They're "college men" or "boys..."

I used to look out at the Corby porch and there would be Father Eugene Burke. After the community breakfast, he would be there with his little coterie telling wonderful stories, one after the other, laughing and laughing, with his arms shooting up in the air, shouting. The priests were so happy; there was such harmony among them then...

Phil, when did we first meet each other? What vacation period was it?...

I remember this photograph. I had been teaching just a few weeks here, when I was told to go down and see the rector. It was Father Lavin who gave me the phone. And it was our family doctor on the line...

Remember the way you used to come in and we would have such nice chats, Phil? It's good for me to be around all the life, the running and yelling of the boys. I have always mixed better with the younger crowd than with my own...

How lucky I am to have run into Hesburgh like that. "Good to see you walking around campus like this," he said. So he knows I'm trying to get well...

I came back primarily on account of you and your little clique. I think I'll graduate with you. As long as I'm here, I expect to get in a good deal of visiting with each of you, some quiet time alone...

I retired in 1962 and was ready to go back to Pennsylvania, but George said, "Hold it! You're going to stay here. There's work for you to do in the alumni office. I can't offer you much in the way of a salary, but I'll see to it that you get your quarters here for the rest of your life."

I had forgotten much of this, but as it began coming back to me I was enchanted by it. When I originally made my journal entries, I never had time to reread what I'd written, but now I took the opportunity to read the journal from start to finish for the first time, and I had an epiphany: in my adolescent zeal to preserve the Professor's stories I had overlooked the most obvious story of all—the story of our own friendship. That story only emerged once I pieced together the little scenes scattered between his anecdotes. I'd begun the journal in order to collect those anecdotes, but now they seemed of secondary importance.

Indeed, the passage of time gave me new insights into the Professor's life. In the last letter I received from Betty Casey, she wrote, "Paul's two sisters, Sarah (my mother) and Mercedes (my aunt with whom I lived as my mother died while I was a child) were both St. Mary's 'girls' (class of 1923 and before in the dark ages). After my graduation in 1951 and for the following 15 years I was a Sister of Holy Cross, leaving during a large exodus in the '60s." Her son was married and working on a film career in Pittsburgh now. "I guess you never really met him but you must have seen the pictures of a red haired toddler in the Professor's room. Paul was crazy about him."

Betty and Tom Casey have since passed away, as have most of the Professor's old friends. Yet I did run into another character in our little drama, after not seeing him for over three decades, as I walked across campus with my parents one day. "Phil, I've been thinking of you," Father Green said. "I heard you were in the area." He turned to my parents. "Phil saved Sorin Hall." We smiled in surprise. "Yes, he did. Before Phil came the students teased the Professor and played pranks on him. But when Phil came and showed him the proper reverence, I think the other students saw that and learned to offer him the proper respect. So your example made a real difference. You saved Sorin Hall."

My first reaction was that he had to be kidding. I couldn't see how anything I ever did had the slightest impact on the character of the hall. Nor did I accept the premise that Sorin had been turned around. At least, I never remember thinking the hall had changed much during my four years. But later, as I thought some more, it occurred to me that we never did have another Sorin Seven, did we? And when I went back to my journal, I found the Professor's last recorded use of the tern *bastard* was in my sophomore year. If this one telltale word was anything to go by, either the worst of the troublemakers had graduated by then, or the rector was instilling more effective discipline, or the Professor was simply too worn out to vilify them anymore. Maybe Father Green was onto something, after all.

For me, the most revealing thing my old rector had to say was that the Professor really had been having a hard time of it. I finally had an answer to the question of whether he had been paranoid about students being out to get him. Now I understood he wasn't imagining things. Just as he told me so often, I was naïve for thinking students wouldn't hound an old man that way. Looking back, I now realized the arrival of my little group must have been a welcome relief to him.

Father Green's comments certainly shook my perspective on the events recounted in my journal, but so, too, have the physical changes to campus proven disorienting. Though the ancient core of campus has been preserved, Notre Dame has erected numerous buildings and pulled down others in the past forty years. A lavish refurbishment of Sacred Heart and the Main Building has returned them to their Victorian splendor, and the Stations of the Cross have been retrieved from their hiding places and returned to their original positions in a structure now elevated to the dignity of a basilica.

Today Sorin Hall is better known as Sorin College. In my day,

the wooden sign atop the porch commemorating the hall's seces-
sion from the university in an anti-war protest was a mere novelty, but today's residents have taken it to heart. Whatever you
call it, the building has been significantly altered. With the two
elms gone, the bricks shorn of their ivy and smartly tuck-pointed,
Sorin looks like it did in old black-and-white photographs from
the 1920s. In addition, the courtyard entrance has been bricked
up and replaced by doors on the end of each wing. Inside, Father
Sorin's statue has been returned to its rightful place and students
now touch his foot for good luck. To replace the fire escapes
with new emergency exits, several rooms had to be destroyed,
including two of the Professor's old ones, 302 and 356 (ironic,
given his fear of fire). To create lounge and study space, other
rooms were knocked out as well, resulting in new numbering
throughout the building.

Room 141 is just where it has always been. Father Malloy
has lived there ever since the Professor died, including during
his eighteen years as president of the University of Notre Dame
(succeeding Father Hesburgh) and now as president emeritus.
According to his memoirs, Father Malloy sees himself living in
the Professor's role "as a grandfather figure and source of continuity." In that role, he gave me a tour of his rooms.

When you open the outer door, you now see straight through
to the biffy window. That old bathroom was removed, resulting
in an enlarged 'sheet' room, which today is no longer semi-public
but private. On your right is the door to a modern bathroom,
constructed by bumping out space from the rector's room next
door. Father Malloy's inner room is a stark contrast to the faded
apartment I knew so well. Red drapery covers the windows, and
the entire room is encircled by bookshelves fitted to the curve of
the wall and stretching a dozen feet high. The ceiling has been
lowered by two feet for lighting and fire fixtures.

Next door, in the chapel, striking changes are just as evident. The old altar has been replaced and there are modernistic Stations of the Cross on panels opposite the stained glass windows. The Professor and I needn't have worried about the windows. Robert Leader's swirling fragments of brown, copper, indigo, and gray now enliven the entire space. In the back of the room, where our Station used to be, there is a plaque honoring the Professor, "Sorin Hall's most beloved resident," whose friends and former students funded the chapel renovation in his memory.

If you look, you can find other places the Professor has left his mark, including some online campus histories that mention him. The University Archives lists various collections of material connected with him, too. Scrolling through them one day, I came across the index to his letters. The names of his correspondents had by now taken on a mythic quality in my mind; they saturated the pages of my journal. Heading the list was Earl "Stretch" O'Connor. Next were Clarence Manion and Paul R. Byrne. I continued reading: Kerndt Healy, F. X. Disney—then my eyes widened in surprise. My name was there. *What was I doing here?* I asked myself. *I don't belong with these names.* I scanned the rest of the column: T. E. Burke, George N. Shuster, John H. Neeson, T. Bowyer Campbell, Paul W. Romweber.

There were half a dozen names I didn't recognize, but by including my name the archives catalog was suggesting I was on equal footing with the Professor's closest friends. Was that a misleading impression, a fluke of some sort? After thinking about it, I finally decided, no, he must have meant to keep my letters. They were dated two summers before his death, so it wasn't a case of just a recent letter or two lying about the room amidst the general confusion of the last months of his life. He must have made a point of preserving them.

In retrospect, perhaps my name *did* belong in that roll call of friendship. Only after reading my journal cover to cover and finding these letters did I come to understand I had meant so much to him. As a young man, I knew my visits were unusual and I'd invested a great deal of time in them, but they seemed like ordinary parts of my day. Only now did those experiences, covered with the patina of history, assume an importance I didn't comprehend at the time. As a freshman, I was content to be a fly on the wall, passively recording what the Professor had to say, but as he wove his tales, I'd been drawn into his web of friendship. Little did I realize that while I was collecting stories he was collecting friends. Is it too immodest to believe I must have been one of the last and best he ever made?

***

St. Mary's Road originates in front of the Grotto, near the banks of St. Mary's Lake, and stretches towards St. Mary's College, just as Father Sorin laid it out for stagecoach. Bowed for drainage and lacking curbs, stripes, or footpaths, the asphalt is just wide enough for two cars to pass. With a field and the lake on one side of me and the lawn of Columba Hall on the other, I begin walking on it. The elevation rises slowly and soon trees on either side of me form a canopy overhead. Left and right I see dense vegetation and can smell the pungent soil of the woods. I hear something rustling in the undergrowth, possibly a groundhog or squirrel, though I have seen rabbits and even a fox or deer on other walks. For several steps, I feel alone in the wilderness, though I am just a few hundred yards from Sorin. In the winter, you can stand here for minutes and even hours in absolute stillness, but now a car comes up from behind and passes me.

Ahead there is a bend in the road, and in the clearing a grassy field on my right and some tall memorials across from it. As I walk, rows of identical concrete crosses come into view. Now I see hundreds of them planted in the grass and enclosed by a low iron fence. Many of them are no longer white but gray-green with grime. In the distance is the section for Holy Cross priests and in the foreground the precinct for the CSC Brothers. Right in front of me—the first thing you see, approaching from this direction—are the graves of three laymen, honorary members of this community. As betokens their irregular status, these crosses are placed at the edge of the cemetery. On one of them, these figures are cut:

Paul I. Fenlon
July 31, 1896
Nov. 7, 1980

Two steps away is Frank O'Malley and just beyond him is Johnny Mangan.

As I look out across this expanse, I see countless bare crosses. The only exception is the Professor's. For several years a clear-beaded rosary has been draped over the post and arms of his cross like a scapular across his chest. Months ago, someone—also unknown to me—added another set of beads. Now I place a third, joining with those anonymous friends my prayer for the last of the bachelor dons.

Notes

Introduction

One of "the giants in Notre Dame history": Edward A. Malloy, CSC, *Monk's Tale: Way Stations on the Journey* (Notre Dame: University of Notre Dame Press, 2011), 55.

He had a "genius for friendship": George Shuster, quoted in Edward Fischer, *Notre Dame Remembered: An Autobiography* (Notre Dame: University of Notre Dame Press, 1987), 59.

"He lived his role longest and most fully": Thomas Stritch, *My Notre Dame: Memories and Reflections of Sixty Years* (Notre Dame: University of Notre Dame Press, 1991), 119.

Most notably at Yale University: Carla Yanni, *Living on Campus: An Architectural History of the American Dormitory* (Minneapolis: University of Minnesota Press, 2019), 7-8, 17-18, 55-56, 117-19, 142-50, 196-97, 218.

Set apart by a priestly aura and lifestyle: For the dons, see Richard Sullivan, *Notre Dame: Reminiscences of an Era* (Notre Dame: University of Notre Dame Press, 1951), 208-9; Stritch, *My Notre Dame,* 101-20; Kenneth M. Sayre, *Adventures in Philosophy at Notre Dame* (Notre Dame: University of Notre Dame Press, 2014), 25.

Notre Dame's lay faculty lived in student residences: See Thomas J. Schlereth, *The University of Notre Dame: A Portrait of its History and Campus,* 2nd ed. (Notre Dame: University of Notre Dame Press, 1977), 164; Howard P. Chudacoff, *The Age of the Bachelor: Creating An American Subculture* (Princeton: Princeton University Press, 1999), 5, 50-51.

And about half were priests: Much of the information in this paragraph draws on Schlereth, *University of Notre Dame,* 122, 153, 162.

287

Chapter 4
Goering and Ribbentrop: Thomas E. Blantz, CSC, *George N. Shuster: On the Side of Truth* (Notre Dame: University of Notre Dame Press, 1993), 206-11.

Chapter 30
White Elms: Peter E. Hebert, *Trees, Shrubs and Vines on Notre Dame Campus* (Notre Dame: Biology Department, University of Notre Dame, 1967), 23.

Chapter 31
Stritch as a friend: This sentence and the previous two rely on John W. Meaney, *O'Malley of Notre Dame* (Notre Dame: University of Notre Dame Press, 1991), esp. 20-21, 50-51, 227, 245-46, 250.

"I'm not a legend; I'm a myth": For the details about O'Malley in this paragraph, see Meaney, *O'Malley of Notre Dame*, 51, 117, 169, 228, 237, 245, 248 (quotation), 249, 260-61.

"Redeem the time": My account of O'Malley here is much indebted to Stritch, *My Notre Dame*, 104-9. For the idea of O'Malley as a guru, see also Meaney, *O'Malley of Notre Dame*, 54 (quotation), 170, 205, 227, 261.

Write-ups in Time and Newsweek: See Meaney, *O'Malley of Notre Dame*, 212; *Time*, Feb. 9, 1962.

Chapter 32
No "greater testimony of love than to live among his students": *Observer*, May 1, 1980, 3, 6.

Chapter 35
"Grandfather figure and source of continuity": Malloy, Monk's Tale, 101.
Laid it out for stagecoach: Schlereth, University of Notre Dame, 54.

Index

Alby's (tavern, South Bend, Ind.),
127-28, 199
alma mater. *See* Notre Dame,
Our Mother
Angsten, Phil, 176
Archives, University of Notre Dame,
22, 76, 107, 149, 221, 258, 275, 283
Ave Maria (magazine), 111, 117

bachelor dons, XIV-XV, 263. *See also*
Professors' Alley *and individual names*
Badin Hall, 110, 217
Baer, Robert, 176
Barnett, Reggie, 223
Bartell, Ernest, CSC, 14
Bell, Jimmy, 143-44
Belloc, Hilaire, 125
Bernhardt, Sarah, 73
Blairsville, Pa., 27, 45-47, 156, 227,
228, 238, 239, 258, 266
Blantz, Thomas E., CSC, 76, 141, 149,
200, 230, 256, 261, 268, 274
Boehm, Paul, 34, 49, 121, 227, 238,
241, 242
Bolger, William, CSC, 83
Bread Loaf School of English
(Ripton, Vt.), 180, 250
Brennan, 'Red,' CSC, 175-76
Brothers of Holy Cross, 72, 102, 285.
See also Maurilius
Brownson Hall, 97-98, 206
Bryan, William Jennings, 229
Buckley, John, 143-46
Burke, Eugene, CSC, 10, 71, 72,
110-11, 199, 212, 215, 264, 279
Burke, Joseph, CSC, 83
Burke, Thomas, CSC, 110-11, 283
Burns, James, CSC, 84-85

Burrell, David, CSC, 14, 155
Burtchaell, James T., CSC, 14, 40, 65,
107, 119-20, 155
Busby, Myron, 34, 135, 171, 187, 230
Byrne, Paul R. (PRB), 62, 119, 132-33,
154, 181, 189, 210, 220, 227, 283

'Cadillac Hall,' 49, 140
Cambridge University, XIV, 263, 271-73
Campbell, T. Bowyer, 32, 66, 119, 132,
202, 210-11, 219, 220, 283
Caparo, Jose Angel, 112
'Captain's Corner.' *See* Sorin Hall,
rooms in
Carey, Joseph, CSC, 72
Carr, Daniel, 143
Carrico, J. Leonard, CSC, 163, 175
Carroll, Patrick, CSC, 165
Casasanta, Joseph, 113, 140, 144-46
Casey, Danny, 29, 197, 239, 280
Casey, Elizabeth 'Betty,' 29, 32, 191,
205, 232, 237, 260-61, 274-75,
277, 280
Casey, Thomas, 29, 79, 191, 230,
260-61, 280
Casper, Dave, 223
Cather, Willa, 250, 251
Cavanaugh, John J., CSC,
(Notre Dame president, 1946-52),
34-35, 66, 114, 118, 140, 143,
146, 209, 214-16
Cavanaugh, John W., CSC
(Notre Dame president, 1905-19),
48-50, 66, 71, 72, 74, 84, 143,
165, 214
cemetery, community (Congregation of
Holy Cross), 140, 203, 249, 274,
284-85

Chesterton, G. K., 104, 116, 123, 125-29, 185, 253
Chevigny, Jack, 114
Clements, Tom, 223
Commonweal, 90
Confrey, Augustine, 112-13
Confrey, Burton, 112-13
Conley, Dick, 95, 96
Conley, Harry, 76, 95
Conyers, Richard, CSC, 104
Corby Hall, 4, 10, 25, 49, 110, 118, 134-35
Corona, Jose, 139, 143, 145
Crowley, Jim, 10, 212
Crowley, 'Putty,' 188
Crumley, Thomas, CSC, 51, 73, 80, 145
Czarboski, Zygmont 'Ziggy,' 97

Dailey, Agnes, 184-85
Danehy, James, 188
Dante Collection, 49, 189
Davis, Charles, 147-48
Devine, Dan, 220
Dickens, Charles, 34
Dillon Hall, 14, 41, 81, 107, 134
Dirksen, Everett, 249
Disney, F. X., 87, 186, 197, 202, 283
Dolan, Patrick, CSC, 24
Doremus, Charles 'Frenchie,' CSC, 106
Dunn, Thomas, 76, 189, 192, 230

Easter Rebellion, 53
Egan, (Monsignor) John J., 29
Egan, Maurice Francis, 71-72
Eisenhower, Dwight D., 90-91, 142

Faccenda, Philip, Sr., 206, 256
Fagan, Vincent, 113
Farley Hall, 125, 131, 248
Farley, John F. 'Pop,' CSC, 24, 40, 74, 85-86, 117, 123-25, 128
Fenlon, Paul, *passim*
  as assistant dean, College of Arts

and Letters, 213, 217
as best man or godfather, 89, 95, 216
burial of, 238, 274, 285
canes belonging to, 34-35, 134, 164, 275
childhood of, 45-48, 243, 259, 278
death and funeral of, 158, 272-74
European trip of, 181-82
friendships of, XII, 27, 66, 229, 239, 241, 253, 259, 274, 280, 283-84
illnesses of, 120-21, 169-72, 187-88, 191-92, 200, 204-5, 230-31, 235, 236, 273-74
letter-writing of, 31-32, 75-77, 195-96
memory of for campus events, 21, 141, 148, 221-23, 273
niece of *See* Elizabeth Casey
parents of, 34, 45-48, 66, 83, 84, 86, 207-8, 234, 235, 246, 259, 266, 274
personality of, XIII, 18, 208, 228, 233, 251-52
physical appearance of, XIII, 34, 76, 159
racehorse named after, 26-27
relationships of
  with alumni, 241, 256, 274, 279
  with Father Hesburgh. *See* Theodore M. Hesburgh
  with Sorin students, 55-59, 80, 107, 116, 121, 199, 226, 233-34, 280-81
  with Holy Cross priests, 263-65, 274. *See also individual priests*
  with nuns, 109-10, 247. *See also* Jean Lenz
religious devotions of, 32-33, 36, 38-40, 66, 190, 206
routines of, 31-36, 267
sisters of (Sarah and Mercedes Fenlon), 46, 48, 84, 207-8, 246, 280
as storyteller, 18, 45, 186, 189, 223-24, 253

as student at Notre Dame, XV, 48-53, 69-74
summers spent by, 109-10, 180-82, 246-47, 264
teaching career of, XIV, 27-28, 67, 83-86, 180, 225, 251-52
tributes to, XIV, 203, 253, 257, 267, 274, 283
watches belonging to, XIII, 35, 57, 76, 77, 158, 266
Fieldhouse, 5, 95
Fischer, Edward, 27, 116, 133, 253
Fisher Hall, 114, 247
Fitzsimons, Matthew, 170, 171, 252-53, 263
Flatley, Lee, 151, 230
Foik, Paul 'Pal,' CSC, 119
Four Horsemen, 10, 116, 212
  See also Jim Crowley, Elmer Layden, Don Miller, Harry Stuhldreher
Frederick, John Towner, 66, 245-46

Gerber, John, CSC, 132-33, 153, 154, 191, 248
ghost of Washington Hall, 139-49, 231
Gipp, George, 12-13, 104-5, 187, 209
Glee Club, 157, 184
'Gold Coast' (Walsh, Lyons, Morrissey, Howard Halls), 51, 109
Grant, Chet, 101-5, 116, 136, 139, 207, 209, 220, 278
Green, Gregory A., CSC, 3, 24-26, 30, 118, 134-35, 185, 187, 280-81
Griffin, Robert, CSC, 192

Hagerty, Cornelius 'Con,' CSC, 53, 177-78, 203
Haggar Hall, 94, 222
Haggerty, Patrick, CSC, 24, 88, 94, 105
Haig, Alexander, 179-80
Haley, J. Arthur, 157, 209
Harkcom, Dale, 227
Harvard University, 180, 230
Hayes, Helen, 230

Hayes, Jimmy, 143
Healy, Kerndt, CSC, 66, 117, 202, 283
Hebert, Peter, CSC, 85
Hesburgh, Theodore M., CSC, 2, 14, 23, 35, 41, 77, 96, 120, 156, 216-17, 247, 271; and Paul Fenlon, 99, 135, 181, 206, 233, 235-36, 238, 241, 248, 255-56, 267
Heston, Edward, CSC, 248
Hicks, Andy (author's brother), 78, 96
Hicks, Mack (author's father), 1, 15, 19, 20, 24, 27-28, 94, 141, 272
Holy Cross Hall, 112
Holy Cross House, 118, 264
Hope, Arthur J., CSC, 111
Hornung, Paul, 1, 5
Hosinski, Helen, 96, 206
Howard Hall, 246
Howells, William Dean, 246
Hoynes, William J. 'Colonel,' 69-71, 111-12, 148, 219, 222, 242
Hudson, Daniel, CSC, 117
Hunter, Al, 77

infirmary (Student Health Center), 205-7, 233, 238
Irving, Thomas, CSC, 95, 279

John Paul I (Albino Luciani), 199
John Paul II (Karol Wojtyła), 206, 275
Johnson, Samuel, 21, 160
Joyce, Edmund P., CSC, 42, 114, 176, 191, 256, 274

Kathleen, Sister. *See* Kathleen Rossman
Kennedy, Walter, 119
Kirsch, Alexander, CSC, 222
Kittredge, George Lyman, 180
Knute Rockne, All-American (film), 157, 209-10
Kostanty, Eddie, 31, 76, 103, 196
Krause, Edward 'Moose,' 2, 66-67, 125, 133, 160
Kunz, George, 223

Lady Chatterley's Lover (Lawrence), 129
Laetare Medal, 89, 230
Lahey, Thomas 'Dopey Dan,' CSC, 111
Lange, Bernard, CSC, 85-86, 142, 207, 257
LaSalle Hotel (South Bend, Ind.), 2, 87
Lavin, Walter, CSC, 207, 279
Layden, Elmer, 94, 101, 210
Leader, Robert, 41, 283
Leahy, Frank, 216
Lenz, Jean, OSF, 131, 171, 248, 274
'Lilacs,' 71, 219
Lujack, Johnny, 30, 222
Lynch, Jim, 223
Lyons Hall, 88, 245, 249-50

Madden, Thomas, 132, 181-82, 210, 220
Main Building, 4, 20, 37, 41, 48, 51, 98, 110, 124, 144, 157, 281
Malloy, Edward A., CSC, 243, 257, 282
Mangan, Johnny, 140, 144, 145, 279, 285
Manion, Clarence 'Pat,' 11, 12, 31, 87-89, 126, 200, 216, 231, 233, 283
    career of, 142
    and ghost of Washington Hall, 139-49, 231
    as orator, 95, 141, 229
    quoted, 128, 132
Manion, Gina, 89, 140, 141, 144, 148, 178, 201, 231, 233, 234, 238
Maritain, Jacques, 113
Maurilius, Brother (Maurilius DeGan, CSC), 144, 146-47
McCarragher, Charles 'Black Mac,' CSC, 24
McCarthy, James 'Mac,' 113, 120
McDonagh, Thomas, CSC, 246-48, 255
McGinn, John, CSC, 51-52, 74
McMahon, Ed, 180
McNutt, Paul, 89
Miller, Creighton, 222

Miller, Don, 78, 200
Miltner, Charles, CSC, 66
Moore, Philip, CSC, 262
Moran, Dennis William, 21, 28, 159, 195, 274
Morris, Hiney, 112
Morris Inn, 34, 157, 197, 205, 249
Morrissey, Andrew, CSC, 84, 89
Morrissey Hall, 132, 210
Mulcaire, Michael, CSC, 177
Murphy, Miss, 34, 274
Murtaugh, Jimmy, 88
Murtha, Sam, 176

Navy, US, 33, 211-13, 249
Neeson, John, Jr., 176, 179-80, 283
Neeson, John, Sr., 179-80
Nelson, Lindsay, 1
Notre Dame Magazine, XIV, 27, 30
Notre Dame, Our Mother (Casasanta and O'Donnell), 144, 157-58, 274
Notre Dame, University of, *passim*
    Catholic character of, 155-56
    graduating classes of,
        1927: 77
        1928: 159, 200
        1931: 30, 176
        1935: 176
    historical development of, XV-XVI, 1-2
    and minims and preps (grade and high school students, respectively), 51, 124, 140

O'Connor, Earl 'Stretch,' 50-51, 154, 283
O'Connor, Edwin, 250
O'Donnell, Charles L., CSC (Notre Dame president, 1928-34), 11, 125-27, 146-47, 161-62, 176-77, 178, 209, 210, 211
O'Donnell, J. Hugh, CSC (Notre Dame president, 1940-46), 157, 166, 178, 209, 211-12, 216
O'Grady, Dan, 128

O'Hara, John F. Cardinal, CSC, 13-14, 26, 41, 105, 113-14, 177
  as resident of Sorin Hall, 13, 42, 113-14
Oliver Hotel (South Bend, Ind.), 48, 52, 74
O'Malley, Frank, XIII, 13, 214, 245, 249-53, 275, 285
O'Meara, O. Timothy, 235-36
O'Neil, Daniel, CSC, 33, 35, 37-39, 45, 66, 98, 118, 187, 201-2, 214, 216, 266
  illness of, 75, 77, 78, 121, 133, 151, 153-55, 197
  death of, 195, 197, 198, 200-203, 230
Orpheum Theatre (South Bend, Ind.), 53
Oxford University, XIV, 70, 113

Paderewski, Ignacy Jan, 164
parietals, 5, 25
Parseghian, Ara, 1, 10, 33
Pay Caf, 31, 96, 250
Payton, Gene, 113
Phelps, Richard 'Digger,' 96
Phillips, Charles, 34, 65, 66, 80, 127, 128, 161-67, 185, 275
Porterfield, David, CSC, 197-98, 201-2, 204, 224, 226, 238, 257, 273
presidential elections, US, 8, 275
'Professors' Alley.' *See* Sorin Hall
Prohibition, 84, 127-28, 174, 199

Reese, Frank, 102
Reyniers, J. Arthur, 221
Riehle, James, CSC, 80
Robinson, Jack, 26
Rockne, Bonnie, 12
Rockne, Knute, 1-2, 9-11, 101-2, 114
  and academic eligibility of athletes, 87, 186, 216
  funeral of, 11-12
Roemer, James, 25, 26
Ronay, Steve, 128, 129

Romweber, Paul, 98, 283
Rossman, Kathleen, OSF, 185
Ruettiger, Daniel 'Rudy,' XVI
Ryan, Joseph, XIII, 98, 214, 250

Sacred Heart Church (Basilica of the Sacred Heart), 4, 32, 211,
  renovations of, 14, 40-42, 281
  Stations of the Cross belonging to, 40-41, 281
St. Edward's Hall, 3, 4, 269, 273
St. Mary's College, 5, 48, 74, 84, 184, 188, 277, 280
St. Petersburg, Fla., 27
Salmon, Louis. J. 'Red,' 207-8
Scherer, Joseph, CSC, 72
Schlafly, Phyllis, 229
Schlitzer, Albert, CSC, 24
Schumacher, Matthew, CSC, 50
Seton, Saint Elizabeth Ann, 34
Shaw, Lawrence Timothy 'Buck,' 85
Sheedy, Charles 'Chic,' CSC, 36
Shuster, Doris, 90, 115, 117, 133, 189, 234, 259-62, 273
Shuster, George, 38, 42, 76, 86, 88-91, 108, 115, 223, 256-57, 262, 279, 283
  career of, 28-29
  death of, 28-29, 156, 202
Sisters of the Holy Cross, 145, 280
Smith, Walter Wellesley 'Red,' 77
Sorin, Edward F., CSC, 1, 4, 105, 107-8, 284
  miniature statue of, 106-7, 282
Sorin Hall, XIII, 3, 4, 7, 20, *passim*
  attic of, 135-36
  basement of ('rec room' or 'subway'), 9-10, 102-4, 174, 226. *See also two-digit room numbers, below*
  bathrooms in, 7, 8,, 35-36, 42, 94-95, 121, 172-73, 212, 250, 282
  chapel of, 7, 26, 36, 39, 41-43, 111, 133, 228, 274, 283
  law classroom in, 70-71, 73, 174

porch of, 69, 70, 115, 242-43, 282
'Professors' Alley' in, XV, 62, 112-14
rector's office in, 3, 7, 39
rooms in
   15 ('Captain's Corner'): 223, 230
   41: 57, 80, 222
   47: 222
   56: 136
   102: 222
   115: 89
   117: 222
   119: 174
   123: 113, 174
   141: 7-9, 42, 65-66, 97, 174,
      231-32, 246, 282
   201, 203: 161
   215: 62
   241: 56, 112, 113
   246, 248: 113
   250, 251, 254: 113
   255: 88
   301: 78, 183, 200, 222
   302: 87, 200, 228, 282
   304: 87
   306: 88
   315: 25-27
   327: 63, 72
   329: 4
   331: 3
   333: 161, 179
   341: 112, 128, 161-67, 174, 185
   355: 11, 64, 83, 89, 109-10, 114,
      162, 213, 246-47
   356: 89, 247, 282
Sorin, Madame, 105-8
'Sorin Seven,' 25-27
South Bend Tribune, 30, 32, 101, 118,
   147, 155, 261
Stadium, 126-27
Steiger, Brad, 140
Steiner, Thomas 'Pop,' CSC, 72, 107,
   214, 255
Stoddard, Mrs., 274
Stevenson, Harry, 146
Stritch, Samuel Cardinal, 205, 214

Stritch, Thomas J., 34, 40, 114, 135-36,
   152, 189, 206, 213-14, 232, 238,
   240, 274
   quoted, 77, 204, 240-41, 258, 274
Student Health Center. See infirmary
Stuhldreher, Harry, 102, 103, 136
Suckow, Ruth, 246
Sullivan, Richard, 32, 159, 163-64, 197,
   246, 256

Time, 32, 217, 253
Toohey, William, CSC, 222

University Club, 34, 240, 249

Vatican II, XVI, 39-40, 43, 246, 248
Victory March (Shea and Shea), 4, 13

Wallace, Francis, 63
Walsh, Adam, 221
Walsh Hall, 3, 12, 14, 31, 51, 73-74, 85,
   109, 124, 142, 145, 177, 214
Walsh, Matthew, CSC, 66-67, 87, 89,
   110
Ward, Leo R., CSC, 246
Washington Hall, 4, 70, 71, 113,
   126, 153. See also ghost of
      Washington Hall
Waters, Daniel 'Chappy,' 113
Weir, David, 113
Wenninger, Francis, CSC, 222
Wilson, Jerome J., CSC, 41, 256
Wilson, Woodrow, 83
Withey, James, 214-15
Woodstock, Ill., 46, 95, 178
World War I, 46, 72-74, 163
World War II, 212-13, 249-50, 259
Wurzer, Hank, 176

Yale University, XV
Yeats, William Butler, 53
Young, Daniel, 146

Zahm, John, CSC, 189